THE
PSYCHOBIOTIC
REVOLUTION

THE
PSYCHOBIOTIC
REVOLUTION

Mood, Food, and the New Science of the Gut-Brain Connection

SCOTT C. ANDERSON

with

JOHN F. CRYAN, PH.D. &
TED DINAN, M.D., PH.D.

NATIONAL
GEOGRAPHIC
WASHINGTON, D.C.

Since 1888, the National Geographic Society has funded more than 12,000 research, exploration, and preservation projects around the world. National Geographic Partners distributes a portion of the funds it receives from your purchase to National Geographic Society to support programs including the conservation of animals and their habitats.

National Geographic Partners
1145 17th Street NW
Washington, DC 20036-4688 USA

Become a member of National Geographic and activate your benefits today at natgeo.com/jointoday.

For information about special discounts for bulk purchases, please contact National Geographic Books Special Sales: specialsales@natgeo.com

For rights or permissions inquiries, please contact National Geographic Books Subsidiary Rights: bookrights@natgeo.com

Illustrations
Scott C. Anderson: 28, 55, 86, 96, 98
Scott C. Anderson and Kiran Sandhu: 119, 126

Photographs
15, © Martin Oeggerli, supported by School of Life Sciences FHNW; 48 (LE), BSIP SA/Alamy Stock Photo; 48 (RT), SCIMAT/Science Source; 93, Omikron/Getty Images; 148, public domain; 160, Haisam Hussein/National Geographic Creative.

Library of Congress Cataloging-in-Publication Data

Names: Anderson, Scott C., author. | Cryan, J. F. (John F.) author. | Dinan,
    Timothy G., author.
Title: The psychobiotic revolution : mood, food, and the new science of the
    gut-brain connection / Scott C. Anderson, John F. Cryan, Ted Dinan.
Description: Washington, DC : National Geographic Partners, LLC, [2017] |
    Includes bibliographical references.
Identifiers: LCCN 2017030130 | ISBN 9781426218460 (hardback)
Subjects: LCSH: Gastrointestinal system--Microbiology. | Digestive
    organs--Diseases--Psychological aspects. | Nutrition. | BISAC: HEALTH &
    FITNESS / Diseases / Nervous System (incl. Brain). | PSYCHOLOGY /
    Psychopathology / Depression. | SCIENCE / Life Sciences / Biology /
    Microbiology.
Classification: LCC QR171.G29 A53 2017 | DDC 612.3/2--dc23
LC record available at https://lccn.loc.gov/2017030130

Interior design: Katie Olsen

Printed in the United States of America
17/QGF-LSCML/1

For my wonderful kids, Brooke and Blake, who constantly inspire me, and their amazing mother (and my awesomely patient wife), Candyce, who stood by me throughout.
—*Scott*

To my beloved Colleen for choosing to live in this microbial world with me, and to our amazing kids, Oisín and Alannah.
—*John*

To my parents, who gave me the opportunity to study medicine; my wife/lover, Lucinda; and my three kids.
—*Ted*

CONTENTS

PREFACE

ARE BACTERIA CONTROLLING YOUR BRAIN? IT SEEMS ABSURD! Bacteria are so ridiculously tiny that you could fit a thousand of them into a single human cell. And yet, microbes seem to have superpowers. Flesh-eating bacteria can mow a human down in mere days. The Black Death brought down entire civilizations. Could such a primitive creature take the reins of our exquisitely evolved human minds? The answer is yes. Just as scientists are learning more each day about the trillions of microbes living inside you, so they are also discovering that some of these microbes can actually commandeer your mind, control your tastes, and alter your moods.

In 2004, I set up a lab for a company in Ohio, and started to design and analyze animal experiments on gastrointestinal (GI) problems like colitis. I did a lot of reading into the scientific literature about the relationship between gut health and disease. An association between gut health and mental health was always noted in these studies. As I focused on articles about gut bacteria that had a psychological angle, I learned of the work of Ted Dinan and John Cryan, two of the leading researchers in this field. In fact, they are the ones who came up with the new word to name the microbes that can improve your mood: *psychobiotics*. These microbes are major players in the *gut-brain axis:* the communication between your gut and your mind.

9

I soon recognized how incredibly productive Cryan and Dinan are, together having written more than 400 peer-reviewed articles in this decade alone. John Cryan is chair of Anatomy and Neuroscience and Ted Dinan is head of the Department of Psychiatry, both at University College Cork, Ireland (UCC). Together they are the principal investigators at UCC's APC Microbiome Institute, where they manage a team of young, bright investigators who have come from all over the world to join them in this groundbreaking research.

Cryan and Dinan are leading a revolution that is upending long-held doctrines in almost every branch of biology—and that can have profound effects on the decisions we make to stay healthy and treat disease. When I decided to write a book about psychobiotics, I knew who my guides should be. I contacted the good doctors by Skype, and we started a dialogue that ultimately led to a delightful fish and champagne dinner in Cork—and the book you are now reading.

In this book, I will be your primary narrator. While I guide you through the basic biology, John Cryan and Ted Dinan will take you into their labs. When they take over the narrative, it will look like this:

> *In neuroscience and medicine, we're conditioned to think of only what is happening above the neck in terms of the regulation of our emotions, but this is changing. Research, including that being carried out by us in the APC Microbiome Institute at UCC, is literally turning this concept upside down. We're beginning to fully realize the importance that gut function and the food we eat have on our mental well-being.*

That's Cryan and Dinan speaking. You will hear their voices throughout, as they bring their research to life. In some cases, they'll be quoting directly from their published research; in other cases, they'll be commenting on promising work in the field. Their psychobiotic theories permeate this book, as do the theories of dozens of other researchers who have been finding a similar connection between gut microbes and the brain. Cryan and Dinan have patiently vetted this entire tome; it has been a wonderful collaboration that we all hope will put our readers into the best possible mood.

—Scott C. Anderson

CHAPTER 1

. . . .

MEET YOUR MICROBES

"If microbes are controlling the brain,
then microbes are controlling everything."

—John F. Cryan

MICROBES SURROUND US AND SUFFUSE US. WE ARE SERIOUSLY outnumbered. A single bacterium, given enough to eat, could multiply until its brethren reached the mass of Earth in just two days. That's a big clue to their superpower: They are excellent at reproduction. They are also profligate interbreeders and think nothing of swapping genes with whoever is nearby. They are so promiscuous that biologists cannot even positively identify many of them. Their DNA is shot through with genes borrowed from other species—even other kingdoms of life. Dose them with antibiotics, and they may just depend on a passing virus to grab a handy antibiotic resistance gene. They can mutate every 20 minutes, while humans try to counterpunch with genetic evolutionary updates every 10,000 years or so. They are genetic dynamos, running circles around us.

Fortunately, life tends to lean toward cooperation, happily forming alliances to advance a shared cause. That, presumably, is why our planet is completely coated with living matter. And that is how, some millions of years ago, bacteria and animals struck up a deal. In return for a moist bed and a warm buffet, beneficial bacteria took up the job of defending us against the madly proliferating *pathogens* in the world. It takes a germ to fight a germ.

And so, in your gut today, you are host to trillions of bacteria. They are online 24/7, duking it out with rogue microbes and even helping you nutritionally by producing vitamins and eking out the last few calories from every speck of fiber. When everything is running smoothly, you pay no attention to your gut. Like your heart or your liver, it's best if these things are on autopilot. Your conscious mind is too busy looking for your keys to be trusted with running these critical organs. Nature has built you a GI tract that can operate completely independently of your distracted brain. In fact, your gut has a brain of its own, to relieve you of those menial gastronomic details—at least until things go wrong.

YOUR MICROBIOTA
....

The community of microbes living in your gut—your so-called *microbiota*—is like another organ of your body. It's a seething alien living inside of you, fermenting your food and jealously protecting you against interlopers. It's a pretty unusual organ by any measure, but even more so in that its composition changes with every meal.

It's not just made of bacteria. Your microbiota is also home to ancient life-forms related to the colorful creatures that tint hot springs, called *Archaea*. It includes the kings of fermentation, the yeasts. It hosts swimming single-celled protozoans, constantly on

Your gut is home to an astonishing variety of life-forms, including protozoans, fungi, bacteria, and viruses (shown here with a bit of fiber).

the prowl. It also includes an even more insane number of viruses, as small relative to bacteria as bacteria are to human cells. Your gut microbiota is spectacularly cosmopolitan, making it a challenging beast to study.

Your microbiota communicates directly with your *second brain,* a phrase coined by Michael Gershon in 1998 to refer to the network of nerves surrounding your gut. A good set of microbes encourages this second brain to keep the feast moving. For good health, including mental health, the food you eat needs to be good for you *and* for your microbiota. This book will help you make better choices by learning about the foods that feed your microbiota best, including what we now call *psychobiotics.*

In 2013, we defined a psychobiotic as a live organism that, when ingested in adequate amounts, produces a health benefit in patients suffering from psychiatric illness. As a class of **probiotic,** *these bacteria are capable of producing and delivering neuroactive substances such as gamma-aminobutyric acid and serotonin, which act on the brain-gut axis. Preclinical evaluation in rodents suggests that certain psychobiotics possess antidepressant or anxiety-reducing activity. Effects may be mediated via the vagus nerve, spinal cord, or neuroendocrine systems.*[1]

Recently we have suggested broadening the psychobiotic concept to include prebiotics—the **fiber** *that acts as food for the psychobiotics.*[2]

Your microbiota is not garrulous, but it can make itself heard. It can make you feel better if you feed it what it wants, and it can make you feel miserable if you don't. One way is through cravings. You may feel that you just have a personal penchant for certain candies, but it might not be up to you at all. It might just be a siren song from the alien organ that lives in your gut. Some part of your microbiota is begging for nougat, and another for chocolate. Together, they guide you—using techniques that we'll discuss in this book—to a candy bar. Soon after you eat it, your microbiota releases sugars and fatty acids, lifting your spirits considerably. Your cravings, it seems, might belong more to the second brain in your gut than the one in your head. Who is really running the show?

Your microbiota can affect your mood as well. Take an obvious case like food poisoning. Your microbiota recognizes the pathogenic intruders and starts to attack them. It tries starving and poisoning them and—importantly—it alerts your immune system. Now kicked into high gear, your second brain prepares to purge your system. It sends you a terse admonition to find a bathroom, quickly. Your mood at that point is acute anxiety. Now imagine that happening day after day. That's what occurs when you have chronic inflammation, often caused by a breach in your microbiotic defenses. Anxiety and depression can become a constant companion.

Nature has wired us to lay low when we have an infection. This is called sickness behavior, and you know the feeling: Leave me alone, but cover me up and bring soup. This makes sense for you, because it conserves your energy to fight the bug. But from an evolutionary point of view, it also makes sense for your roommates, who will benefit when you retire to your own quiet space and stop spreading the contagion.

Endured for any lengthy period of time, sickness behavior is better known as depression. Depending on the levels of inflammation, you can suffer from alternating periods of depression and anxiety. You may think of these maladies as strictly a brain problem, but there are actually *two* brains involved—and a gland or two.

Sickness is one of the unsubtle ways that your microbiota can influence your moods. It may be a shock to the ego, but you are not alone in your body, and your microbiota is right now making plans for your future. By manipulating your cravings and mood, it gains control over your behavior.

This book explores the amazing gut-brain connection and shows you how to gain the upper hand. Your gut may be in charge right now, but it's never too late to recondition it. Remember, your microbiota is renewed every hour or so. The turnover is huge, and you may be able to divert it with some surprisingly easy tricks.

You've let your gut run your life long enough. It's time for an intervention. We'll show you how to get back in the driver's seat.

IS THIS BOOK GOING TO BE DEPRESSING?

No, just the opposite! Here, you'll find out how psychobiotics can help you to live a happier, healthier life. Even if you don't have depression or anxiety, this mind-boggling research is showing that a better-balanced gut can improve *anyone's* mood. It can even improve your thinking and boost your memory. Far from depressing, this is an uplifting story that can help millions of people afflicted by depression or anxiety.

There is more than one way to be depressed, of course: Loss or other kinds of psychic trauma can depress you. At first blush, external events like this don't seem to be related to your gut microbiota, and initially they usually aren't. But the gut-brain connection is a two-way street. Despair, anxiety, and depression can lead to negative changes to your microbiota, called **dysbiosis**. That disruption can channel anxiety and depression right back into your brain. It creates what most of life tries its best to avoid: a positive feedback loop, otherwise known as a vicious cycle.

Today we have an epidemic of depression without an obvious external cause. We also have an epidemic of gut problems. These two are strongly associated, a phenomenon called *comorbidity*. Research continues to reveal connections between gut health and other diseases, both mental and physical. Depression accompanies many of these diseases, including Parkinson's, Alzheimer's, irritable bowel syndrome (IBS), inflammatory bowel disease (IBD), obesity, psoriasis, arthritis, multiple sclerosis (MS), autism, and many more. These diseases sometimes start with depression or anxiety—and sometimes they end with them.

Our research has shown us that it's like Downton Abbey: *You have two communities living together in the one house. They need each*

other to survive, but they go around more or less ignoring each
other. It's only when things go wrong downstairs that the real drama
occurs upstairs.

Research keeps unearthing connections between seemingly
unrelated gut and brain diseases. What do skin diseases like psoriasis and eczema have to do with brain problems like multiple sclerosis (MS)? The surprising connection is the gut microbiota. Even
seemingly intractable conditions like autism may be improved with
psychobiotics. Normal social bonding may depend on a healthy gut.

Interestingly, you can induce depression with a tiny amount of
a pathogen's cell wall. This is evidence of a bacterial war that has
gone on long enough that our ancestors evolved genes to deal with
them directly. Your immune system can detect these bacterial
molecules at very low levels. This is part of your *innate* immune
system, and it doesn't require any training. It just reacts, and it does
so with alacrity.

But you have another immune system that is more subtle and that
requires training: Your *adaptive* immune system is deliriously complex. This adaptive system—working closely with your microbiota—
can protect you against pathogens that it has never seen before. That
is truly a remarkable feat. It's not perfect, though, and can inflict some
serious collateral damage. In this book, you'll learn how to fine-tune
your adaptive system to bank the fires of inflammation.

Your genes contain the blueprint for all the proteins that make
up your body. Some genetic diseases like sickle-cell anemia or
Huntington's disease are inevitably progressive and difficult or
impossible to treat. But many other diseases with a genetic component, like cancer, autism, or schizophrenia, may be modifiable. That
treatment starts with your microbial genes, which outnumber your
human genes by an amazing 100 to 1. It's a little humbling, but to

an outside observer, you are a hybrid creature that is genetically only one percent human.

That genetic abundance is due to the rich diversity of microbes in your gut, consisting of thousands of species, each with a unique set of genes. Because these microbe populations can change from meal to meal—and because you have control over those meals—Mother Nature has given you a way to adjust your gene pool. This book will show you how to put nature on your side, simply and safely.

MICROBIOTIC MARVELS

The science of the gut-brain connection is often counterintuitive and full of surprises. Here you'll discover dozens of completely unexpected gut-brain connections. For instance:

- Babies need gut bacteria to develop properly. In studies in which mice pups are raised in a germ-free environment, they tend to be more anxious and have certain cognitive deficits. To develop the appropriate wiring, the brain needs gut microbes to be healthy and balanced—and that needs to be established early. Provided too late, the microbes cannot reverse the effect.
- Your gut can act as a brewery and get you drunk. For a long time, this seemed unbelievable, and the victims were suspected of sneaking booze. Scientists finally found yeast that could grow in the small intestine and produce enough alcohol to make you blotto. That was an unexpected gut-brain connection that was cured with antifungals and ended a continuous hangover.
- Bacteria live *inside* the tissues of your veggies. Washing them only gets the surface clean. Fortunately, these microbes mostly

seem benign or even beneficial, but it also casts a new light on the raw food movement. How do these microbes affect your mind?

- Mind-bending microbes can make animals do things that are dangerous or even deadly. A microbe of the genus *Toxoplasma* can make mice become aroused by cat pee. It's hard to overstate what a bad life strategy this is, but it works well for the microbes: They will, with this gruesome mind trick, inevitably find their way into a cat. Once there, the toxoplasma can complete its nefarious life cycle.

- Only one percent of your genes are human, and those genes are fairly stable, but your microbial genes—the other 99 percent—are in constant flux. Measured by your genes, you're a different creature each and every morning.

- Is our civilization actually built for the benefit of microbes? Happy people tend to be more social, and the more social we are, the more chances our microbes have to exchange and spread.

How can mere microbes pull off these impressive stunts? It may have something to do with the startling fact that these unassuming creatures speak the same language as our own vastly evolved brain cells.

In our studies, we have found that many bacteria are capable of producing some of the most important neurotransmitters in the human brain, like serotonin, dopamine, and GABA. We don't think these bacterial neurotransmitters go straight to the human brain, but we do believe that these bacteria are capable of producing substances that impact our brain function through the vagus nerve—which directly connects to the brain.

GOOD HEALTH DEPENDS ON HEALTHY BIOFILMS

· ·

We underestimate these tiny creatures at our peril. So-called single-celled bacteria can in fact form great citylike complexes composed of several different species living harmoniously in a *biofilm*. It sounds exotic, but you step on biofilms every time you walk over a lichen-covered rock. The biofilms in and on your body are related to lichen, and share their features of resilience and togetherness.

Biofilms are marvelously complex. They have pores for pumping nutrients, acting as a basic circulatory system. They maintain a protective coating—a primitive skin—that holds water in. The various species communicate with each other, using signaling molecules, including *neurotransmitters*. They concentrate digestive *enzymes*, creating a rudimentary alimentary system. At that point, microbes are no longer really single-celled; they have in essence become a hardy, multicellular organism.

These biofilms are everywhere, from your mouth down to your anus. In your mouth, you know it as plaque. In your intestines, a pathogenic biofilm might be behind Crohn's disease. These biofilms are unavoidable. Fortunately, you can put them on your payroll. You can spread a biofilm throughout your gut that is a stalwart defender, a tough adversary of pathogens. Properly established, a compatible biofilm can lead to a lifetime of gastronomic bliss, unburdened by inflammation and its frequent companions, depression and anxiety.

A microbiota that is unbalanced and that provokes an immune response is called *dysbiotic*. It can lead to inflammation, which is a significant contributor to depression and anxiety. Worse yet, it is a major predictor of mental decline, making dysbiosis important to everyone, regardless of mood. Depression is associated with brain atrophy. So your depression is not only setting you back today, but could have even worse long-term effects. We'll show you how to dial down gut-based inflammation as a way to reclaim the health, both physical and mental, that you deserve.

How do we know that microbes can control mood? Much of it comes from animal studies, which will be the frequent evidence presented in this book. This is medical research on the cutting edge, but as the human studies start to come in, they are echoing many of the animal findings.

> *In our lab, we were able to show that we could transfer "the blues" with gut microbes. We transferred fecal matter from human patients with major depression into rats and noted that they, unlike the controls, became depressed, too. Mood was not only transferable by fecal microbes but also from humans to rats, demonstrating that psychobiotic effects are, to some extent, independent of species.*
>
> *That suggests that a given microbiota may be able to affect moods. So if you have to get a **fecal transplant**, in addition to having the donor worked up for infectious disease, you might want to get a good psychological profile of him or her, just in case.*[3]

In another study with healthy adult males, the results had some unexpected effects on the mind.

> *We gave healthy male subjects some psychobiotic bacteria, and they became less anxious. The effect was large enough for them to perceive less **stress**. These healthy men also underwent an intelligence test. We found a statistically significant improvement in cognitive function, particularly memory. This was a study in which we managed to find in humans exactly what we have found in animals.*

That builds a wonderful bridge between mice and men, but no one expects to see all the rodent studies being applied directly to humans. There are plenty of differences, even if we all love cheese. Some bacteria that are common in mice are rarely seen in humans and vice versa. But at least as a proof of principle, the connection is promising. These studies showed something else: Psychobiotics can improve cognition even in healthy adults.

This book is full of hope, not only for people with depression or anxiety but also for people suffering from a number of debilitating illnesses—and, in fact, for everyone who wants to improve their mental health and well-being. The story of how microbes interact with your mind is nothing short of astonishing.

When we give psychobiotics to mice, they become a lot more chilled out and relaxed. They behaved as if they were on Valium or Prozac. We looked at their brains and there were widespread changes. The question is how? How can bacteria in your gut communicate with your brain?

The answers are not obvious; you cannot just pop probiotics and expect magic. A lot of products on the market today promise to help you on the path to gut health, but research has not shown all of them to be effective. This book will help you make choices among the many products that are making promises out there. It turns out that you can take back control of your body with a simple, all-natural diet and specific microbial foods and supplements. Amazingly, for many people these changes can be as powerful as any medication.

CHAPTER 2

MANKIND, MICROBES, AND MOOD

"No man is an island, entire of itself."

—John Donne

SOME OF YOUR DEEPEST FEELINGS, FROM YOUR GREATEST JOYS to your darkest angst, turn out to be related to the bacteria in your gut. That outrageous proposition implies that you might be able to alter your mood by adjusting your bacteria. Just why this is so—and just how you can adjust these bacteria—are at the core of this book.

The first theories about the gut-brain connection go back to the 18th-century French anatomist Marie François Xavier Bichat, who discovered that the gut has its own nervous system, independent of the central nervous system. It isn't organized in a lump like the brain but rather as an intricate double-layered lacework surrounding your entire gut like a tube sock. Bichat also, far ahead of his time, saw the connection between emotion and the gut, and situated the passions in the "epigastric center," as he called it.[1] At the end of the 20th century, the concept was dusted off and better defined by Michael Gershon, who dubbed the intestinal nervous system the "second brain" in a book with the same name.[2]

Along with Bichat, Gershon realized that the gut is closely involved with mood. When your gut is running smoothly, your brain is calm. But when *pathogens*—microbes that are dangerous—threaten your health, spikes of anxiety are delivered to your brain. That pathogen angle brings a third player into the gut-brain scenario: the microbiota.

As a counterbalance, you have your own homegrown microbes that are friendly. These are your **commensals**, from Latin, meaning "together at the table." If these friendly microbes also keep your mood on an even keel, they are called *psychobiotics*. Taken together, these tamed microbes constitute your microbiota, which is there to shield you against the wild pathogens of the world. They are like domesticated dogs that you feed and care for so that they will defend you against their callous cousins, the wolves.

Despite its autonomy, your second brain maintains a pretty constant communication with your first brain. A large part of that conversation concerns your microbiota. Astonishingly, your microbes themselves can talk to both brains using chemicals similar to neurotransmitters (the communication molecules of your brain) and other molecules like hormones, fatty acids, **metabolites**, and cytokines. (More on all those later.) Pathogens also secrete chemicals like these, some of which cause your immune system to hit the panic button. These alert signals are mainly fired off in the gut, which is the largest component of your immune system. This is because the gut is a highly specialized tissue whose challenging job is to suck nutrition out of food without also sucking in pathogens.

Most of the action of gut immunity is local: Immune components called natural killer cells concentrate their fire on pathogens in the immediate neighborhood. However, if pathogens leak through the lining and get out of your gut, your immune cells will follow them into your blood system and spark a systemic inflammation—a condition often called leaky gut. You don't always understand it as such, but inflammation signals your first brain that something is wrong and may cause you to seek out a quiet place with warm blankets to recover. That's sickness behavior, and it has a lot in common with depression. Like depression, it's not a choice: Your brain will force the issue, unless something preempts it.

Both of your brains are able to receive messages from your microbiota. These are mostly communiques about the state of pathogens in your gut, but there are also signals about improper movement of food and other anomalies. If everything is running well, both brains are happy, and the first brain rarely intrudes on the second brain's business. That leaves the second brain on auto-pilot throughout most of the digestive system. You—meaning your first brain—are allowed a little bit of conscious input at either end. You can move your tongue and swallow at the near end, and you can control your sphincter at the far end. Everything in between is pretty much out of your control. That's one less thing you need to worry about, which is always welcome, but it eliminates a lot of important inside information. Without definitive cues from your gut, you often have to guess what's wrong with you. If you just feel a general malaise, you may not place the source of your worries where it often belongs: in your gut.

That's a big problem. Gut issues like IBS and IBD are highly associated with depression and anxiety, but the connection is often missed. Curing the underlying GI problem can often resolve the mental issues. But without a clear signal from the gut, people don't

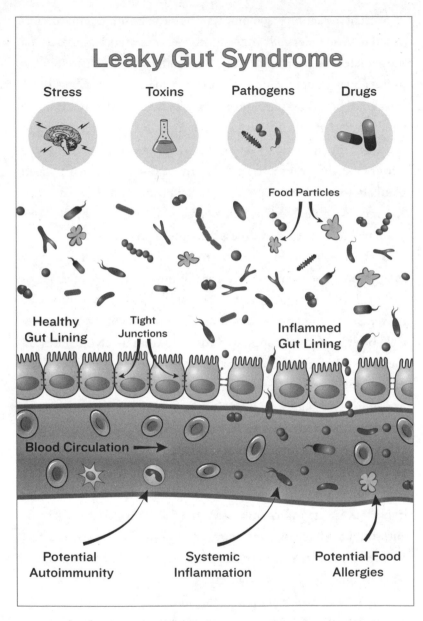

The condition called leaky gut results when stress, toxins, pathogens, or drugs damage the intestinal lining and allow pathogens to leak into your circulatory system.

always get the proper treatments. If you go to a psychiatrist for anxiety or depression, the doctor rarely asks you about your gut issues—but that is likely to change as the connection between the gut and the brain becomes better understood. Dealing with gut problems may not cure all cases of depression or anxiety, but it can ease the burden.

DISCOVERING THE NATURE OF MICROBES

Bacteria were here first, so we have to learn to live with them. They cover almost every surface on the planet with a thin, usually invisible scum. They live (slowly) in glaciers. They eke out an existence in rocks miles under the ground. They thrive in the deepest ocean trenches. They even float through the air, in every breath you take.

Bacteria, when they were discovered by Antonie van Leeuwenhoek in the 1600s, were mere oddities, tiny creatures wiggling around in a miniature water world of their own. Even though Leeuwenhoek looked at his own spit through his high-powered homemade microscopes and marveled at the diversity of what he called "animalcules," they didn't seem to be very relevant to the human story. Leeuwenhoek was secretive about his microscopes, and when he died, microbiology died with him.

It wasn't until the work of Louis Pasteur and Robert Koch in the 1850s that microbes became a hot topic again. These two worked out the germ theory of disease, and many fanciful theories of life, like spontaneous generation, crumbled in the face of their evidence. Pasteur and Koch knew from their research into fermentation that most microbes were beneficial, but the germs involved in disease got all the attention. For the next hundred years, when most people thought about bacteria, they thought about pathogens. The battle was on to kill them off.

At the beginning of the 20th century, a French pediatrician named Henri Tissier determined that babies were born sterile, only picking up bacteria with the final squeeze down the birth canal.[3] Looking at baby poop, Tissier discovered that babies fed on mother's milk had a population of unique microbes he called *Bifidobacteria* because they bifurcated into a "Y" shape. These had been first described by Theodor Escherich, who published a paper on the gut bacteria of infants in 1886. Escherich had a good eye, and he also spotted a rod-shaped bacterium in baby poop that would soon be named after him: *Escherichia coli*, better known as *E. coli*, arguably the most famous pathogen of all time (a sobering reminder that we don't always get to specify how we will be remembered). But many species of bacteria can be subdivided into even smaller subcategories, called **bacterial strains,** and, as we shall see, most strains of *E. coli* are model citizens and don't deserve all of that bad PR.

Tissier was able to culture the *Bifidobacteria* that Escherich had first spotted in baby poop. He had two experimental groups of babies: bottle-fed and breast-fed. In the poop of children reared on cow's milk, Tissier didn't find *Bifidobacteria*. These babies were also not as healthy and often suffered diarrhea; in fact, bottle-fed babies at that time were dying at seven times the rate of breast-fed babies. Tissier decided to treat the bottle-fed babies with *Bifidobacteria* and had some amount of success. It was an early attempt to produce a formula to emulate mother's milk, a quest that continues to this day. The *British Medical Journal* (now just *BMJ*) praised Tissier's work. In a 1906 review of his discoveries, it enthused that *Bifidobacteria* "may restore the intestine to the virginal condition of that of a nursling at the breast, and restore within us the true golden age of digestion."

We are going to be talking enough about *Bifidobacteria* that we can nickname it *Bifido*. When we use it in a species name, we can shorten it even further to simply *B*. One species, *B. longum,* has the largest DNA of any *Bifido* species, partly because it codes for a large internal protein machine designed to digest human milk. At this point we need to marvel at nature for creating a tiny bacterium that dines on, and helps us to dine on, human milk. This is the amazing leverage of coevolution, where two creatures living side by side for millennia end up creating complex molecules designed to help each other. Far from nature as a bloody horror show—red in tooth and claw—this is more like nature as a buddy movie.

Tissier couldn't know that *Bifido,* along with other microbes, were not only helping with digestion but were also educating the baby's immune system. Without that basic education the immune system can mistakenly attack beneficial bacteria and even the baby's own cells. That can lead to inflammation and may plant the seed for depression and anxiety as the baby grows. Depression and anxiety can have many roots, but this one may start to grow even before the baby is born.

Tissier was right about *Bifido,* but he was wrong about the sterility of a newborn baby. In his day, it just wasn't possible to see all the microbes that coat almost every surface imaginable. Given what we know today, it seems naive to imagine humans without microbes. Indeed, Pasteur, who spent years fighting bacteria, nonetheless felt that they were essential for the health of all animals. But his was a lonely voice, and in the waning years of the 1800s, researchers tried to prove Pasteur wrong by creating germ-free chickens. It took a decade of failure before Max Schottelius was finally able to breed germ-free chickens, but his results seemed to vindicate Pasteur: All his chickens were sick and could only be made well by inoculating them with bacteria.

A few years later, in 1912, Michel Cohendy was able to raise germ-free chicks by sterilizing the eggs and incubating them in an antiseptic chamber. They lived well for 40 days and proved that it was possible to live germ free. It was a game changer. If chickens could live without them, what good were the bacteria? Perhaps all bacteria *were* pathogenic.

THE DREAM OF A GERM-FREE WORLD

In 1928, Alexander Fleming discovered penicillin, one of the first **antibiotics**. Fleming was a wonderful scientist, but tidiness was not high on his list of strengths. It wasn't unusual for him to take a stack of petri dishes, fuzzed over with bacterial cultures, and shove them into a corner. One day he noticed that an old dish had some mold growing in it. He also saw that all the bacteria around the mold patch were dead. There was a clear moat surrounding the **fungus**. People think that the moment of discovery is marked by shouts of "Eureka!" but more often it is along the lines of what Fleming actually said, which was, "That's funny . . ."

Fleming recognized the mold as *Penicillium,* and he dubbed the substance that created the moat "mold juice," which had a pleasantly humble ring to it. Months later, after further testing, Fleming gave it the more scientific sounding name "penicillin." It turned out to be able to kill a wide range of bacteria. The world began to wonder: Could germs be completely eliminated? The idea of living in a sterilized world—a world free of disease—was tantalizing. People fantasized about a future in which children would be brought up as superkids, liberated by their germ-free environment. Without bacteria, they would never be sick and could live for hundreds of years. It was a vision of purity, a sparkling biological utopia.

The importance of germ-free animals went beyond simply proving Pasteur wrong. It was realized that they might be useful for research as well. Mice and rats are the preferred animals in the lab, but experiments on their microbiota were getting harder to replicate. Even though the mouse strains were carefully specified, different labs kept getting different results. The problem was that each mouse supplier had different chows and thus their mice supported different bacteria. A germ-free mouse could solve the problem.

Germ-free mice were finally created in the 1940s by delivering them via C-section in sterile conditions and then raising them in a sterile environment. From this pedestrian beginning, a world of unexpected biology was spawned. Researchers led by Russell Schaedler were among the first to use the germ-free mice.[4] These mice are understandably difficult to work with, because direct human touch or even a stray puff of air can contaminate them, but their consistency made it worth the trouble.

Success with mice gave researchers the confidence to try germ-free techniques with other animals, and soon there were—as hard as it is to imagine—germ-free farms growing germ-free pigs. But these farms didn't scale well and were ultimately unsuccessful. Microbes, it turns out, are impossible to eliminate on anything remotely farm-size. Out of this, however, came new ways of excluding at least a few pathogens, leading to faster growth of the animals. Over time, even this proved too difficult to maintain. When antibiotics became more broadly available, these experiments were abandoned.

In 1971, the ultimate germ-free animal was created: a human. David Vetter was born with severe combined immunodeficiency (SCID), and his doctors were ready. They had, in fact, anticipated his condition, as his parents had a 50-50 chance of passing down the genetic defect. In an act of remarkable hubris, they convinced the parents to conceive a child, reasoning that a marrow transplant from his sister could cure any SCID. When he was born, however, his sister turned out not to be a match, and David would live the rest of his life in a plastic dome. He became famous as the "boy in the bubble."

The doctors had hoped to learn what happens to germ-free humans, but the setup was not appropriate for any reasonable findings. David didn't take long to realize that he was doomed to be cut off from the world, and he started questioning his life. He was depressed, but whether that was from being germ free or just because he lived in a plastic bubble with no physical human contact is debatable. By the time he was 12, medicine had advanced enough to try a marrow transplant from his sister, even though the match wasn't perfect. Sadly, she had an undetected virus, and within weeks of the transplant, David was dead. In David's final days, his mother was able to touch his skin for the first time in his life.

The public was taken aback by this human experiment that had gone so wrong, and at a stroke, it seemed, we awoke from the dream of a germ-free world. David, freed from germs, was not a superkid. The microbes, it seemed, had won a reprieve.

Much of what we know about the microbiota and its effect on the mind comes from the germ-free (commonly called GF) mice Schaedler and others pioneered. GF mice have become a gold standard, but they have issues, some of which were anticipated. It was well known that animals depended on bacteria to create certain vitamins, so the GF mice needed supplements. But other issues were unexpected: Their cecum, a little pocket off of the colon that normally contains billions of bacteria, swelled up. The phenomenon could be deadly and made it difficult to breed them. Their gut lining was leaky. In addition, due to the lack of challenge by normal bacteria, their immune systems were stunted.

On the up side, they were slim, even when challenged with fatty or sugary diets. This indicated just how important the gut bacteria were to their metabolism. Without microbes to help digest their food, they simply couldn't absorb as many calories as a normal mouse. To compensate, the GF mice needed extra chow.

But before you try a germ-free diet plan, keep in mind that without a microbiota to protect them, GF mice live on a dangerous knife-edge. Whereas it may take a million *Salmonella* bacteria to affect a normal mouse, a GF mouse can be brought down by a single bacterium. Even normal commensals can kill a GF mouse, because there is no community of microbes to balance the population.

Schaedler realized that his GF mice were too problematic for most researchers. They were hard to raise, hard to ship, and not representative of ordinary mice. But there was a workaround: With germ-free mice, you could introduce one microbe at a time, or any given ratio of multiple microbes.

Schaedler developed a mix of bacteria that allowed the mice to develop an immune system that could better defend against arbitrary infections. The mix has changed over the years as scientists have gotten better at culturing bacteria, but the basic idea is the same: These mice have a known microbiota and so are better to experiment with. There are now catalogs of mice fed with specific bacterial mixes for research purposes, making it much easier to compare results across many studies. These mice are called **gnotobiotic** ("known life"). Having only a dozen or so microbes, they are not much more normal than GF mice, but compared with an ordinary lab mouse with thousands of unknown gut species, they are refreshingly simple.

GENES AND THE MICROBIOTA

In the 1980s, when scientists invented a new generation of machines that could pick up every single gene in a blob of microbes, the game changed. Suddenly, you didn't need petri dishes anymore. You could directly detect DNA. It was a paradigm changer. With modern gene sequencers, hundreds of thousands of new genes, many representing brand-new species of bacteria, fungi, and viruses, have been discovered—and many of them have been found on supposedly sterile ground.

In 2004, Nobuyuki Sudo and colleagues published a landmark study with GF and gnotobiotic mice that excited the gut-brain research community.[5] They compared the brains of GF mice with those of normal mice and showed that those of GF mice are different, resulting in an exaggerated response to stress. They also showed that a normal stress reaction could be restored if a healthy microbiota was reconstituted—but only if the reconstitution was done before the mouse was three weeks old. There was a threshold beyond which there was apparently no turning back.

The microbiota, they found, plays an important role in the formation of stress circuits. The study also found that GF mouse brains had a reduction in a molecule that boosts brain cell production, which might lead to cognitive defects. In other words, bacteria appear to play a role in brain development.

The idea that the microbiota could have such an impact on the brain, and that GF mice could be so effective in this line of research, was a game changer. It inspired us to undertake our own research using GF mice. Among other things, our studies showed that levels of serotonin (a "feel-good" brain chemical) in GF mice were elevated to a degree similar to that found with some traditional antianxiety medications.[6] *The idea of manipulating the microbiota to control anxiety became an enticing possibility.*

GF mice are no more natural than the boy in the bubble. They can be content in their sterile world, but it's an unreal world. Natural animals have been prepared by millions of years of coevolution to come to some sort of truce with their inner microbes. But the truth is, as good as the microbiota is at fighting off pathogens, these abilities may come at a price. For all animals, commensal bacteria represent a trade-off: They protect us, but they may also establish a low level of inflammation that leads to an ever smoldering anxiety. There may be no escape from this baseline disquietude that simply reflects a life shared with microbes.

THE BATTLE OF THE MICROBES

From his moldy petri dishes, Fleming had discovered that microbes battle each other and that it's possible to harness this natural antipathy to protect us against infection. But there was a downside. As Fleming learned more about the battle of mold versus bacteria, it became clear that if you didn't have enough penicillin, or if you took it away too quickly, the bacteria became resistant and could no longer be killed by it.

We tend to think of bacterial resistance as a recent phenomenon, but it was well understood within months of the discovery of antibiotics themselves. Fleming made sure to publicize this nasty side effect, but the healing power of antibiotics blinded people to it— and compared to the enormity of the problem that antibiotics solved, resistance seemed a small price to pay.

Resistance or not, penicillin was a fabulous weapon in the war on disease, and its discovery led to hundreds of other antibiotics. It's hard to overestimate their value. Millions of lives have been saved, and untold suffering has been cut short with Fleming's antibiotic "mold juice." Penicillin, along with the hundreds of other antibiotics discovered in its wake, represents one of the biggest breakthroughs in the history of medicine.

But most antibiotics are broad-spectrum, killing a wide variety of microbes. As long as you think all bacteria are bad, that scorched-earth treatment sounds great. But it turns out that most bacteria are not bad. In fact, your good bacteria rival your own immune system when it comes to killing pathogens. Indiscriminate dosing can damage friendly microbes—and we're only now realizing how great that damage can be.

Salmonella, for instance, gets a justifiably bad rap for making people sick. But when your good bacteria are doing their job, you can handle quite a bit of *Salmonella.* After antibiotic treatments, however, you may become defenseless against it. Most of the people who succumb to *Salmonella* infections are people who have an injured microbiota, either from age, disease, or antibiotics. *C. difficile,* another disease-inducing bacteria, is the same: Your normal flora keeps it in check. It's only after antibiotics kill off your good microbes that *C. diff* can really bloom. Similarly, *E. coli* makes the news on a regular basis as a nasty food-borne pathogen, yet it is also found commingling with healthy microbes. Whether a bacterium is considered pathogenic, then, depends a lot on its environment. But when they do act as pathogens, these bacteria can cause anxiety and depression.

It's not just bacterial pathogens that take advantage of an antibiotically compromised gut. Yeasts are notorious for stepping in when commensal bacteria are knocked down. *Candida* is a yeast that loves the intestinal environment. It puts down rootlike tendrils, which, like a weed flourishing in a sidewalk crack, can pry open the spaces between gut cells and cause systemic damage. Under siege by *Candida,* your gut may become pocked with holes and start to leak food bits into your bloodstream. Your immune system may then attack the out-of-place food particles, in the process setting up food allergies, which are often linked to anxiety and depression. It is not uncommon to have allergies disappear when yeast infections are cleared up.

MICROBES AND IMMUNITY

The immune system is the interface where mankind meets microbe. When pathogens invade your body, they can move between your cells or directly into your cells. Your immune system tracks down the extracellular microbes and kills them. It also locates any infected cells, which may contain thousands of bacteria, and kills them— along with their unwelcome tenants.

Bacteria trade genes and mutate so often they might seem to be an elusive target for your immune system. How do you track a shape-shifting microbe? You look for structures that haven't changed. Certain features seem so vital to some species that they have retained them for eons. Humans—and our primate ancestors—have fought some of these pathogens for so long that we've permanently etched the genes for recognizing them into our DNA. That is how your innate immune system works, providing a built-in response to ancient bacterial enemies. Many cell types are involved in the innate response, including the evocatively named **natural killer (NK) cells.** NK cells stab holes into bacteria and pour in toxins, dissolving them or causing them to commit suicide. Many of these antibacterial genes are found in the DNA of all animals—and even plants. That entirely different kingdoms of life share similar immunity genes is striking testimony to the long, nasty but successful history of pathogen infections.

Other bacterial fingerprints are new and have never been seen by your immune system. Bacteria divide quickly, and each division can generate mutations. In the evolutionary race, bacteria leave us in the dust. How can your immune system be expected to keep up? The answer involves what scientists call adaptive immunity.

Adaptive immunity was first recognized some 2,500 years ago, during the Plague of Athens. In the middle of a war with Sparta, Athens was afflicted by a plague, probably typhus, which wiped out some 20 percent of the population. Death was typically quick, taking about a week, but some people survived. It was soon discovered that those who survived were no longer susceptible to the disease and, thus protected, were conscripted to take care of the others. This was a perfect example of adaptive immunity where, once exposed, the body remembers a pathogen and can then quickly flush it out of the system. Because it takes time to learn about a novel pathogen, the adaptive system is not as fast as the innate system upon first contact. But after the initial schooling, both systems are marvels of rapid deployment.

The first instance of adaptive immunity could be called the immunological big bang. Some half a billion years ago, a lamprey-like fish developed something called jumping genes. These are genes that can move from one spot to another in your DNA. This is somewhat disconcerting: DNA is supposed to be stable; it's how we maintain our species while passing down traits to our children. But jumping genes occur often in nature, and one of them found its way into one of these ancient fish.

This jumping gene happened to plunk down into the middle of the genes that make **antibodies**, the Y-shaped molecular tool of immunity. The bottom post of this molecule is typically attached to an immune cell, while the top part of the Y has a kind of microscopic Velcro that sticks to a specific type of bacteria. That specificity is limiting: You need a new gene for each microbe, which is pretty much impossible. And then jumping genes came to the rescue. Suddenly, instead of making a single antibody, the jumping gene allowed millions of variations to be created.

All cells—from human cells to bacteria—have a peach-fuzzy surface composed of short strands of sugar and protein molecules. These help the cells to communicate, to stick to other cells, or just to provide support. But these membrane molecules also expose cells to discovery by immune factors. These foreign molecules are called **antigens**, which trigger an immune response. Some of the most potent antigens come from the cell walls of pathogenic bacteria.

This is where the antibody variations come in. With millions of different shapes, one or more of these variations are bound to fit a pathogenic antigen. When they do, they stick to the antigen, and sometimes that's enough to disable it on the spot. Other antibodies act like flags that say, "Eat me," and they cause their victims to get swept up by other immune cells and consumed. These interactions represent the way the body's immune system responds to disease-inducing antagonists.

Immunity, when it works, is a marvelous balancing act, able to distinguish friend from foe, ready to eradicate never-before-seen pathogens, but at the same time, warmly welcoming a wide variety of beneficial bacteria. Importantly, it has to refrain from attacking your own cells as well. But how can immune cells recognize your own cells? The interesting answer is that they learn it in self-school. After coming up with a novel, randomly created antibody, a juvenile immune cell is screened against a library of human markers. This happens with **B cells** in the bone marrow and **T cells** in the thymus, a gland under your breastbone. Immune cells that bind to any part of this human library may be sent back to the randomizer for a new set of antibodies—or they may be killed. In this way, any of the random antibodies that stick to your own cells are filtered out. The rare ones that escape this screening process are dangerous: They can cause autoimmune diseases, like multiple sclerosis or rheumatoid arthritis, with attendant depression.

Something fortuitous came along with jumping genes: immune memory. Certain immune cells, namely those that managed to produce effective antibodies, end up being kept around by your immune system. The next time the same pathogen shows up, these cells are recruited, whereupon they multiply rapidly and quickly shut down the attack. This is the origin of the adage, "What doesn't kill you makes you stronger." Indeed, you are far better protected the next time around, which is also the theory underlying vaccines: A dose of a killed pathogen will cause a memory to be stored by your immune system, ready to spring into action with a repeat appearance. You can still get infected, but you'll clear it up so fast you may not even notice it.

BAD-GUY MICROBES

Some bacteria are irredeemably bad. Syphilis is one of them. Most people know that Europeans took many diseases with them when they explored the New World in the 1400s. Fewer people know that some diseases went the other way. Syphilis was apparently carried back to Europe by none other than Christopher Columbus. The bacterium responsible is called *Treponema pallidum,* and it started out far nastier than it is today. Pustules would break out all over the victims' bodies, and their flesh would start to rot off. Death mercifully claimed its sufferers within months.

Bacteria that kill their hosts quickly have less of a chance to spread, and mutations that moderate their virulence tend to take over. By the mid-1500s, the disease had evolved into what we recognize today as syphilis. If left untreated, it can cause mental issues including irritability, memory problems, and depression. *Treponema pallidum* thus became one of the first bacteria known to influence mental health and mood. It would not be until the successful manufacture of penicillin during WWII that syphilis was finally brought to heel.

To this day, new examples of bacteria implicated in depression are being discovered. In May 2000, the town of Walkerton, Ontario, was flooded after a heavy rain. The town's water supply became contaminated with *E. coli* and *Campylobacter jejuni* from a nearby farm. More than two thousand of the townsfolk became seriously ill. Six people died. The town basically shut down. And then it was noticed that hundreds of these people, after recovering from their original infections, came down with IBS. They also became depressed.

Stephen Collins, a professor at McMaster University in Hamilton, Ontario, took the two-hour drive to Walkerton to see if there was a way to snatch some good research out of the misery. Collins and his colleagues followed the infected people and found some genetic changes that seemed to be persistent. These people had leaky guts and abnormalities in the genes that are supposed to recognize pathogens. Because their genes had been affected, Collins realized that they could be dealing with a chronic condition—a kind of semipermanent environmental change to DNA that is called **epigenetic**.

For eight years researchers followed this group of unlucky Canadians and found that many continued to have intractable IBS.

Collins recognized this as postinfectious IBS, which was first seen in soldiers who had picked up dysentery during World War II. About one-eighth of IBS cases start this way, and, ironically, those who are treated with antibiotics fare the worst, long-term. Collins also discovered a significant association between IBS and the mental conditions of depression and anxiety.[7]

Interestingly, Collins found that preexisting depression doubled the risk of contracting IBS. This observation underlined the dual nature of the gut-brain dialogue. In some ways, it acts like a positive feedback loop, a vicious cycle that can be hard to break. The initial infection causes the immune system to move swiftly to eradicate the offending bacteria. But in some people, the immune response fails to wind down after eliminating the pathogens, leading to IBS. We'll discuss the Walkerton epidemic in greater detail later in the book because it vividly demonstrates how bacteria can, over a period of time, induce depression.

Collins was joined in the research project by Premysl Bercik, also of McMaster University. Bercik took fecal matter from IBS patients and transplanted it into mice. The mice subsequently developed anxiety-like behavior, demonstrating that gut microbiota can affect mental states and that, intriguingly, these states can be transferred from one animal to another—even one species to another.

Bercik also tried fecal transplants between mice with specific behavioral traits and found that some of those traits transferred with the feces. When they took feces from an exploratory mouse and transferred it into a timid mouse, exploratory behavior transferred, too. It was another early indication that behavior and mood can be affected by gut microbiota. The idea that anxiety can be transmitted via fecal transplant took most scientists completely by surprise.

LEARNING TO LIVE WITH YOUR MICROBES

It's hard to overstate how important friendly microbes are to your health. They cover every inch of your skin and are particularly numerous in your colon. We're talking about *pounds* of bacteria, tens of trillions of the tiny creatures, but that's what it takes to protect us from the even greater numbers of microbes that surround us.

Like the bubble boy, you could take away all of your bacteria and still survive. Outside your bubble, however, you wouldn't like it much. Those missing bacteria were your first line of defense against pathogens; without their protection, you would constantly be sick. You wouldn't be germ free for long, but without a balanced microbiota, those germs would be mostly pathogenic. Even if you scrubbed every last microbe off your skin and flushed all the microbes from your gut, you would still be permeated with bacteria, because they can also live *inside* your cells. It isn't easy to get inside a cell, but once ensconced, life can be pretty good for a microbe. Without a bubble to live in, you would be unlikely to make it past infancy. This is germ warfare, and you need a balanced microbiota to even stand a chance.

There is another, very important way in which you coexist with bacteria. Because your good microbes fight the bad microbes, you need to tell your immune system to leave your good guys alone. This happens early in life, before you are two years old, as your microbiota primes your immune system and tells cells called regulatory T cells to accept a core group of microbes as part of your gut population. These commensals insinuate themselves intimately with your immune system. Some of them, for instance, produce **butyrate**—a fatty acid that is a preferred food of the cells lining your colon, which induces your immune system to calm down. We have made hundreds of beneficial arrangements like this with our microbiota over millions of years of partnership. It has been a wildly successful enterprise, but not without a few glitches here and there.

Thus, the education of your immune system is one of the first jobs of a healthy microbiota. Without that tutoring, your immune system would destroy *all* your bacteria, not just the pathogens. From the time you are born, your bacteria gain the grudging acceptance of your immune system, which learns not to go on high alert when it sees a few isolated *E. coli*. This schooling lasts until you are weaned, and then your immune system seems to get pretty well locked in.

For invaders never seen before, your adaptive system is at the ready with hunter and killer cells constantly on call. Regulatory cells called T-regs keep these hyperactive immune cells at bay and exert a calming effect on them. Under the right circumstances, a T-reg exposed to a commensal bacterium can learn to accept it. It's a long-lived lesson, and these T-regs will protect your good bacteria for life. An educated T-reg tells your immune system that, when it comes to your commensals, these are not the bacteria it is looking for.[8]

Some bacteria are host-specific, and not all human commensals properly educate the mouse immune system.[9] Nevertheless, there is still more commonality between animal-bacterial relationships than difference, and several studies have shown that most human microbes perform as expected when transferred to mice.[10]

In our lab, we collected fecal samples from 34 depressed human patients and 33 healthy controls. We found that the microbiota of the patients with depression was less diverse than the controls.

46

We then transferred these samples to rats. The rats that received fecal matter from depressed patients showed symptoms of depression and anxiety, while the controls did not. This suggested to us that the microbiota may play a causal role in the development of depression, and might present a target for treatment and prevention of this disorder.[11]

Animal studies such as these indicate a significant association between microbiota and mood, whether you are a rodent or a human. If you don't properly educate your immune system, you could constantly be hitting the alarm and attacking your normal commensals. That seems to be a major factor underlying GI issues like IBD.[12] It may happen from bad early immune training or, as happened to the people of Walkerton, from a major infection that somehow messes with immune memory. If your immune system is continuously on alert, you'll develop chronic inflammation, which can lead to depression and anxiety.

Bacteria are not only on your skin and in your guts: They are embedded in your very flesh. Some of them are there to take advantage of a warm cell. Others are there to kill you. And yet, without some of them, you could die. You likely have a thousand different species of bacteria living in and on you right now. Some of them are the first line of defense against pathogens—the *really* nasty bacteria. Bacteria produce toxins, mostly to kill off competing microbes. We are sometimes innocent victims of the cross fire, and the result can range from inconvenience to incontinence. The amount and severity of the toxin is one of the markers that distinguish friendly commensal bacteria from pathogens.

In this book, you will read about many species of bacteria, but two major genera will grab the spotlight: *Bifidobacteria* and *Lactobacillus.* We've already nicknamed the first genus *Bifido,* and here

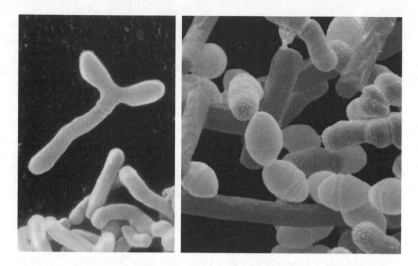

Y-shaped Bifidobacteria *(left) and yogurt bacteria including rod-shaped* Lactobacillus *(right) are proven psychobiotics and some of the first bacteria a baby consumes.*

we name the second genus *Lacto*. They will often be shortened to the first letter when we talk about different species, like *B. breve* for *Bifidobacterium breve* or *L. acidophilus* for *Lactobacillus acidophilus*. (If these two sound familiar, it is because they are popular in many fermented foods, especially yogurt.)

When you are born, *Bifido* species predominate, but over time, *Lacto* species start to take over. These two genera are largely considered to be probiotics, and research is also showing them to have psychobiotic properties as well. Over time, humans have welcomed these and other beneficial bacteria. They serve us well—they help us produce important vitamins, like B$_{12}$ and K—but by depending on them, we often leave ourselves vulnerable to their whims. If we don't make proper accommodations for the good microbes, we may suffer the consequences, not only GI problems but also depression, anxiety, psychosis, and dementia. As much as microbes seem to have the upper hand, however, we are still nominally in charge. The diet you choose, as you will learn, goes far to determine which bacteria you end up living with.

VIRAL COMPLICATIONS

Viruses vastly outnumber bacteria in the gut. Some viruses, called **bacteriophages** (or just phages), can destroy bacteria. In fact, phage therapy has been used for decades as a type of antibiotic treatment. They can also cause benign bacteria to go rogue. The toxins for diphtheria, pertussis, botulism, Shiga, and cholera are all virally induced. Sometimes viruses just modify behavior in bacteria. *E. coli* can be infected by a phage, for example, that helps it to stick to your cheek and form plaques. Other viruses cause bacteria to invade the cells lining your gut.

Despite their many influences, viruses are poorly understood. Whereas plants, animals, and bacteria can be neatly categorized into family trees, viruses are harder to sort out. Part of the reason is that they have a tendency toward promiscuity. They can pick up a gene from one bacterium and then inject it into a completely unrelated microbe. This is called transduction, or horizontal gene transfer. This makes these DNA-swapping viruses difficult to classify because many of their genes are not really their genes at all. This gives viruses a surprising amount of leverage in the evolution of life.

Gene transfer doesn't just happen to bacteria, but to all creatures, usually mediated by a virus. If it happens to a sperm or an egg cell in an animal, that gene will get passed on to the next generation. If it turns out to be useful, it can become a permanent change, handed off to succeeding generations. In your own DNA you will find hundreds of these viral genes, and by comparing the viral genes in other related species, you can even figure out when these additions were made. For instance, if a viral gene is found in the DNA of both humans and chimps, then it must have been added before the two species split, at least five million years ago.

Viruses can also act as a kind of backup mechanism, although not always to our benefit. When you dose yourself improperly with antibiotics, you may fall victim to *antibiotic resistance*, in that the bacteria that aren't killed outright become immune to the antibiotics. Viruses play a role here as well. They can transfer antibiotic resistance genes from completely different species into the besieged bacteria. This neat trick means that bacteria can run lean most of the time, with a minimal gene kit, and then count on viral messengers to replenish them with antibacterial resistance in times of need.

Because of this genetic plasticity, it can be hard to pin down not only viruses but also what we mean by a bacterial species. Today we use DNA testing as a definitive fingerprint for identifying bacteria, but what does that mean if viruses can ferry DNA between cells with apparent abandon?

YOU ARE A UNIQUE ECOSYSTEM

Everyone presents a distinctive environment for bacteria to colonize. You may have genetic inclinations that affect your gut environment. We each have a unique exposure to bacteria through dirt, pets, food, and other aspects of our environment. So your microbiota is as unique to you as your fingerprints. This is why it's unlikely that any single probiotic or psychobiotic will work for everyone. You will need to experiment to see what works best for you.

You have at least one hundred times more microbial genes than human genes. Each gene codes for a protein, and each protein contributes to the functioning of both the microbe and the human. Their collective efforts and the ways they interact represent an astounding complexity. Not everyone gets the best assortment. Some people are stuck with bad microbes that may plague them for their entire life. Some of these bacterial genes may predispose you to depression or anxiety. This is your baseline allotment, and it is tricky (but not impossible) to change it.

As odd as it seems to group your genes with those of your microbiota, there is good reason to do so. The world is full of bacteria on every surface we touch and in every morsel we bite, and they are evolving at a head-spinning rate; your hardwired human defenses are simply incapable of keeping up. While you read that last sentence, several completely novel bacterial strains likely popped up somewhere in or on your body. The only way to fight such a shape-shifting foe is to recruit your own shape-shifters.

That is the origin of our microbiota, and it has been passed down from our ancestors, along with our human DNA, mostly from mothers, not fathers. For millennia, we have coevolved with our friendly microbes, passing them down with birth and bringing them with us when we travel the world. We hang on to a core population while we simultaneously let a certain percentage of them change quickly, day by day, with each new meal and with each new living circumstance. This is the deal we made long ago: We will supply them a place to live, and they will help us fend off the nasty vagaries of the world. It's a two-way street. We depend on our microbes, but they also depend on us. Our commensal microbes are now so associated with us and so dependent on us that many of them can live nowhere else on the planet but in and on our human bodies. If it weren't for our microbial inheritance, they would become extinct. And if it weren't for their protective abilities, so would we.

THE MAJOR MICROBIAL PLAYERS

There are 100 trillion bacteria in your gut, composed of at least 500 species. The bulk of them, some 98 percent, come from about 40 species divided into just four big groups (phyla). Their relative predominance in the human microbiota is represented by the following percentages. Bacteria in gray are typically pathogenic. Bacteria in boldface are the major psychobiotics.

Firmicutes		64%
	Lactobacillus	
	Streptococcus	
	Staphylococcus	
	Enterococcus (E. faecalis)	
	Faecalibacterium prausnitzii	
	Clostridia (C. difficile)	
Bacteroidetes		23%
	Bacteroides	
	Prevotella	
	Alistipes	
Proteobacteria		8%
	Enterobacteriaceae (Salmonella, E. coli, Klebsiella, Shigella)	
	Campylobacter (C. jejuni)	
Actinobacteria		3%
	Bifidobacteria	
TOTAL		98%

With modern civilization's highly processed foods, broad-spectrum antibiotics, and enhanced hygiene, we may be tipping the balance away from this long-term association—and actually placing that relationship in danger. It is possible that this microbial shift underpins the swift and otherwise inexplicable increases in obesity, autoimmune diseases, depression, anxiety, and many other health problems that we see today.

You are not a single creature, but rather a collection. Many of your most human aspects—your moods, your cravings, even the shape of your body, may actually be crafted by your microbes. It's a little humbling, but with this knowledge comes the chance to reassert control. To do that, you'll need to learn the language of the microbes.

HOW MICROBES ORDER PIZZA

Bacteria can talk to you. The intricacies of this conversation make the Internet look quaint. There are 4 billion Internet users, but you have 10 *trillion* bacteria in your gut alone that are all sending messages to each other—and to you. Your gut can talk to your brain using several biological networks, but we don't always get a clear channel. Your brain can talk back to your gut through these same channels. Only a tenth of your nerves are dedicated to this back channel, but it represents an important additional technique (along with psychobiotics) to help you gain control over the microbes in your gut.

Studies have shown that cognitive behavioral therapy (CBT) can help people suffering from IBS. Research is under way to determine what the mechanism is behind this intriguing brain-gut connection. It is exciting to think that we could solve our gut issues with talk therapy, thereby improving our gut, reducing inflammation, and resulting in even greater improvements in mental health—a virtuous cycle. A vicious cycle can also be established: Stress can negatively impact your gut microbiota, which in turn can make you more anxious. As well as stress, brain damage can also disturb your microbiota, which can affect your recovery from stroke and injury.[13]

Techniques for "talking back" to your microbiota are the crux of our story. You can change the composition of your gut overnight, just by eating different foods. This is a natural consequence of the extreme plasticity of your microbiota, which can reorganize itself in minutes to deal with novel foods. In the coming chapters, you will discover more about your intimate relationship with your microbiota, and more importantly, how you can control that association to mitigate depression and anxiety.

Gut microbes produce all manner of chemicals to talk with each other and to your gut; that information is relayed to your brain primarily via the **vagus nerve**, which is a long wandering nerve from the brain to all your bodily organs. The problem with this communication is that it has very few words. It's mostly "okay, okay, okay, hungry, hungry, full, okay, okay . . ."

You are designed so that many of your systems—like your heart, lungs, and gut—are on autopilot. You only know what's going on down there when you have a major problem. But you can tune in to the subtler signals coming from your gut. Your microbiota has needs and over your lifetime has learned how to tell you about them. When you wake up craving a doughnut, where do you think that idea came from? Your cravings are often just committee memos sent up from your gut microbes. They contain a complete list of the carbs, sugars, and fats they are looking for.

Here's an example of how that works. Some microbes, especially our friendly *Bifido* species, produce butyrate, which feeds and heals the lining of your gut. Butyrate can make its way to the brain, where it can induce a good mood, dampen inflammation,[14] or encourage the production of a brain-growth hormone.[15] All these changes can improve your mood and even help you to think better.

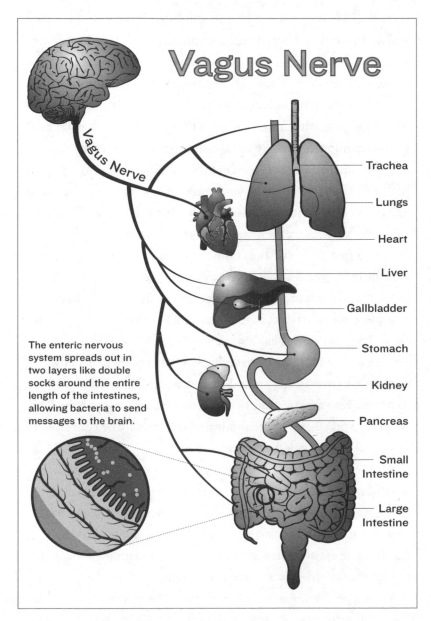

Vagus Nerve

Vagus Nerve

Trachea

Lungs

Heart

Liver

Gallbladder

Stomach

Kidney

Pancreas

Small Intestine

Large Intestine

The enteric nervous system spreads out in two layers like double socks around the entire length of the intestines, allowing bacteria to send messages to the brain.

The vagus nerve is a major two-way conduit between your brain and your internal organs, including your gut.

Your *Bifido* thrive on the fiber in your diet. If you feed them fiber and find your mood improving, over time you will start to yearn for the fiber that makes you feel good. That is a simple Pavlovian way to create a craving. Your *Bifido* has conditioned you to feed it. It's not just butyrate. Some bacteria, like *Lacto* species, go even further. In studies with people suffering from IBS, it was found that some *Lacto* species actually manipulate the opioid and cannabinoid receptors in the brain, acting almost like a shot of morphine.[16] Like the addiction to a runner's high, this kind of reaction can lead to cravings for whatever food your *Lacto* microbes prefer. You might think your cravings are all in your mind, but chances are they begin with the bacteria in your gut.

Germ-free mice like sugar more than conventional mice, and their taste receptors are altered to crave it.[17] Sugar is an exceptional energy source, but conventional mice have a diverse microbiota that requires other important food sources that compete with sugar, like fat and protein. In this light, sugar cravings can be seen as a consequence of a dysbiotic gut. That is likely related to the sugar cravings of people in mental hospitals. Sugar cravings have also been seen in people who are stressed.[18] This could be an attempt by the body to load up on energy-dense foods that can quickly be converted to muscle action, a typical stress response.

Cravings undergo a major change in people who have gotten a stomach bypass to lose weight. They have a completely different microbiota and brand-new cravings.[19] In fact, much of the weight loss attributed to a smaller stomach is actually due to other factors, including changing tastes. Studies are starting to indicate that much of that may be due to the altered microbiota.

Each type of bacteria has its own food preferences. Bacteroidetes have a thing for fat, *Prevotella* enjoy carbs, and *Bifido* are fiber lovers. They each have their own way of asking for an appropriate meal, and they also have ways of thanking you.

Some bacteria don't go for subtlety. Many species of *E. coli* are model citizens in the gut, but others are strictly pathogenic, such as *enterohemorrhagic E. coli* (EHEC). As long as enough sugar is around to placate it, EHEC will play well with your other gut buddies. But if the sugar runs out, EHEC turns rogue and digs in to your gut lining, potentially causing bloody diarrhea.[20] That's a terrible way to ring the dinner bell, but it gets your attention. If you have EHEC, candy actually acts like a medicine.

This kind of behavior is called bacterial virulence. *Shigella flexneri* is another microbe that complains about a lack of sugar by becoming virulent.[21] These are pathogens, but the same principles seem to apply to commensal bacteria as well. If they don't get what they want, they can make a fuss. When that happens, you may not know it directly, but they have ways of making you uncomfortable until you give them what they want. It's that funky feeling that makes you suddenly crave a candy bar or other snack. You may not know why, but you know there is a bonbon-size hole in your gut, and it quickly becomes your job to fill it.

For such tiny, simple creatures, bacteria have an astonishing array of tricks. If your gut is healthy, there will be a cosmopolitan bustle of microbes with no one species dominating. That means that no one species can exert too much control. A dysbiotic gut, on the other hand, has less diversity. A few domineering microbes can rule the land, calling out orders for specific foods on a regular basis. You may be able to override these cravings with your superior willpower, but your microbes won't go down without a fight.

Our cravings seem like an integral part of our psyche. We are chocolate lovers, we are pizza people, we are meat and potato eaters. As long as we feel it's part of our personality, we are unlikely to make any changes. That's just who we are. But when you think of your cravings as microbial longings, it may be easier for you to take back control.

57

TAKE CHARGE OF YOUR MICROBIOTA

Have you ever been told that "It's all in your mind"? That is often the distressing medical attitude toward patients who have issues that vaguely involve the gut but definitely affect the mind. There's a limit to what doctors can test for, and if your disease doesn't bubble up out of that test suite, you're in head-scratching territory. Good doctors will admit that they just don't know. If you have such doctors, count your blessings and never let them go. But other doctors might tell you it's psychosomatic—all in your head. If they cannot diagnose it, you must be making it up.

In fact, some kind of microbiota assessment would be a good adjunct to any medical exam—and any psych exam as well. The reality being revealed by psychobiotic research is that many issues we think of as purely mental are actually directly related to gut dysbiosis. Unfortunately, there are still very few tools to probe the health of your microbiota, so it can be difficult to demonstrate that something real is at work and that it's not just your imagination. Recent work done at the University of California, San Diego, has shown that a computer can discriminate healthy from dysbiotic guts, so help may soon be on the way.[22] In the meantime, you may just have to take this assessment into your own hands—and this book will help you.

Many of the personality quirks that you think of as "just the way you are" may actually be vague messages from your gut. They affect your mood, even if you cannot put your finger on their origin. Realizing what is brewing in your gut—and how much influence your microbiota has—gives you the upper hand. Your microbes may outnumber your own cells, but you can outsmart them. Besides, that mass of microbes has been your constant partner since you were about the age of three. Without really knowing it, you've figured out how to feed your particular beasts and integrated them into your life. If you're healthy, that is working for you.

But if you're feeling depressed, anxious, or just plain funky, it's very likely your gut that's behaving badly—and you *can* do something about it. You can change the composition of your gut bacteria just by feeding the good guys and starving the bad. That doesn't mean that the old regime won't try to reassert itself, because it will. Isolated pathogens can hide out in every crevice of your gut. They are always going to cry out, but you can choose to ignore that smooth-talking request for a candy bar and show your gut who's the boss. In the following chapters, you'll learn how to take back the reins.

CHAPTER 3

YOUR MICROBIOTA, FROM BIRTH TO DEATH

"My mother groaned, my father wept:

into the dangerous world I leapt."

–William Blake

YOUR INVOLVEMENT WITH MICROBES STARTS EARLY AND changes dramatically as you grow. This chapter follows you and your microbiota from a gleam in your parents' eyes to the bitter end. It is a surprising relationship that, like all good ones, gets richer with time.

FROM EGG TO BLASTOCYST

In the ovary, at the beginning of menstruation, a dozen or so eggs start to grow, in anticipation of fertilization. One of them is destined to become *you*. Each egg is swaddled in its own follicle, a structure in the ovary that is a Russian doll of different cell layers, one inside the other.

From the moment these eggs start jockeying for position, they secrete estrogen to prime the uterus for when a sperm finds its target. The estrogen also makes its way through the circulatory system to the *hypothalamus,* a part of the brain that controls much of the autonomic nervous system, including mood. The hypothalamus communicates with the woman's pituitary to produce other hormones, like luteinizing hormone (LH). The estrogen is also picked up by her microbiota. After some four million years of partnership,[1] the mother's body and certain gut bacteria have worked out a way to recycle estrogen. A dysbiotic gut may not respond properly to the estrogen, which can lead to problems down the road for both mother and child.

Over the next five days, the selected follicle that cradles future-you goes into overdrive, growing and swelling with fluids. At the same time, it puts out another surge of estrogen, once again driving the hypothalamus to secrete more hormones into the bloodstream. At some point, these hormones start to affect the microbiota of the vagina, favoring *Lactobacillus* species, and the pH starts to dip as lactic acid is produced. This is one of the first stages of the maternal microbial preparation, which culminates in your mother's passing on your microbial inheritance.

The ovary, meanwhile, is bulging with the selected follicle. In a feedback loop, the LH that the pituitary secreted causes the egg to burst out of its follicle where, alarmingly, it finds itself floating freely in your mother's abdomen. Fortunately for the drifting egg, finger-like projections from the nearby fallopian tubes fan the area to sweep up the tiny ovum. If all goes well, the egg is gently ushered into the fallopian tube. There, both cilia and peristaltic motion push the egg down the tube and toward the uterus. It has only a day or so to find a mate, or it will be shed, along with the special uterine lining that was set up to receive it.

In the middle of all this plumbing—if all goes well—a sperm cell shows up. Although your dad only gets a cameo in this story, his sperm comes with an entourage of bacteria. Seminal fluid turns out to be ideal culture media. It has a fairly neutral pH and it's chock-full of carbs. Bacteria love it, and they splash around with sperm in the same fluid.[2] It's an open question how much these bacteria contribute to your future microbiota. There is telling evidence of a connection between the seminal microbiota and the vaginal microbiota of sexually active couples, and this may be the one way a father can pass down his microbiota to his children.

When the sperm and egg finally meet up, it's not exactly intimate. The sperm has to elbow its way into the egg proper. Microbes, good and bad, may join the nuptials. There are plenty of reasons for eggs and sperm to not hit it off, and one of them may be a microbial incompatibility, also known to underlie some couples' infertility. For these people, a dose of antibiotics can often clear the way for making babies.

In this area of study, as in many others, scientists have used fruit flies as research subjects. In one study, when female fruit flies were given antibiotics, their sex appeal evaporated. Male flies lost all interest. But when a healthy microbiota was reestablished, the males perked up and copulated in earnest. In a classic study in 1989, Diane Dodd took these findings a step further. She separated flies into two groups. One group was raised on maltose and the other group on starch. When these two populations were allowed to mix, the maltose flies preferred to mate with other maltose flies, and the starch flies similarly chose other starch flies.[3] Eugene Rosenberg and his colleagues extended this study to show that the flies' sexual preference was due to their unique microbiotas; when they were given antibiotics, those preferences disappeared.[4] This result tells an important story: Microbes can affect mating choice.

When the sperm fertilizes the egg, you become a zygote with a brand-new mix of chromosomes. A similar mixing may be happening with the contributing microbes. So far our love story seems more like a war epic. In the process of making you so far, nature has killed off dozens of eggs, billions of sperm, and trillions of bacteria. It's an untidy process that plays out as a form of evolution, writ small.

Thank goodness for those of us with a Y chromosome, we are essential to the process. But this is pretty much the only positive contribution your dad will make to the growing embryo. In many animals, including some worms, aphids, wasps, fish, amphibians, and reptiles, the male is actually optional. If one isn't around, the mother can execute the whole business on her own in a process called parthenogenesis. If you had any doubts about why it is called Mother Nature and not Father Nature, this should dispel them.

As a fertilized egg, you continue your trip down the fallopian tube, where you start to split into multiple embryonic stem cells. To stay on course, you are encouraged by waving cilia. Soon, you arrive and implant yourself in the lining of your mother's uterus. At this point, you are no longer a simple fertilized egg; you have become a blastocyst.

MAKING A PLACENTA

Thus ensconced, you start to create a placenta. Here again, a microbiota of sorts seems to establish itself, although many scientists suspect these bacteria are pathogenic only. After all, the womb has long been thought of as a citadel designed to protect the vulnerable fetus from exactly this kind of contamination. A big surprise here is that the bacterial load, which is fairly light, seems to have originated from your mother's mouth and may contain pathogens. How these bacteria travel to the placenta is a mystery, although researchers speculate that they come from your mother's blood, which typically contains small amounts of mouth bacteria. Every time someone brushes their teeth—especially if their gums are bleeding—a small dose of these microbes leaks into the bloodstream. Studies on placental microbes are somewhat controversial, and so we need to maintain some skepticism that these bacteria might be beneficial.

Still, it's clear that any woman considering pregnancy should take good care of her mouth. Because the colonization of the placenta can happen early, it is important to clear up any gingivitis or periodontal disease *before* pregnancy begins. At this point in life, the proper cultivation of the baby's gut bacteria may be a life-or-death proposition. This is one of the first turning points in the development of a baby's microbiota, and it can have long-term consequences.

The discovery of *E. coli* in the baby's meconium is a strong indicator that somewhere along the line, the baby is getting exposed to microbes and the uterus is a plausible place for this exposure. Interestingly, the mouth-to-womb connection may go both ways; pregnancy may induce changes in the oral microbiota of the mother. As pregnancy proceeds, the populations of oral bacteria climb, and their composition changes.[5] Perhaps the uterus designates the task of recruiting beneficial bacteria to the mouth, which then sends the approved recruits back to the womb. This may be a primary way that what a mother eats during pregnancy can have an effect on the baby. A lack of protein, for example, can lead to problems that can last into adulthood.[6] The connections between a mother's microbiota and her baby's health are still being worked out.[7]

DECLARING GENDER

....

We like to think of embryos as little people, but they're not. Embryos, for instance, have twice the reproductive plumbing, containing both female and male precursors to reproductive organs. Genetically, an embryo is destined to be male or female, but physically, the embryo is ready to swing either way. From a biological perspective, you are a hermaphrodite for the first two months of your life.

How this plays out may be important to your future mental health. Many mental issues, from depression and anxiety to autism, are sexually biased. Men are four times as likely to have antisocial personality disorder or autism, while women are almost twice as likely to have depression.[8] These gender differences are poorly understood, but they clearly have a big impact on the brain.

Meanwhile, at this stage of pregnancy, your mother's gut microbiota is changing to accommodate feeding you. Remarkably, these changes look a lot like metabolic syndrome, a kind of prediabetes, inducing weight gain and insulin resistance.[9] Between the first and third trimester, the number of bacterial species drops and those that remain seem to favor putting on fat. This means that there must be some kind of mechanism that prods the gut microbiota toward extracting extra energy from food to take care of you. The same mechanism, triggered at the wrong time, could lead to obesity, gut dysbiosis, and even type 2 diabetes.

For the next eight or nine months, you incubate, feeding on maternal blood containing immune cells and antibodies—and possibly being exposed to a weak microbial soup. Mysteries abound about the extent of the bacterial inoculation in these early stages of human development. Exactly how much exposure you get to microbes and what kind of microbes they are—even whether they are beneficial or pathogenic—will be discovered by new research in the next decade. Much of it will be indirect knowledge, because performing experiments on healthy babies, much less developing embryos, is understandably off-limits.

The idea that beneficial microbes could be passed down by mothers is shocking to many doctors and scientists, who have long held that any bacteria associated with embryos are universally pathogenic and can result in preterm birth. But these days, researchers keep finding microbes wherever they look. It may not be just the placenta that harbors bacteria, either: Even in completely normal babies, investigators have found evidence of bacteria in the umbilical cord,[10] amniotic fluid,[11] fetal membranes,[12] and meconium.[13]

BIRTH

Next up: birth. Here it gets real; you are moments away from bursting out of your amniotic sac and into a world crawling with microbes. You get a healthy dose of bacteria while being squeezed down the birth canal. Your mother developed a distinctive vaginal microbiota as pregnancy proceeded. Certain *Lactobacillus* species became dominant, and the population became less diverse, which might be a way to minimize your exposure to bacteria that are not relevant to your gut. You are swathed in this bacterial blanket before you ever poke your head out of the womb.

The amniotic bubble having popped, you become exposed to the world. On this big day everything is cold, dry, and infectious. You, of course, are naked. You have no real consciousness yet, and you won't remember this day, but you know enough to cry.

Birthing can be an untidy business, and you may pick up your mother's fecal bacteria as well. Many animals pass on their microbes through mother's poop. This is your first legacy, a microbial starter kit, pre-owned and passed down from your mom, her mother, and her mother before her. Unless you get violently ill or end up on an antibiotic regimen in the first days of your existence, your body will form a memory of this first bacterial initiation that will likely last for the rest of your life. This bacterial appetizer is there, among other reasons, to teach your immune system what to expect. Because it comes from your mom, if she's in good health, you'll have a head start on life.

If you were born by cesarean, you missed a lot of that messy stuff. Instead, you were whisked away to a nursery where you picked up a bacterial population unique to your nurse's skin and your hospital. Depending on the hospital, that can be a bad thing— or a terrible thing.

Some studies have shown that children delivered by C-section may lack important *Bacteroides* species for up to the first 18 months of life, making them more likely to suffer from asthma and allergies. New studies suggest that babies born by C-section react differently to stress, and may even be more susceptible to depression and anxiety—all hypothetically correlated to gut and microbiota health.[14] Not all studies are so downbeat, though: New research has shown that at around six weeks, the microbiota of most of these children has normalized,[15] with some of that due to breast-feeding.

There are also known differences between the gut bacteria of full-term babies and preemies, which may reflect the microbiota in the mother's placenta or the amount of time the baby spends in the womb. After birth, the mother's vaginal microbiota undergoes a rapid and significant change, dropping the *Lacto* species that had multiplied during pregnancy. These changes persist for up to a year after pregnancy.[16]

WIRING THE BRAIN

As a newborn, you cannot talk, and most of what happens to you won't be remembered. That's probably for the best. Birth is traumatic. But your brain is rapidly sprouting neural branches while simultaneously pruning them, and challenges to the brain at this early stage can profoundly alter development.

The reason you don't remember anything before you were six months old is partly related to the insulation on the wiring of your brain. **Neurons** are brain cells that act a little bit like wires, in that they conduct electrical signals. Like wires, they need to be insulated or they can short-circuit. That insulation is provided by layers of fatty myelin. A lot of that myelination happens in the womb, but the process isn't completed by the time you're born. Before myelin fully develops and wraps around the neurons, signals are slow and flooded with cross talk, and it's unlikely that you can either lay down memories or retrieve them. Your brain is still a work in progress.

The myelination proceeds from the center of your brain to the outer layers over a period of several years. It's like a stain slowly spreading from the core brain stem out. As a consequence of this continuing construction work, people cannot remember anything that happened to them before the age of three, although there may be exceptions. Salvador Dali said he could remember living in the womb, but Dali also had a famously active imagination. It's not that you don't have a memory at that age; you do. It just isn't being laid down with much permanence. Newborns can remember certain things like colors and simple shapes for up to 24 hours, but not much longer.

As you get older, the duration of your memories increases, but by the end of your first week, you've likely already forgotten what it was like to be born. And then, around the age of seven, you start to forget your earliest memories. This is called infantile amnesia, and it explains a lot of fogginess about your past. That memory lapse has also provided a convenient but mistaken rationale for repressed memories.

Your *amygdala,* on the other hand, is wired, insulated, and good to go as soon as you pop out of the womb. The amygdala is responsible for processing emotions and some kinds of rapid decision making. It's a kind of starter brain, primitive and without nuance, but capable of very basic reactions to the outside world. A healthy baby benefits from all kinds of normal stimuli, but can suffer from bad events. These can set your amygdala on high alert and possibly affect you for the rest of your life. And yet, because you're not fully wired, you likely won't even remember the insult that left you anxious.

These bad events can involve your microbiota. The early studies Nobuyuki Sudo did on germ-free mice showed that when raised in a sterile environment, the mice seemed more exploratory than ordinary mice. That sounds pleasant enough—until you consider that tiny prey animals survive better with a little anxiety. Importantly, their stress response went back to normal when they were fed *Bifido* bacteria.

In our lab, we found that germ-free mice have abnormal amygdalas, with unusual neurochemistry.[17] *An abnormal amygdala is linked to anxiety, depression, and autism. Some of the genes involved with activating neurons seem to be enhanced in these germ-free mice. These alterations may have a long-term effect on behavior and attitude. The changes appeared to happen early, as the effects weren't seen in germ-free mice that had been given probiotics after weaning.*

As well as the amygdala, our studies have also shown that a germ-free mouse may have an unusual **hippocampus,** *a seahorse-shaped part of the brain that is involved with both memory and emotion.*

We noted some dramatic changes in nerve cells, including different kinds and shapes of neurons as well as the growth of more new nerve cells than in normal mice. Somehow, the microbiota is controlling the growth of important memory and anxiety centers of the brain.[18]

We have also demonstrated that extra myelin is formed in the brains of germ-free mice. We found that myelination—especially in a region of the brain known as the prefrontal cortex—is regulated by the **microbiome.**[19] *The prefrontal cortex is an important area for top-down regulation of the stress response and is involved with depression, schizophrenia, and autism.*

We found that these changes could be reversed by providing the mice with a conventional microbiota after weaning, suggesting that the microbiota is a potential target for myelin-based psychiatric disorders.

It makes sense that early exposure to microbes would lead to a change in your immune system, but the effect of microbes on brain development seems more surprising. Why are bacteria needed to develop a properly functioning brain? Mouse studies are suggestive: Germ-free mice are loners, but when they're colonized with a normal microbiota, they become socialized. Is this a way for hopeful microbes to induce us to explore our world so that they can meet new potential hosts?

BREAST-FEEDING

We have long comforted ourselves that breast milk is pure and antiseptic, but we now know it is a microbial balm for your vulnerable baby gut, full of bacteria. Mother's milk contains sugars that a baby cannot digest, which seems like a waste of maternal energy—but these sugars aren't for the baby. They are prebiotics designed to feed the accompanying microbes in mother's milk. And the microbes, in return, produce food for you in the form of fatty acids like butyrate. That makes mother's milk both a prebiotic and probiotic drink—a combination of microbes and the food microbes want—a sort of homemade kefir. These prebiotics not only feed the starter microbiota, they also reduce the release of the stress hormone cortisol, keeping you happy and content.

Children who are breast-fed tend to have a superior microbiota from early on. Formula can be a lifesaver, but most formula contains neither probiotics nor immune factors from the mother. Someday, researchers may create a probiotic mix that will improve the baby's microbiota, but it won't easily replicate the shifting levels of prebiotics and probiotics that breast milk passes on to the baby.

The first milk, produced right after delivery, is called colostrum and is packed with hundreds of species of bacteria. It is also full of maternal white blood cells and antibodies to establish a newborn's foundational immune system—kind of an immune system transplant, designed to provide instant protection for your defenseless body. For such an innocuous-looking substance, milk packs an astounding immunological punch.

In anticipation of birth, your mother's intestinal lining underwent a change to allow certain roving immune cells called *dendritic cells* to better sample the gut population. These cells grab microbes and ferry them through the lymph vessels that are woven throughout the gut. This is a second circulatory system in the body that cleanses the tissues of unwanted substances. The lymph then carries the dendritic cells to the mammary glands.[20]

The payload of these immune cells makes it into your mother's milk. Milk is food, but more importantly, it's an efficient way to plant and fertilize the baby's own microbial garden.

Over time, the immune components of the milk change, reflecting your own growing immune system. After the first week of breast-feeding, the numbers of white blood cells drop dramatically when both you and your mother are healthy. In some cases, your mother may get an infection, such as mastitis, that gets passed on to you. When this happens, your mother's system adds copious numbers of white blood cells to her milk, getting them into your body where they can chase down the infection.

Many more microbial assaults are in store. As a baby you are subject to thousands of kisses and hugs, each leaving a bacterial residue that is folded into the bustling community of your own microbiota. Over time you develop the bacteria that will travel with you for the rest of your life. You will eat dirt. The cat will lick you. You will lick the cat. You progress through major life events like nursing, weaning, and the introduction of solid food. Your gut bacteria even seem to anticipate the switch to solid food by boosting populations of carb-loving bacteria. If this seems like a lot of trouble to go through, it's because it's absolutely vital to your health. Without a well-balanced microbiota, your life will be hobbled. You reach a major turning point by the age of two, and yet you are too young to know what you're doing. Now your gut is pretty much established, and you had nothing to say about it.

While your gut bacteria are working out their living arrangements, your immune system is also blossoming. Somehow, and quickly, your good bacteria and your immune system come to an arrangement where they don't try to destroy each other. Immune cells produced by your bone marrow and thymus gland, including the regulatory cells called *T-regs,* target specific pathogens and arbitrate inflammation.

When T-regs realize that your own cells are being killed in an immune reaction, they have the job of stepping in and breaking up the fight. They are important players in the baroque world of immunity. As a baby, your thymus is highly active while you build up your unique collection of antibodies and T-regs. As you get older, your thymus shrivels, and you might find it harder to fight off pathogens. That can lead to chronic inflammation and depression as you age.

Detecting pathogens with antibodies is a big part of immunity. But you still have to give a pass to the *desirable* gut bacteria. You don't have a built-in blueprint of all your friendly bacterial antigens like you do with your own cells. There is no thymus gland equivalent to screen your microbiota. Somehow, a growing child's immune system must learn to give a pass to a bunch of newly acquired microbes. It seems that the immune system, for the first couple of years of your life, does so by lowering its guard. During this brief period of trust, your system assumes that its environment is okay, and it learns to tolerate what it finds in its gut. Depending on how you were raised, that may or may not be a correct assumption.

Oddly enough, not that much is known about the beneficial bacteria in your gut—the spotlight has been on the pathogens. So, although we know a lot about *E. coli* and *C. difficile,* we know frustratingly little about the humble commensals that have lived with you from birth or even before. But at least we now know that breast milk has a lot to do with seeding the baby's commensal microbiota, and the immune cells have been trained to tolerate them.

After around six months of breast-feeding, the bacteria in your mother's milk start to change. Instead of bacteria that are expert at digesting milk sugars, the new milk microbiota starts to look a lot like your mother's own oral bacteria. This transformation helps prepare you for solid food, because a lot of the work of digesting starts in the mouth.[21]

WEANING

By the time you are weaned, your immune system has learned a lot, and it should have made peace with your developing microbiota. A well-trained immune system leads to mental health, but a poorly taught immune system can lead to chronic inflammation, depression, or anxiety. All these players in your microbiota have learned a lot, but school is still in session.

The environment, lavish with microbes, has much more to teach. Many of these lessons are passed on by your family. Warmly swaddled in mucus, your siblings' microbiota are ready at a moment's notice to educate you. A sneeze, a poke in the eye, a wet finger in the ear; these are just a few of the methods by which you inherit bacteria from your clan. The firstborn misses out on many of these microbial anointments.

The Hygiene Hypothesis

In 1989 David Strachan, a British epidemiologist, reported in the *British Medical Journal* his analysis of 17,414 British kids born in March 1958. Looking at data on the kids 23 years later, he was able to analyze the incidence of hay fever, asthma, and eczema—all allergic diseases caused by an overactive immune system. Those who suffer from these illnesses have very sensitive immune cells that overreact in response to pollen or benign bacteria. These immune cells go into high gear, inflaming normal tissues as collateral damage. They secrete proteins called ***cytokines*** that summon more immune cells to the site of the inflammation. These new recruits overreact as well, spraying more cytokines in a frenzied feedback loop called a cytokine storm. Unless something can break the feedback loop, the situation gets serious and can even result in death by anaphylactic shock, as the person is essentially attacked by his or her own immune system.

Strachan found one thing that correlated perfectly across those who suffered from these diseases: They came from small households. The fewer the kids, the greater the allergies. And the first-borns were worse off than their siblings. What was happening?

Strachan realized that children were being vaccinated by their older siblings. Early exposure to hand-me-down microbes somehow quiets the allergic reaction. The second-born become immune-tolerant: Their immune system learns to live and let live. The firstborns don't have the luxury of a tested microbiota, typically passed around via sibling snot, to tutor their naive immune system. That lack of education leads them to overreact when exposed to new microbes.

This observation, which came to be called the hygiene hypothesis, implies that cleanliness actually has a negative influence on normal development, and it has had a big impact on how people look at bacteria. Rather than being pathogenic or at best marginally useful, a certain set of bacteria may actually be *essential* for the proper development of your body's defenses. It is the job of these microbes to train your immune system, and without them, your system stays naive and prone to overreaction. For a parent, it means that letting your kids make mud pies could be a smart move—and at an early age. It is difficult to teach an old immune system.

As a result of the hygiene hypothesis, researchers started paying more attention to the good bacteria living in and on the body. We've since realized that bacteria aren't just tolerated by the immune system: They're comrades. Microbes work with the immune system in your gut to add an extra layer of protection. Certain favored bacteria not only get along well with your own cells but also give grief to pathogens, competing with them for food or poisoning them.

Microbe-Rich Mucus

The epithelium, or skin, of your gut mostly consists of absorptive cells called *enterocytes*. Tightly bound together by proteins, these cells take in nutrients from your food and stop bacteria, which are swarming in your gut, from getting into your bloodstream. This translucent tissue just a few cells thick is remarkably resilient, tough yet permeable to absorb nutrients but keep problem microbes out. It's a difficult balancing act.

Some of the absorption is simple; ions can be pumped directly through pores in the enterocyte membranes. Small molecules can get through the cracks between the enterocytes. Certain fatty molecules can "melt" right into the cells themselves. Other larger molecules may use molecular portals in the enterocyte membrane to escort them inside. These techniques allow you to take in nutrients, but they can be subverted by microbes as well. Your gut, in other words, has the unenviable goal of making an impenetrable wall that is also permeable. Pathogens often exploit the inevitable glitches that result from trying to reconcile these incompatible goals.

From your mouth to your anus, your GI tract is covered with the well-known polymer known as mucus. It's the slime that flows out of your nose when you're sick: That is your body's indiscreet way to flush bacteria and viruses out. When you wipe a toddler's nose, billions of microbes are being ejected. Toss the tissue!

Slimy and sticky, mucus provides a layer of protection on top of the enterocytes. Mucus in the gut comes in multiple formulations. First a network of sugary strands stuck tight to the enterocytes provides an excellent physical barrier against microbes. On top of that is a second, less dense mucus layer full of a microbial buffet of sugars. Embedded in this second mucus layer is your most important defense against pathogens: other bacteria. Like picking the class bully to be your bodyguard, your gut chooses certain bacteria to protect against the onslaught of other, far worse bacteria, and the mucus matrix anchors these chosen bacteria.

The bacteria selected for the job are right at home in your warm mucus. Like a gingerbread house, the sugars in your mucus provide a home that can be eaten. When it feels the need for extra protection, your gut produces extra mucus to attract more microbes to the front lines. These are your royal guard, the most trusted bacteria in your system, and they have coexisted with humans for millennia.

During the early years of your life, your immune system needs to be educated to leave these protective bacteria alone. If your immune system kills your guardian bacteria, pathogens can directly attack your gut. They can eat holes in your gut lining, letting bacteria into your bloodstream and provoking a systemic immune response. Without your guardian bacteria, you may find yourself fighting a continuous low-level guerrilla war. Untreated, a condition of chronic inflammation can develop, leading to IBS and IBD (Crohn's and ulcerative colitis)—diseases that often come with anxiety and depression, which may be nature's way to keep you home, where you are less likely to encounter the pathogens to which you are now vulnerable.

FROM TODDLER YEARS ON

Your gut, your microbiota, and your immune system have pretty much ripened by the age of two, trained to work together, if you are lucky, in a healthy relationship in which your microbiota fights pathogens, doesn't invade your gut, and doesn't provoke your immune cells. A team like that is hard to disrupt, and you may enjoy a healthy childhood. But there are threats to be reckoned with, most critically broad-spectrum antibiotics, which can decimate your gut bacteria, wiping out whole legions of beneficial bacteria that may never recover. These microbes are involved in proper programming and development of the brain, so their loss early in life can have drastic consequences. On the other hand, antibiotics can save a child's life, so it all needs to be considered in the right perspective.

Although the basic framework of your microbiota is set by age two, it is still a dynamic situation. As you grow, there will still be changes, and there is an overall drift away from *Bifido* species. They will always be there, but in smaller numbers as the years go by.

THE TEEN YEARS

Ah, to be a teenager again, says almost nobody. Yet here you are, stuck in the days of frenemies, sexual awakening, drugs, acne, junk food . . . and dicey microbes. Few teenagers think about it, but the microbiota plays a surprisingly important role in adolescence.

From birth to toddler years, the foundations of your brain structures are laid. The teen years bring continuing transformations as your hormones start to change and as many of the seeds for future depression and anxiety are planted. Of particular importance to mood during this time of life are drugs, food, and stress. Drugs directly affect your mood, and some of them—especially alcohol— are known to kill brain cells. Teenage diets, typically laughable, lead to a rash of gut problems. And stress affects the teenage brain and microbiota alike.[22] Meanwhile, the long project of myelinating your brain continues, spreading out to the frontal lobes, where executive decisions are processed. Depending on your particular microbiota, your myelin may be thicker or thinner, potentially even affecting how you think and make judgments.

Teenagers are actually no worse at making decisions than younger children, but with many more ways to implement them, the consequences of those decisions can be far more dangerous. Meanwhile, adolescent hormones are raging, the parts of your brain involved in processing anxiety are still developing, and your microbiota is subtly changing as well. Life stressors such as sleep deprivation, lousy eating habits, and continued courses of antibiotics motivate these changes—which might explain why the peak age for psychiatric problems is 14 years old. Even healthy teens are susceptible to emotional instability. In retrospect, it's lucky you ever make it out of your teenage years. There's good news and bad: You can make a difference, because this may be the last time in your life that you can make durable changes to your microbiota. But if a bad set of microbes gets established, you may have to fight for the rest of your life to keep the upper hand.

Eating habits can make a big difference. The ramen and popcorn diet is doing you no favors. As a teen, you should be eating plenty of fiber and other foods with psychobiotic properties, as you'll learn about later in this book. If you're the parent of a teen, try to help. Remember that your teen is still quite malleable, and sensitive to microbial intervention. This is one of the pivotal periods in life, and even a small intervention can lead to great psychiatric resilience down the line.

GETTING OLD

As you age, your microbiota still continues to change, but it is hard to make generalizations at this point because there is so much variation. Studies done in different countries have produced widely varying results, showing how even the definition of old is different from country to country. In Italian studies, 70-year-old subjects were not that different from youngsters. No distinct changes were seen until they looked at centenarians. Among Irish study subjects, though, gut

Age	Firmicutes	Bacteriodetes	Proteobacteria	Actinobacteria	Other
Baby (breast-fed)	15%	10%	25%	48%	2%
Baby (formula-fed)	40%	3%	9%	45%	3%
Baby (solid food)	33%	45%	1%	0%	21%
Toddler (healthy)	33%	45%	1%	0%	21%
Toddler (antibiotics)	20%	75%	1%	0%	4%
Adult (healthy)	72%	20%	1%	5%	2%
Adult (obese)	68%	15%	10%	5%	2%
Elderly	68%	20%	5%	5%	2%
Centenarian	65%	14%	1%	20%	0%

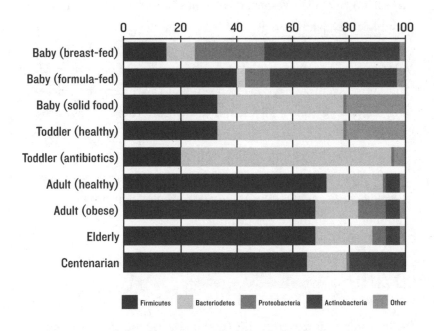

As you age or get sick, the proportional bacterial content of your microbiota changes, as the charts above convey.

microbes started to change at age 70. What makes the difference? Probably dietary differences between the two populations.[23] There is evidence that you can improve your microbiota even in old age by adopting a Mediterranean-type diet and eating more fiber.[24] It's never too late: A good diet can keep your gut happy, increase your health span, and improve your mood, all at the same time.

These choices make a difference in the quality of life. Your microbiota can affect your immune function, your inclination to get cancer, and your cognitive abilities. In other words, a good microbiota can enhance not just your life span but also your health span.[25] In old age, as in childhood, antibiotics take a toll on your microbiota, further knocking down levels of beneficial *Bifido*.

Studies show how aging and diet have an interesting relationship to each other. The Western diet, with high levels of fat and sugar (think icing), leads to high levels of Firmicutes, whereas a diet rich in fiber (think beans and greens) leads to an increase in Bacteroidetes. These are the two most prevalent groups of bacteria in your gut. Aging seems to have an effect similar to a Western diet, increasing the proportion of Firmicutes in the gut. These changes relate directly to the hardiness or frailty of the individual, with diversity of microbes decreasing as illness increases.[26] Community living encourages microbial diversity and thus an increased health span. Playing cards and dancing as you get old may be more than entertainment; it can make you healthier.

DYING

After a happy and eventful life (we hope), you die. But surprisingly, you die by pieces. Your cells don't all die at once, and many of them continue to metabolize and produce proteins. These proteins are attempting to stave off pathogens, trying to fire up immunity and inflammation. They can continue to fight, even though doomed, for up to four days.[27]

Meanwhile the party in your gut goes on, with last-call bacteria continuing to rave as long as there's still food left. After you pass, you may still pass gas. For hours. Death, as it turns out, is not as dignified as we might wish. To add insult to injury, some of your bacteria turn to consuming you, even as your last straggling cells put up a feeble resistance. But without an immune system to intimidate them, they are free to eat the place down.

Embalming stops that decay by killing everything. But if you just drop dead in the forest, some of your microbes may find another host, that is, you may be eaten. But your main microbial defenders— your royal guard—will likely wither and die alongside you. They were the tightest of partners and they just cannot live outside of that special human gut they called home. That brutal reality is why they worked so hard to keep you healthy.

If you are a member of the Y chromosome gang, this is the end of your microbial line. If, however, you are an X chromosomer and a mother, you have passed on a good portion of your microbiota already. Your legacy will live on in your children. The circle of life rolls on.

CHAPTER 4

A VOYAGE DOWN YOUR ALIMENTARY CANAL

"The real voyage of discovery consists not in seeking new landscapes, but in having new eyes."

—Marcel Proust

LET'S FOLLOW A FEW MOUTHFULS OF FOOD THROUGH THE twists and turns of your GI tract. It will be like whitewater rafting, only with acid instead of water and a lot darker. On this intestinal odyssey, we'll follow some good food like lentils and yogurt, as well as some deliciously toxic food like candy and doughnuts.

YOUR MOUTH

First up: the mouth. For most of us, this is the only part of the GI tract that we've really seen in any detail. Unlike your skin, it doesn't have a tough keratin layer, but rather a vulnerable-looking pinkness

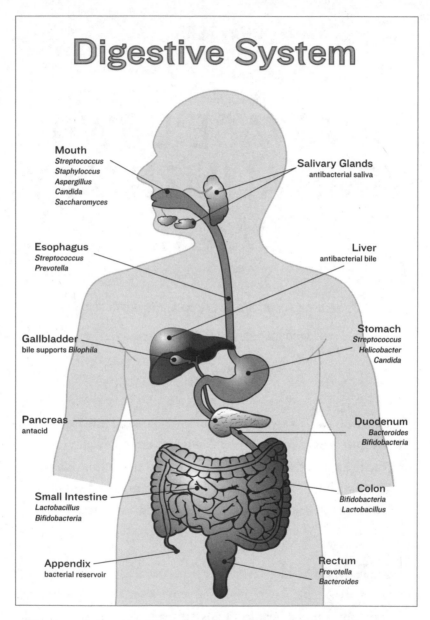

*Here is our tour map of the human digestive system, from mouth to anus,
including the bacterial story for each organ along the way.*

to its surface. This is the first hint that your gut, which is designed to absorb nutrients, is worlds apart from your skin, which is designed to keep things out. Accordingly, the microbes in these two environments are utterly different.

As well as bacteria, your insides are full of fungi and viruses and even a few protozoans swimming about. Your mouth provides accommodation to hundreds of species of bacteria, including a fairly rough crowd of *Streptococcus* and *Staphylococcus,* bacteria known to cause disease. In a healthy person these are generally not troublesome, being held in check by other bacteria. Your diet, however, determines a lot about which bacteria will thrive, and that in turn determines a lot about your mood.

One of the most basic things that happens here in your mouth is simple starches—think white sugar—are broken down by your saliva into component sugars such as maltose and dextrose. One pathogenic member of the *Streptococcus* genus, *S. mutans,* lurks in your mouth and turns these sugars into acids that eat away at the enamel on your teeth. When you feed candy and other sugary treats to *S. mutans,* its numbers bloom, your teeth suffer, and you become an annuity for your dentist. This is the first of many reasons to limit sugars and simple starches (such as white bread, baked potatoes, and cake) in your diet.

Still, at this point, your taste buds are telling you that doughnuts are pretty wonderful, and your sugar-loving bacteria are responding by rapidly reproducing. Our evolutionary history, which included very few pastries rolling across the savanna, didn't prime us for glazed doughnuts. We are inadequately prepared for this temptation, and that is a problem, because the bacteria that crave sugar are not the ones that support a good mood. Short-term bliss, yes, but in the long term a sugar-centered microbiota can potentially make you anxious and depressed.

A bite of food triggers fountains of saliva at the back of your mouth. Saliva has enzymes that quickly start breaking down simple starches and fats, but it contains something else important to our story: home-brewed antibiotics. This is a part of your innate immune system, and many pathogens are immediately killed right here in your mouth thanks to the copious flows of saliva. You will produce about two quarts of saliva today (gulp!), and it will help to wash down billions of dead bacteria.

Some bacteria live in your mouth, but others are just transients here, on their way to the small intestine or colon. Where do these travelers come from? Many, including fungal spores, are the ultimate drifters, actually floating in the air. Open your mouth and they simply waft in. Others come with your food, despite your having washed things before you eat them. Some foods are associated strongly with pathogens (like chicken with salmonella), so we cook them to sanitize them. Other microbes live inside the foods you eat raw, such as salad vegetables. Because they are inside the tissues, you cannot wash them off. These bacteria are called endophytes, meaning "inside the plant," and the good ones represent one of the benefits of eating veggies. In essence, vegetables are a kind of probiotic all by themselves. Some of these endophytes may be pathogens. If things are working well, they will be quickly killed by your good bacteria or your immune system. Others may be more benign and may get along well enough to make a home in your mouth and settle down—perhaps for your entire life. These are your commensal bacteria. The implication of commensal is that you derive no real benefit in return for letting these bacteria join you at the table. This simplistic concept is changing as new studies find that we do, indeed, benefit from many of these bacteria, making the relationship more symbiotic than merely commensal.

Your mouth is a complex habitat with dozens of enticing hiding places. Each gum fold and tooth gap is host to a thriving bacterial community. Did you forget to brush your teeth this morning? A single one of your teeth could be harboring a billion bacteria. Are you feeling smug because you remembered to brush? Congratulations, you've reduced those numbers to more like 100,000—the population of South Bend, Indiana. On each tooth.

How can you have so many bacteria even after a thorough brushing? It comes down to the way your bacteria organize themselves into tough biofilms, also known as plaque. These are communities of bacteria that manage to hang tight, even against the exuberant scrubbing of a toothbrush. When they find a comfy habitat, these bacteria modify their secretions, creating an organic glue that holds large microbial communities together. Once a biofilm is established, it is difficult to dislodge.

Every niche in your mouth supports a unique ecosystem. Astonishingly, these oral communities are established within minutes of your birth and perhaps even before you are born, typically seeded as you are squeezed down the birth canal. That ecosystem is further embellished by mother's milk and kisses from every relative and baby-smoocher you run across for the next couple of years. Once established, they can maintain their character for the rest of your natural life.

The cheek side of each tooth has a different microbiota than the tongue side. The molars in the back host different microbes from those on your canines and incisors. Each of these microbial communities is exquisitely tuned to its particular environment. Proximity to salivary glands means a wetter and slightly less acidic environment that favors a specific set of microbes. Your body's left-right symmetry holds true among the bacterial communities in your mouth, to the point that if your back left molar has an infection, the odds are good that your back right molar will soon have the same infection.

Near the gum lines we see that microbes have formed what look like bacterial bushes sprouting from the surfaces of your teeth. Long filaments of the species called *Corynebacteria* make up the limbs of the bush, and other bacteria cluster on these branches. Safely toward the inside of the bush are anaerobic (oxygen-hating) bacteria seeking shelter from the oxygen in your mouth. Toward the outside of the bush, spherical oxygen-tolerating coccus bacteria hang off the branches like berries. These microbes communicate using hundreds of chemical signals, and if you could tune in, the conversation would be deafening. Bacteria talk to members of their own species, but they also talk to different species and even different kingdoms of life swarming inside your mouth, including viruses, the fungal fur that coats your tongue, and the tiny one-celled creatures swimming through your saliva.

The Drama Going on Inside Your Mouth

Commensal microbes secrete chemicals that are off-putting or even lethal to other members of your teeming oral microbiota. In fact, you depend on certain friendly bacteria to battle the more pathogenic ones, and as we tour your gut, we will see far more examples of good bacteria than bad. They are mostly—like 95 percent—good.

The battle is not just between bacteria. Bacteria and fungi tend to push back on each other as well, and in the absence of bacteria—often due to antibiotic use—your mouth fungus can run amok, turning your tongue black with thrush. Fungal infections tend to be tenacious. We used to think of fungi as strictly pathogenic, but we are realizing that fungi are just other members of the community, cooperating with other microbes until the balance is upset.

Research on fungi is surprisingly thin, but they are everywhere. On the bad side, a big player is *Candida,* which can get out of control and raise havoc throughout the body. On the good side is a strain of *Saccharomyces,* which can act as a psychobiotic. There are also some scary fungi that nevertheless seem to have struck a truce with the immune system, including *Aspergillus, Fusarium,* and *Cryptococcus.* Most people have at least a dozen different species of fungi in their mouth, and many of them survive the trip to your colon.

While we're near the tongue, let's look a little deeper at the taste buds. These are small clumps of sensory and supporting cells that stud your tongue. To those of us who love flavorful food, these buds are a joyful part of life. But from an evolutionary perspective, our tingles of excitement with a curry or spicy Mexican dish are beside the point. Taste buds also alert you to poisons and pathogens. Many of them are bitter or have bitter by-products, and you have millions of taste buds designed to detect bitter flavors and then secrete antimicrobial chemicals, just in case. The antimicrobial action of bitter taste receptors is probably their prime directive; letting you enjoy the taste of coffee and grapefruit is just a lucky by-product.

When bacteria form biofilms, they deliver a chemical invitation to other like-minded bacteria. This bacterial solicitation has a bitter taste, and when your bitter buds sense it, they produce nitric oxide, a gas that is lethal to bacteria. This happens within seconds of sensing the bitterness. If you are pregnant, your oral bacteria can travel all the way to your baby's placenta. This is an important pathway for passing on your microbial heritage, but if your oral microbiota is unbalanced it can lead to premature delivery, dysbiosis, and depression later in your baby's life. This important connection between mouth bacteria and the developing fetus is a remarkable example of the intimate relationship between humans and microbes.

It may be a little disconcerting that bacteria can gain such easy access to your internal organs. If your gums are damaged or diseased, they will provide little resistance against aggressive bacteria, which can slide between the damaged cells and shoulder their way into the bloodstream. This bodily invasion by oral bacteria has been associated with cancer, arthritis, and heart disease. These assaults also trigger a strong immune response, and the consequent inflammation can lead to depression—a direct way that pathogens can cause mental distress.

Antibiotics disrupt and may permanently damage the original healthy community of your oral microbiota. Over-the-counter probiotic supplements can help reestablish a successful community in your mouth, especially those containing *Streptococcus salivarius*. You may blanch at the idea of sucking on a strep lozenge, but there are many species of strep, some of them beneficial. That's because the war between bacterial species is strongest between the closest players. It takes a *Strep* to fight a *Strep*. It turns out that *S. salivarius* produces a narrowly targeted antibiotic (called a **bacteriocin**) that chokes out *S. pyogenes*, the pathogen that causes strep throat and rheumatic heart disease. That makes *S. salivarius* a type of psychobiotic in that it outcompetes a pathogen that can lead to depression and anxiety.

All these bacterial interactions take place while your teeth chew up your food and your tongue pushes it to the back of your throat for swallowing. Whatever probiotics and psychobiotics you hope to grow in your colon have to make it past this first stage of digestion—and the trauma to come.

We now head past your uvula, a cartoonish piece of flesh dangling in the back of your mouth that is as poorly understood as the appendix (which we will encounter later). The uvula, like so much of the tissue wrapping your gut, can produce mucus and prodigious amounts of saliva. Some scientists think that in humans it may help to lubricate your voice box, helping us to be the chattiest animals on the planet.

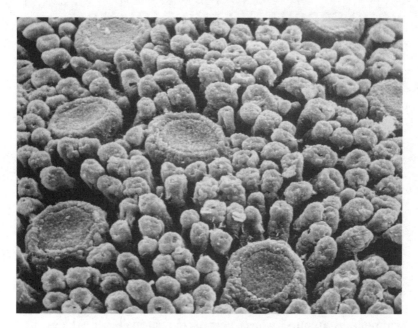

Taste buds, the larger circles seen above, are found on your tongue, but taste receptors are scattered throughout your entire gut as well.

To the left and right, we can see the tonsils, acting as twin guards at the beginning of your gullet. These glands of the lymphatic system are looking for pathogens in your food (and in the air you breathe), and they are the first obvious sentinels of your immune system. When they sense pathogens, they swell up with immune cells. As we shall see, the immune system can sometimes get overeager, and this is a place where that is easy to observe. Swollen tonsils can result in a sore throat, and that swelling can ultimately block the throat. When that happens, they need to be removed.

There's no time to dwell on the tonsils, though. We're headed for a precipice at the end of the mouth and are about to be shoved over the cliff by a strong pulse of your tongue. With little fanfare, we plunge into the darkness of your esophagus.

YOUR ESOPHAGUS AND STOMACH

When you swallow, your epiglottis closes off your trachea, keeping you from inhaling your food. The epiglottis seems to be proof that evolution has a perverse sense of humor. Many animals manage to keep their breathing tubes completely separate from their food tubes, but mammals get to suffer the indignity of gagging every time they fail to close their epiglottis when food is on the way.

Your food is squeezed down your esophagus, an eight-inch tube that empties into your stomach. As in the rest of your GI tract, a coating of mucus and bacteria covers a layer of rosy skin, behind which is a complex mesh of nerves, veins, arteries, and lymph vessels, loosely bound together by elastic connective tissue that lets your gut shrink and expand as food passes through. All of this is wrapped by an outside layer of muscle responsible for the pulsing muscular contractions, called *peristalsis,* that force food down your throat. Peristalsis happens throughout your entire GI tract, mixing your food as it moves it along, all under the control of your *enteric nervous system* (ENS)—the gut's nervous system, which is large and complex enough to be called the second brain.[1]

Now we are in the territory where gastroesophageal reflux disease (GERD) happens, a condition affecting the esophagus that is undergoing a major resurgence in the Western world. GERD occurs when stomach acids flow backward into your esophagus, causing "heartburn." This, in turn, affects the kind of bacteria that live in this part of your digestive system. Untreated GERD can lead to cancer and other problems. And the process goes both ways: If you suffer from anxiety, you may be extrasensitive to the acids splashing up from your stomach. People with anxiety are three times more likely to have GERD. No one knows why the incidence of GERD is growing so much faster than that of other diseases, but new research is finding an association with the gut microbiota. It isn't clear if the change in bacteria noted in people with GERD is a cause or effect of the disease, but either way, some researchers are looking at probiotics to help treat the condition. People with anxiety are three times more likely to have GERD, so from a psychobiotic point of view, this connection to mental health is important.

Your esophagus serves as a simple conduit for food to pass from your mouth to your stomach. There, powerful acids—as strong as battery acid—tear into your food, and then, within minutes, other secretions buffer the mix, bringing it to a pH of about two, similar to lemon juice. Specialized cells lining your stomach secrete these digestive acids. Stomach acids are released in response to seeing or smelling food, with your vagus nerve sending a signal to start the secretions. Food in your stomach itself acts as a further signal to produce more acid. Extra mucus, along with a little bicarbonate, is also released to keep your stomach from digesting itself.

It used to be thought that stomach acids were only to help digest proteins, but it is becoming clearer that the acids also kill pathogens. Only a select group of microbes, including *Candida, Helicobacter,* and *Lactobacillus* species, can handle the acidity in your stomach. So at this stage of digestion, millions of bacteria are dissolved or damaged by stomach acids. Any probiotics or psychobiotics you consume—your friendly bacteria—must pass through this chemical gauntlet to make it to a spot they can call home.

If you have gastric ulcers, this is where you will see them. They look like wounds, anything from pimples to bruises to craters. You might also see lurking *Helicobacter,* a corkscrew bacteria that was shown to cause ulcers in 1982 and has suffered from bad press ever since. *Helicobacter* uses its corkscrew shape, powered by its flagella, to burrow into the mucus layer lining your stomach. It is always orienting itself away from the acid, driving itself right into the mucus and up to the cells lining your stomach. It squirts out a bit of glue and sticks itself to the lining. There it sets up shop, eating mucus and spawning numerous sisters. Ulcers can result, and they can become inflamed, sometimes in response to stress. The condition itself can cause anxiety, too, which can, unfortunately, compound that stress: an unfortunate cycle.

But there's another side to the *Helicobacter* story. Like most microbes, *Helicobacter*'s bad side comes out when it's unbalanced by other microbes. In fact, most people with *Helicobacter* don't have gastric ulcers. *Helicobacter* may actually be beneficial, protecting against allergic diseases like asthma and perhaps even protecting against esophageal cancer. This may be a part of the early education your microbe provides to your immune system. However, as studies by Martin Blaser have shown, *Helicobacter* can also lead to gastric cancer in older patients, so it is not without issues. Some people can benefit from wiping out their *Helicobacter*,

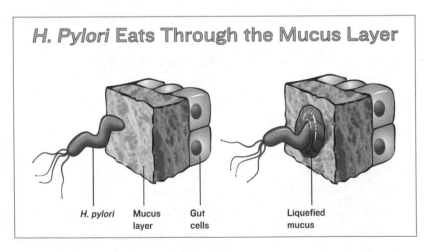

The bacterium named Helicobacter pylori *secretes acids that liquefy mucus, allowing this pathogen to drill right up to the gut lining, where it can then take up residence.*

but many may come out ahead by keeping them around. Nothing is simple in the world of the microbiota.

As well as providing the acid treatment, your stomach muscles massage your food to help expose more of it to digestive fluids and gastric enzymes, as well as acids. At this point, the food is barely recognizable. To mark its change of state, it is renamed chyme (pronounced *kime*), from the Greek for "juice." If you've ever vomited, you know just what it looks like. Although many bacteria have been killed by this point in the journey, there is still a surprisingly thriving world of microbes mixed in with it. Your stomach has now done all it can do, and it's time to move on to the intestines, where these microbes face new challenges—and opportunities.

YOUR SMALL INTESTINE

When your food has been sufficiently mixed and macerated, it passes through a fleshy valve called the pylorus into the narrow tube of your duodenum, the first section of your small intestine. It's called small because of its small diameter—about an inch—even though it's really quite long, winding some 23 feet before it channels into your large intestine.

Your duodenum is not set up to handle the strong acids of your stomach. Directly after passing through the pylorus we can see what looks like a pimple in the wall of your duodenum. It is actually a duct that allows bile and pancreatic juices to be squirted onto the acidic chyme. Pancreatic juices contain multiple enzymes to further digest chyme, but they also contain bicarbonate to neutralize the gastric acids. It's your own personal antacid dispensary. From here on down your GI tract, your stomach juices will continuously be buffered and neutralized, and enzymes will take over the job of digestion.

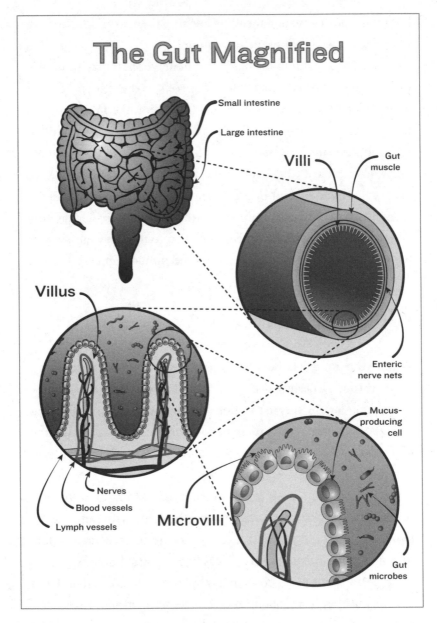

The Gut Magnified

- Small intestine
- Large intestine
- Villi
- Gut muscle
- Villus
- Enteric nerve nets
- Mucus-producing cell
- Nerves
- Blood vessels
- Microvilli
- Lymph vessels
- Gut microbes

Digestion requires a large surface area to absorb nutrients. The area of the intestinal lining is increased by villi, minute surface projections, and further multiplied by thousands of microvilli covering each villus.

Now your gut lining looks furry, thanks to millions of fingerlike projections called **villi** whose job is to increase the surface area available to absorb nutrients by a factor of 20 or so. That's pretty impressive, but like a fractal, every villus is in turn covered by a layer of cells that each brandish their own **microvilli.** These tiny protrusions further increase the surface area to yield about 400 square feet, about the size of a small apartment. That provides plenty of space to absorb nutrients. A single layer of these epithelial cells is all that separates the chyme from your bloodstream, making it easy for water, salts, and sugars to be quickly absorbed and pass from the digestive system to elsewhere in your body. It's a useful plan but an absurdly thin protection against bacteria.

From here through the rest of your small intestine, these mucus-coated villi provide a warm, sticky home to billions of bacteria. Each villus is a complex structure containing blood vessels, nerves, lymph ducts, and muscle cells. Under the control of your autonomic nervous system, the muscles move your villi, and the swaying of billions of these tiny fingers, along with peristalsis, helps to move the chyme along.

Now the bacteria in your food start seeking out places to call home. Those that lack a means of locomotion are just along for the ride, but others have flagella—tiny flippers—and they can motor right up to their destination, navigating by detecting chemical gradients, which guide them toward or away from mucus. If they sense they are headed away, they put their flagella in full reverse, causing the whole bacteria to tumble in some random direction. If they are still headed the wrong way, they tumble again. Sooner or later, they will—purely by accident—orient the right way. When they do, they put their flagella into forward gear and power up. Some two-thirds of bacteria have flagella, and as we look closer at your gut lining, we see an otherworldly vista of squirming bacteria, corkscrewing and flopping around, angling for a good position on your gut lining. It's mostly haphazard and it looks a little silly, but it gets the job done— and, thank goodness, most of these creatures are friendlies.

At this point, your gut is still pretty acidic, which turns out to be an ideal environment for several *Lactobacillus* species. Before they can settle down in their new home, however, they have to swim through an intimidating series of defenses set up by your body. Their venture isn't helped by the fact that they cannot hide very well: They have molecules made of sugars, proteins, and fats that stud their surface and give them away. These are antigens, and they come in millions of shapes and sizes. Each type of bacteria has a unique set of antigens, like a fingerprint. Some of these fingerprints are so important that we have antibodies for them, hard-coded into our DNA. As soon as we are born, without ever having seen a bacterium before, we automatically know how to fight some of the worst pathogens on the planet. Roving immune cells in your body have built-in pattern recognition for standard pathogen parts, like bits of cell wall or snippets of flagella. When any of these patterns is recognized, the patrolling cell will alert other immune cells, and they all move in for the kill.

Enter the Phagocytes

What does the drama look like? A floundering bacterium, coated with antibodies, tries to hide in the mucus. Then, from between the cells lining your gut, a translucent tentacle reaches out. At first tentative, it touches the bacteria and senses the antibodies. Suddenly, the tentacle enlarges and reveals itself as a single cell, shaped like an amoeba, oozing out. It's the beat cop of your immune system, called a ***phagocyte*** or "eater cell."

Phagocytes slither over and between the cells lining your gut, constantly on the prowl. Phagocytes are fascinating cells, independently mobile, cruising for bacteria and then devouring them.

They act like alien invaders, not the well-structured tissue you might expect in your body; they are human cells with permission to travel. This one recognizes the antibodies and responds by wrapping itself around the hapless microbe and dissolving it on the spot.

Looking closer, we see another phagocyte doing something different. Instead of dissolving a bacterium, this phagocyte wraps it up and sticks it in a protective *vacuole*, a kind of fluid-filled cellular balloon. Then it slips between your gut cells and out of sight. This phagocyte takes its trophy and crawls down to the lymphatic vessels in the deeper gut tissue. There it enters your lymphatic system and once inside, it can move through your entire body, presenting its prize to whoever wants to inspect it. It may even be able to display it to your brain, making phagocytes important players in the psychobiotic story.

Back in your gut, another phagocyte scene is unfolding. Y-shaped antibodies have paired up, connected at their bases, forming a molecule that looks something like a dog bone that can connect two bacteria together. When a group of bacteria land in a pool of mucus filled with these antibodies, they can get glued together into a ball that makes them easier for a phagocyte to target.

We spot one of these bacterial balls rolling along the mucus layer, unable to navigate in such an uncoordinated group. Squeezing out from between your epithelial cells, a cruising phagocyte detects the ball and closes in for the kill. Flowing around the ball, it simply envelopes the entire thing. What it does with its catch depends on other signals in the area, meaning that phagocytes perform some calculations before deciding what to do.

First, the phagocyte forms a vacuole around the ball. The bacteria are still alive, crammed inside the phagocyte. Luckily, right nearby is a lysosome—a naturally occurring cell structure, basically another vacuole, this one filled with enzymes. The phagocyte merges the bacteria-filled vacuole with the lysosome. The enzymes spill and go to work, dissolving the entire wad of bacteria in minutes.

Bacterial Survival Techniques

It's a difficult road for bacteria to follow, but they have no choice. If they stay in place, they can starve, be killed and eaten by their fellow microbes, or simply get flushed out and away. Getting to the mucus layer is the hardwired goal of every commensal microbe. Near the lining of your intestine, we can see that some lucky bacteria are already snuggling into the mucus and procreating: They split in two, doubling their population every 20 minutes or so. At that rate it doesn't take long to create a large family of clones.

Down in between your villi, the bacterial communities change as we go deeper, analogous to the changing flora and fauna we would see as we descended a mountain. This is because the deeper into the villi, the higher the oxygen level. Cells near the base of the villi produce oxygen, designed to discourage anaerobes—bacteria that hate oxygen and are often pathogenic. At the base of the villi are pockets called crypts, and at the bottom of the crypts are cells continuously secreting molecules called *antimicrobial peptides* (AMPs) that diffuse up through the mucus, killing pathogens on the way.

Species of bacteria change with distance along your gut and with depth into your villi and crypts, adding extra complexity to the patchwork of microbes coating your intestines. Species change with their proximity to the intestinal lining as well. The humblest nook in your gut can house millions of bacteria with hundreds of species, all codependent and happy.

Digestion Happens

If there are fats in your food, like the milk fats in yogurt, your duodenum will detect them and signal your liver and gallbladder to secrete bile acids to break the fats down. These acids are another bacterial killing ground for many species, but other bacteria, so-called *Bilophila* (for "bile-loving"), do well in this environment—especially when saturated fats are involved—and that is not necessarily a good thing. These bacteria can trigger an immune reaction, which may help to explain some of the inflammatory diseases (and associated depression and anxiety) that plague many people on a typical Western—hence, high-fat—diet.

One of the functions of your duodenum is to absorb iron from your food. Doing this early in the digestive process denies certain bacteria the iron they need to thrive. Billions of microbes that entered with your meal are starved of iron and scalded by acid. This bacterial massacre shows why probiotics need to contain many billions of active bacteria: It's not easy making it through these parts of your gut. On the other hand, sturdier bacteria seize the opportunity to eat their dead comrades, which causes their numbers to swell.

The duodenum runs into the jejunum, and you wouldn't really notice it except for a constriction where a muscle attachment is made. The jejunum has longer villi and more folds than the duodenum, so it is better at absorption, but not much change is apparent. Antacids are secreted in the duodenum, though, and so the jejunum is considerably less acidic and more inviting to bacteria. It is so pleasant for bacteria, in fact, that this is where we see diseases like small intestinal bacterial overgrowth (SIBO), which often correlates with IBS, celiac, and Crohn's disease. SIBO involves an overeager bacterial community that acts more like the densely populated bacterial mats found much farther into the GI system, in the colon. This overload of fermenting bacteria creates gas that causes bloating and abdominal pain. And as we are beginning to hear again and again, SIBO and its brethren are all significantly associated with anxiety.

SIBO has many possible causes, and so it probably doesn't have a single easy solution either. One thing sufferers can do is reduce sugar consumption, starving the out-of-place bacteria back to reasonable numbers. That may help, but each case is unique. Although the bacteria are abundant, the gut lining itself generally remains intact, which makes SIBO and IBS difficult to diagnose. Behind that surface, though, the overloaded tissues may develop a low-grade inflammation that can affect one's mood.

Researchers have been investigating the use of probiotics to treat SIBO and IBS, and they have had good results with the *Bifido* species *B. longum* in reducing symptoms such as distension and discomfort. It also improves mood, suggesting *B. longum* is an effective psychobiotic as well. Different strains (subdivisions of species) have proven salutary, but not always with the same effect. This points to a problem not just with psychobiotics, but also with probiotics in general: Each species can have quite different effects, and those effects may even change with their surroundings. When it comes to microbes, easy answers are elusive.

The jejunum then turns into the ileum where, particularly toward its lower sections, we see mounded groupings of cells, called Peyer's patches, connected to the lymphatic system. These patches include immune cells, like B and T cells, whose job is to kill pathogens. B cells make antibodies that they use to label the pathogens while T cells, along with the ever-present phagocytes, help to vacuum up the tagged bacteria. Considering how much effort is put into killing them, it's a wonder that any microbes survive at all. But many of these bacteria have coevolved with mammals over millions of years and have figured out schemes to either evade or cooperate with your immune system. Some of these strategies were worked out when you were a baby, as your microbiota educated your immune system. From the time you start to eat solid food, you develop a core set of bacteria that may stay with you for life—or at least until you take antibiotics and kill them off. Even then, many microbes in your custom microbiota will usually return because they are able to hide out deep in the crypts of your intestines.

Toward the end of the ileum, the amount and variety of bacteria steadily increase. The acidity level has fallen and the environment is improving for the psychobiotic *Lactobacillus* species in your yogurt. *Lactobacillus* is so common in this story that we will nickname it *Lacto,* or just use the letter *L.* Common species include: *L. acidophilus, L. casei, L. delbrueckii,* and *L. bulgaricus,* all found in yogurt, and all of which can live in this part of your gut. Other psychobiotic *Lacto* bacteria—including *L. rhamnosus, L. lactis,* and *L. helveticus*, found in cheese, kefir, and buttermilk—feel at home here. *L. brevis,* found in fermented foods like sauerkraut and pickles, also fits in well with this company.

In the Company of Others

Yeast can also take up residence here in the lower portion of the ileum. In fact, some of the same yeast used to brew beer, *Saccharomyces cerevisiae* (meaning "sugar fungus of beer"), is found in the small bowel of most people. In rare cases, overgrowth of *S. cerevisiae* can lead to auto-brewery syndrome, in which people actually brew beer in their gut and get inebriated. It's a cheap drunk, but the hangovers are profound. These people often end up depressed, which may have as much to do with the fungal infection as the recurring hangover. Antibiotic treatments can exacerbate the condition, because they kill bacteria that are actually helping to manage the yeast population. Antifungals, along with bacterial probiotics, may help.

S. cerevisiae also affects a larger group of people: those who have developed antibodies to it. This is a kind of allergy—an immune overreaction to the yeast—and it is associated with many of the most prevalent gut syndromes, including Crohn's, celiac, and colitis, all of which are fellow travelers with depression and anxiety.

Candida is another yeast that can live harmoniously in your gut until its population gets out of control. Again, that can happen when antibiotics kill off the bacteria that keep its numbers in check. This occurs often enough in hospitals to make it a major cause of mortality. *Candida* can also be involved with the same syndromes associated with *Saccharomyces* and noted previously.

Something very important happens at the far end of the ileum, thanks to the microbiota within. This is one of the places where you absorb vitamin B_{12}, a large, complex molecule essential to your health. Oddly enough, neither plants, fungi, nor animals can produce it. Only bacteria can synthesize vitamin B_{12}. It's an important vitamin: B_{12} protects against brain atrophy and is critical for maintaining a healthy nervous system. In fact, a deficiency of vitamin B_{12} can lead to mania and psychosis. A healthy gut includes a good population of the *Lactobacillus* bacteria that produce B_{12}, contributing to their psychobiotic properties.

At the far end of the ileum, specialized tissue absorbs the bile acids that were secreted earlier. Your chyme has now been prepared for the next stage of digestion. It is full of fiber and is largely stripped of pathogens. Up ahead we spot a porthole that will take us to the next part of our alimentary journey: your colon.

YOUR LARGE INTESTINE

We saw only subtle changes in the scenery as we traveled through the various sections of your small intestine, but as we get to the large intestine, things look quite different. Your small intestine doesn't just widen to become the large intestine. Instead, the ileum enters through a valve that opens an inch or two from your colon's terminus, leaving a dead-end pocket called the cecum with a wormlike tail: the appendix. Scientists still debate the utility of your appendix, but it is chock-full of bacteria, so perhaps it serves as a reservoir of good microbes that can be called on to repopulate your colon after a nasty bout of food poisoning (or antibiotics) has decimated your normal gut microbiota. In herbivores, the cecum is large and swollen with bacteria that break down grasses and leaves. A horse's cecum, for instance, measures four feet long and holds eight gallons. The human cecum is puny by comparison, but like a horse's, it's likely a way station for the digestion of fiber as well.

Your colon is where the bacteria rule—in unfathomably large numbers. They cram themselves into close-knit communities that fill every crack and crevice. Roughly a thousand different species here form neighborhoods, find shared goals, and seek out the perfect location to set up housekeeping. Some of these species are found nowhere else on the planet. We are their only home, and if we don't treat them right, they literally have no place else to go. The standard American low-fiber diet, coupled with a steady drumbeat of antibiotic treatments, has come close to wiping out certain bacterial species in the Western world. It is possible that we are driving some microbial species to extinction. If some of these have psychobiotic properties, we could be affecting our collective mood without realizing it. The disappearance of beneficial microbes could, in fact, be a major contributor to the alarming rise in anxiety and depression seen around the world.

We skirt the side pocket of your cecum and enter the cavernous channel of your colon. It has what looks like a vaulted ceiling, constructed of a series of domes that runs on into the distance. When a river narrows, it has to move faster to convey the same amount of water in the same amount of time. Likewise, your chyme picked up speed when it was injected into the small intestine from the large-bore stomach. Now, pouring into the spacious colon, your fast-flowing chyme slows down considerably, and during this leisurely transit, more water and salt are wrung out. And the surviving bacteria beget more bacteria.

The texture of your gut here is different. Although your small intestine was covered in furry villi, your colon is thickly pitted with crypts and covered with a familiar layer of mucus. On closer inspection, we can see two distinct layers of mucus here. A viscous inner layer sticks tightly to the crypt-pocked surface, and a less gelatinous layer lies on top of that. As the chyme flows over the looser outer layer, some of it rubs off, creating islands of mucus that are carried along with the flow. These might look inviting to a mucus-loving microbe, and it's not impossible to see this as an intestinal decoy: a slick way to escort certain pathogens right out of your gut.

It's a harsh job being an epithelial cell in the intestines. There is the constant abrasion of food going by, and bacteria are always trying to breach the cellular membrane. A cell can only take about five days of this punishment before it sloughs off, and with it go whatever bacteria had managed to latch on. For a bacterium, colonizing a gut cell is often a Pyrrhic victory. It may gain territory only to see it break off and sail away. Once detached, the cell—and all its hangers-on—becomes part of the chyme that either gets flushed out or eaten by other bacteria.

Peering down into one of these crypts, we see an environment similar to the crypts in the small intestine. Oxygen levels increase as you descend. At the bottom of each crypt is a wondrous sight: a dozen or so stem cells—our body's primal cells, able to develop into any tissue—continuously dividing into new epithelial cells. Outside of the bone marrow, stem cells are hard to find, but here they are, important and active. The continuous loss of cells in your gut means that these stem cells are working day and night to keep your gut lining fresh, pushing the older cells up the wall of the crypt and out, where they get carried away.

By now, all the easily digestible sugars have been broken down and absorbed in your small intestine. What remains are those complex sugars called **oligosaccharides**—or, more simply put, fiber—that cannot be digested by any of the acids or enzymes that have been employed so far. If you didn't have gut bacteria, these complex sugars would just pass out of you. But fiber is manna for the microbes living in your large intestine, and they squeeze out a surprising amount of useful fuel that can then be absorbed by your gut. The process of breaking down these complex sugars is called **fermentation,** accomplished by both bacteria and yeast.

Large folds in your colon provide protective caves for various microbial communities. Ulcers can be found in this area, often because of a bloom of one pathogenic species or another. Ulcerative colitis (UC) is one of the nasty infections that can occur here. UC is like an extension of Crohn's, but located farther down your gut. UC's cause is still unknown, but studies are starting to implicate microbes, among them *Pseudomonas aeruginosa*. UC is also related to an overactive immune response, which can cause inflammation even in the absence of microbes, further complicating our understanding of the condition. Both Crohn's and UC involve inflammation, which is often associated with anxiety and depression, highlighting a gut-brain connection. Some studies show good results treating UC with the yeast called *Saccharomyces boulardii*. If further studies substantiate them, *S. boulardii* may make it into the pantheon of psychobiotics.

Moving through your colon, the chyme becomes more viscous. The bacteria that made it through your small intestine are now rapidly multiplying. The extra size of your colon means that there is plenty of time and room for the chyme to slowly inch by, bubbling and fermenting as it goes. This is the source of flatulence, which is actually a sign of a properly functioning microbiota.

The Cast of Characters in Your Colon

With plenty of fiber to eat, warm mucus to snuggle into, a perfect pH, and low oxygen levels, this part of your colon is a bacterial paradise, and many of the bacteria thriving here have psychobiotic properties.

Bifido is prevalent here, including the psychobiotics *B. longum* and *B. breve*. *Bifido* have been with you since you were born; your mother's milk included these bacteria to enhance its digestibility. Now, as the *Bifido* proliferate in your large intestine, they help squelch your anxiety via your vagus nerve. If you cut that nerve, anxiety can return.[2] We will return to this gut-brain connection later in the book.

Clostridia, another class of bacteria that thrives in your colon, includes some bad guys and good guys. You are better off without the pathogens *C. botulinum* and *C. difficile,* both of which can cause serious distress and disease, but other species of *Clostridia,* like *Faecalibacterium prausnitzii,* are benign, even helpful. They eat oligosaccharides and excrete the fatty acid butyrate, which is a favorite food of the cells lining your colon. Their largesse is not an accident. *Clostridia* and our gut cells have been sharing the same dark space for millions of years, and they each know just what the other one likes. In gratitude for the butyrate, your gut cells secrete more mucus, a welcome medium for the bacteria, and this accommodation between human and bacterial cells is a big win for both parties.

Butyrate, along with other fatty acids, plays an important role in health. It's responsible for improving glucose tolerance and can soothe immune cells. For instance, *F. prausnitzii* can reduce bowel disturbances, including Crohn's, by using butyrate to mute your immune response. Butyrate also modifies certain genes in your brain, encouraging cellular repair and potentially leading to better mental health. These epigenetic changes may even affect how your brain responds to antidepressants—a result that might be leveraged to allow lower doses of antidepressants in favor of psychobiotics.

Another old friend found in your colon is *Lacto*. We saw these microbes in your small intestine, where they proved their mettle by being one of the first to make a home in that acidic environment. But *Lacto* species are very versatile players, and you will find *L. acidophilus, L. brevis, L. casei, L. helveticus, L. rhamnosus*, and others forming fertile colonies in your colon as well. These species all have psychobiotic properties.

Your colon pampers the bacteria that produce vitamins that humans cannot normally synthesize. *Bifido, Lacto,* and *Propionibacteria* can all produce B vitamins, including B_{12}, thiamine, riboflavin, niacin, biotin, and folic acid. A shortage of these vitamins can lead to depression, so here is yet another major psychobiotic contribution made by these microbes in your large intestine. And that's not all: Bacteria like *E. coli* help produce various forms of vitamin K, important in blood clotting. You can find it in green vegetables, but the bacteria in your gut make the bulk of what you use. Babies without a good bacterial system in place may not be able to get enough vitamin K, and it is common to give newborns a shot of it to get them started. There is also some evidence that vitamin K can reduce anxiety.

Bacteria in your gut secrete other essentials, including neurotransmitters, the chemicals that your nerve cells use to communicate. These are surprisingly small molecules that move easily around the body, but they cannot make it past the **blood-brain barrier** (BBB), the intricate cellular interface that keeps the environment of your brain and your body separated. It's astonishing that bacteria can produce neurotransmitters at all. The bacteria don't have a brain or nervous system, so why do they need neurotransmitters? These chemicals may facilitate interbacterial communication, but in the meantime they are sending messages to your gut and your brain.

The nature and condition of neurotransmitters affect your mood, and most pharmacological drugs address depression and anxiety by treating your neurotransmitters. The fact is: Your bacteria naturally produce neurotransmitters in a volume that rivals that provided by prescription drugs. Although it's still not clear how these neuroactive molecules get to your brain, if we can control the type and amount of them secreted by your bacteria, we might have a more natural treatment for mood disorders. Neurotransmitters, and the bacteria that produce them, play a key role in psychobiotic therapy.

For instance, *Lacto* and *Bifido*, two of the bacteria genera abundant in your colon, both produce GABA (gamma-aminobutyric acid), a key neurotransmitter that can have a tranquilizing effect, dialing down your anxiety. This is one of the more promising pathways for psychobiotic treatment. In one study, these bacteria, especially *L. rhamnosus* (provided in a probiotic mix), produced a result similar to that of Prozac, but without the side effects. GABA has a calming effect on your immune system as well, and may be useful in treating conditions such as IBD. How does the GABA make it to your brain? The vagus nerve is involved; if you cut it, the effect disappears.

In the colon, *Streptococcus* and *Escherichia* species produce serotonin—the "happiness" neurotransmitter that is an important player in mood and provides the guiding rationale for selective serotonin reuptake inhibitors (SSRIs), a class of drugs designed to maintain serotonin levels in the body and now the most popular type of drug prescribed for mood disorders.

We could soon see pharmaceutical SSRIs augmented or replaced by psychobiotics. It's not an unreasonable expectation, because some 90 percent of the body's serotonin is found in the gut. That's because your gut—the second brain—uses the same neuroactive chemicals to compute and process information as the first brain does. Serotonin plays a major role in digestion, because it's the main neurotransmitter behind peristalsis. In fact, a quarter of people who take SSRIs end up with changes in gut motility. In low doses, Prozac can be used to treat the gut, helping ease constipation by encouraging peristaltic motion.[3] It isn't too much of a stretch to posit that some of the success of SSRIs has to do with their effect on the gut.

A close look at your gut lining helps to show how the serotonin system works there. Among the normal gut cells, we see the ***enterochromaffin cells*** (ECs) that stud your entire gut lining, commonly called speckled cells because when they are stained, you can see multiple dark spots in them, like raisins in a cookie. These spots are granules containing serotonin. ECs are sensitive to attack by bacteria or physical jostling, and if disturbed, an EC will eject its cache of serotonin, exciting the nearby nerves, which then stimulate your gut muscles to start a peristaltic push. The more bacteria and the more jostling, the greater the peristaltic signal. With enough stimulus, everything can exit your gut in a matter of minutes. At that dramatic moment, in a rush of diarrhea designed to purge your pathogens, no one thinks of serotonin as the happiness molecule.

By the time we reach this part of the intestinal journey, most of the food you ate several hours ago has been digested—chewed up, broken down, dissolved, and otherwise harvested for all its worth—and the bacterial levels have exploded. From the straggling fraction of bacteria that survived all the acid, bile, and antimicrobials in upper reaches of your digestive system, a respectable population is heading out the other end, in the form of poop. In fact, up to 60 percent of the dry weight of your poop is composed of bacteria. You were an excellent host.

Looking Back on the Journey

That brings us to the end of our voyage. On this gastronomic cruise, we visited all the dark corners of your GI tract. We saw villi growing upon villi, and realized how ridiculously thin and tender your gut lining is, especially considering that it is under continuous assault by a menagerie of microbes. We encountered probiotic and psychobiotic microbes that turned out to be important companions, protecting that flimsy gut lining, day and night. We saw more mucus than we ever wanted to.

Perhaps you learned something about the gut part of this gut-brain puzzle, which turns out to be critical for your happiness. Whether you feel sick to your stomach or just have the butterflies that accompany anxiety, you can point to your gut and know that it is valiantly trying to fend off the worst pathogens nature can throw at it, even as we sabotage it by eating pathogen favorites such as doughnuts and ice cream.

In the following chapter, we'll look closer at the very intimate connections between your gut and your brain. If you think things are full of intrigue here in your gut, you'll be amazed to see how this all fits in with your brain.

CHAPTER 5

THE GUT-BRAIN AXIS

"Nature is everywhere gothic, not classic.
She forms a real jungle, where all things are provisional,
half-fitted to each other, and untidy."

—William James

Now that you've met the leading microbial players in your gut, including both psychobiotics and pathogens, let's look at how they manage to converse with your brain. Taken together, these intricate and interconnected channels of communication make up the powerful gut-brain axis that is where the psychobiotic revolution takes place.

Accumulating data now indicate that the gut microbiota communicates with the central nervous system (CNS) through neural, immune, and endocrine pathways—and thereby influences brain function and behavior. Studies in germ-free animals and in animals exposed to pathogens, probiotics, or antibiotics suggest a role for the gut microbiota in the regulation of anxiety, mood, cognition, and pain. Thus, the emerging concept of a microbiota-gut-brain axis suggests that modulation of the gut microbiota may be a winning strategy for developing novel therapies for complex CNS disorders.[1]

There are three main communication channels between your brain and your gut: your nervous system, your immune system, and your endocrine system. The circulatory and lymphatic systems also play supporting roles, but these first three are dominant. Each system is used differently by the microbes that affect your mood. Each has its own unique chemical language, but they also need to coordinate with one another, and so they have some signaling molecules in common as well. These systems interact with each other, making it difficult to discuss any of them in isolation. (William James was right—nature is untidy—but let's give it a try.)

To keep the conversation lively between your second and first brain, the three main systems of communication have the following primary tasks and chemicals they use to accomplish them:

- The *nervous system* relays information to and throughout your brain. It communicates using chemicals called neurotransmitters. Its communication style is fast and point to point, but short-acting.
- The *immune system* is at the ready to rally a defensive response against threats to healthy homeostasis. It uses the protein molecules called cytokines to signal distress. It can communicate quickly, but its urgent chemical effect can be harsh enough to cause tissue damage.
- The *endocrine system* monitors and manages growth and metabolism. Its component glands communicate by secreting *hormones* into your blood and thus sending signals

throughout the body. Its operations are slower, more moderate and systemic, but longer-acting than those of the other two systems.

We're going to see all of these systems in action with a case study in which they each make an appearance. But before we can do that, we need a little more background. Here's a quick overview of each system separately.

THE NERVOUS SYSTEM

The nervous system has two major divisions: the central nervous system (CNS), composed of the brain and spine, and the peripheral nervous system, less well known but just as important. The peripheral nervous system divides into four parts: somatic, sympathetic, parasympathetic, and enteric. To achieve optimal gut-brain health, all four parts are operative, in balance, and in communication with one another and with the CNS.

You use the *somatic* nervous system whenever you voluntarily do anything: walk, talk, wave your arms, look up, look down—all the many things you decide to do (or not to do). In the context of psychobiotics, the somatic system matters because you maintain voluntary control over what you eat (or don't eat)—and thus, you exert some nervous system control over your microbiota.

The *sympathetic* nervous system is the part often nicknamed "fight or flight." When stresses cross a threshold and press your brain and body into action, this system takes over, whether or not you want it to. When that happens, the sympathetic system takes priority; when it's activated, in other words, all other systems get put on the back burner. The stresses that activate this system can be

external—anything from a tiger attack to a frustrating traffic jam—
or internal—tension held in muscles or, pertinent to psychobiotics,
food habits that trigger continued inflammation in the gut.

The *parasympathetic* nervous system has a nickname, too: "feed
and breed." This system is what life is really all about. Eat, drink,
and be merry—and don't forget to have babies to keep the species
going. When the parasympathetic nervous system is chugging
along, you achieve a state of health, happiness, and balance we all
strive for. The psychobiotic revolution—and the point of this
book—promises that you can learn things and make decisions that
will convert an abused sympathetic response into a happier parasympathetic response, where life is good.

The *enteric* nervous system is the one that operates in your gut,
your second brain. It is intimately connected with the rest of the
nervous system but operates with its own set of rules. This system,
including your microbiota, holds the keys to dismantling any
chronic stress responses you may be experiencing, and to returning
your body to a healthy homeostasis. Tune in to the messages of your
enteric nervous system, and you'll find the way to put yourself in a
cheerier groove.

Becoming more aware of your enteric nervous systems may
not be easy. Sympathetic, parasympathetic, and enteric—all three
of these systems operate on autopilot, so typically you don't even
think about them. Your gut is remarkably independent, and it
doesn't really need your brain to tell it what to do. Peristalsis and
other gut movements are under local control, so much so that
you can cut all the gut's nerves to the brain and it will still pulse
with purpose.

Your gut is wired to your brain through your spine and through
your vagus nerve, but the vagus is the primary two-way communication channel for mood, so it's the one we pay the most attention

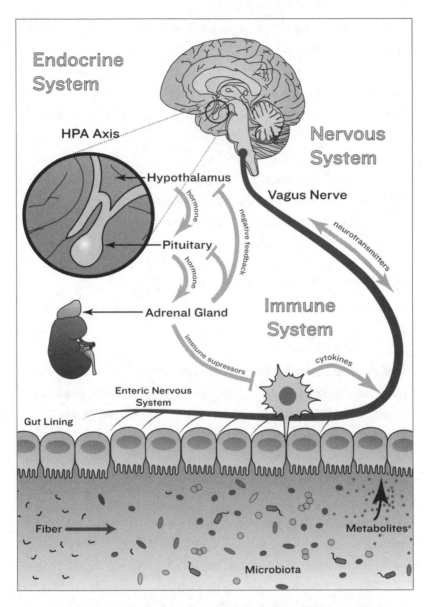

Gut-brain communication occurs through multiple channels, including the nervous system (using neurotransmitters via the vagus nerve), immune system (using cytokines via the blood system), and endocrine system (using hormones such as cortisol via the blood system).

to when discussing psychobiotics. It winds down from your brain through your torso, stopping by your lungs and heart on the way to your gut. The name, from the same root as "vagrant," means wandering, which perfectly describes its meandering path through the organs of your torso. Where it joins the gut, it sends nerve fibers out like a branching vine to reach all parts of the digestive system, from top to bottom.

Signals travel throughout the nervous system thanks to molecules we call neurotransmitters. Surprisingly, these same chemicals are found in plants as well as animals and bacteria, thus playing a role in all the kingdoms of life. In each of these cases, they act as signaling molecules, just as they do in the brain. They are the short, common words in the language of life. Considering their multiple uses, these molecules probably deserve a name other than neurotransmitter.

Inside the webbing of the enteric nervous system, bacteria busily make chemicals to communicate with each other—and they use many of the same neurotransmitter chemicals that the nervous system employs. The bacteria in your gut both secrete and respond to neurotransmitters including *dopamine*, *serotonin*, and *GABA*, all of which can have antidepressant properties in the brain. It's likely that this is one of the primary ways gut bacteria influence your mood.

The exact mechanism, however, isn't clear. Although your brain uses neurotransmitters to send messages, it doesn't want a lot of background noise to disturb its delicate signals. That's one reason why there is a blood-brain barrier (BBB)—a complex structure protecting the precious organ from all that's around it. The BBB blocks most neurotransmitters from your gut—and the rest of your body as well. For the same reason, there is a barrier between your blood and your gut-brain as well. Still, research shows that these neurotransmitters *do* have an impact on the brain and usually the vagus nerve is involved. But the details are still being worked out.

Why do bacteria churn out so many neurotransmitters? One theory is that these bacteria want to control your cravings. This makes perfect sense, really: If you feed *Streptococcus* (just to take a single example of a sugar-hungry microbe) with doughnuts, it chows down and then produces dopamine. It doesn't take long for you to connect those doughnuts to your happiness, and a new craving is established. A species of bacteria has used its own neurotransmitters to coerce you into delivering special foods to it.

Three Mood Centers

Where your spinal cord enters your brain, there is a swelling called the brain stem. There, in several special centers, neurotransmitters that control your mood are produced. One mood center is called the locus ceruleus (LC)—a fancy Latin name that means "blue spot." The LC produces noradrenalin (norepinephrine), which causes you to wake up and pay attention. In response to stress, the LC alerts your amygdala, which processes fear. If the stress continues or increases, you will move from being alert to feeling anxious and even panicked.

Another mood center is actually a small cluster of nodes in the brain stem called the raphe nuclei (RN). *Raphe* is Latin for "seam," and indeed these nuclei form a ridge, or seam, down the center of the brain stem. The RN produces serotonin and distributes it to the amygdala, the hypothalamus, the LC, and the forebrain, affecting wakefulness, cognition, and mood. When this mood center isn't functioning properly, it can cause sleep disruptions and changes in your perception of hunger and pain. It can also cause depression.

A third mood center is the ventral tegmental area (VTA), which produces dopamine. This neurotransmitter is involved with the brain's reward system. When you win the lottery, a rush of dopamine floods your brain, and you feel happy. Dopamine is involved with emotion, motivation, and addiction. Problems with your VTA can lead to anxiety and depression.

Many other centers around the brain stem all interact with each other, sending complex messages throughout the brain, sometimes lifting and sometimes crushing your mood. It's all interconnected, and many of these connections are still under study in research labs around the world. The basics are known without question, though: Neurotransmitters like serotonin and dopamine can make you happy, and their lack can make you depressed or anxious. And microbes make them.

YOUR IMMUNE SYSTEM

Your immune system includes nodes and lymph vessels that extend throughout your body. When you get a cut, immune cells rush to the rescue, and their activity produces the familiar heat, redness, and swelling of inflammation. It's a battle you need to win locally before it becomes systemic.

The immune reaction starts at the site of an infection and can grow from there. Cruising immune cells discover foreign bacteria, using antibodies to tag them. Antibodies are the main tools of the immune system, attaching themselves to specific molecules called antigens that exist on the surface of a pathogen. Once tagged, they can be rounded up or simply destroyed. The system uses cytokines to spread the alarm and coordinate the response of other immune cells. Cytokines are small proteins, so they are mobile and therefore good for sending signals from one cell to another. Whenever a pathogen is detected, cytokines are produced by the heavy-hitter immune cells. But the cells lining the gut can also produce cytokines—which means that virtually every cell of the GI tract can trigger an immune response. Immune factors like fatty acids and cytokines activate **microglia,** the immune cells in the brain, which will fight pathogens but may also lead to anxiety or depression.

Microbes can also produce cytokines. Some of these microbes can talk directly to your immune system, which can be bad news or good news. The bad news is that pathogenic microbes can encourage inflammation. The good news is that psychobiotic microbes will lower inflammation, either directly or indirectly, by helping to heal the gut lining that became inflamed.

Acetylcholine plays a role in this healing. It is a neurotransmitter used throughout your entire nervous system, including your enteric system. Acetylcholine commands marauding immune cells to stop overreacting to microbes. Stimulating the vagus nerve causes acetylcholine to be produced, which, along with cortisol, suppresses the immune system.[2] Many bacteria, including *Lacto* species, can also produce acetylcholine, and they may thereby gain access to the powerful levers of the immune machine. They effectively inject themselves into your homeostatic system, and that is a major aspect of their psychobiotic effect.

Because so many cell types secrete cytokines and so many cell types receive them, it is a fantastically complex system. Some cytokines are inflammatory and others are anti-inflammatory. If the scales tilt chronically toward the former, depression and anxiety can set in over time. In fact, research has shown that just injecting certain cytokines can induce depression.[3] Immune cells produce cytokines when pathogens show up. These signals quickly reach nerve cells in your gut and are then conveyed to the brain through the vagus nerve, providing information about the type and severity of the inflammation.

Your immune system thus serves as a key channel for microbe-brain communications, conveying information about microbial action going on in the gut to several parts of the nervous system at once and thereby meeting the microbial challenge head-on. It's faster and more direct than an endocrine response. The end result, if the pathogen is deemed nasty enough, is a purge, including vomiting and diarrhea. It's an unsubtle way to deal with pathogens, but it works.

This is the balancing act that your immune system maintains: It must be ready to kill invaders or infected cells at a moment's notice, and at the same time it must give similar-looking healthy cells a pass. And when it determines that the infection has been routed, your immune system then needs to calm down and morph back into a watchful state.

Unfortunately, it doesn't always work that way. The inflammation experienced as the immune system responds to pathogens may give rise to psychological problems. And it can also go the other way: Stress can change the effectiveness of your immune system responses as well.[4] Your immune system has been using antibodies as if they were "Wanted" posters identifying foreign microbes. But under stress, the antibody traffic slows down—one of your immune system's ways to conserve energy for the most essential tasks. That lowers the level of scrutiny, allowing pathogens to sneak through and gain a foothold. Once there, they can cause infection or make your gut develop leaks.

In short, your body hobbles your immune system while it deals with stress. For the short term, that may be a wise choice. If you are running from a tiger, your ulcer will have to wait. But if the stress persists and the stress reaction goes on too long, that resulting leaky gut may itself cause further inflammation, initiating a deadly positive feedback loop. The sicker you get, the sicker you will get, raising depression to a new level.

YOUR ENDOCRINE SYSTEM

The vagus nerve plays a key role in all these bacterial interactions. It connects to the brain through a specialized chunk of nerves, a portion of the brain called the hypothalamus, meaning "under the thalamus." About the size of a kidney bean, the hypothalamus is part of your limbic system—the ancient neurological circuitry shared by birds and crocodiles all the way up to mammals. It is central to your mood, motivation, hunger, and sleep.

The hypothalamus is a cross between a brain and a gland, and it bridges the nervous system and the endocrine system. It can reach out past the BBB with specialized nerve cells that sample your blood to detect signs of inflammation.

In your gut, immune cells snip off identifying bits of bacteria that act as ID tags for both beneficial and pathogenic microbes and carry them through your blood and lymphatic systems. Your hypothalamus responds to both good and bad bacterial tags, but it has a strong and prolonged response to the pathogen tags. It conveys alarm signals to your pituitary and adrenal glands. These three organs—the hypothalamus, pituitary gland, and the adrenal gland—constitute the **HPA axis,** a primary network for communication between the gut and the brain. When inflammation is detected, the HPA axis releases cortisol, among other hormones, to respond to the stress. This response is instrumental in mood regulation, and many people with depression or anxiety have a

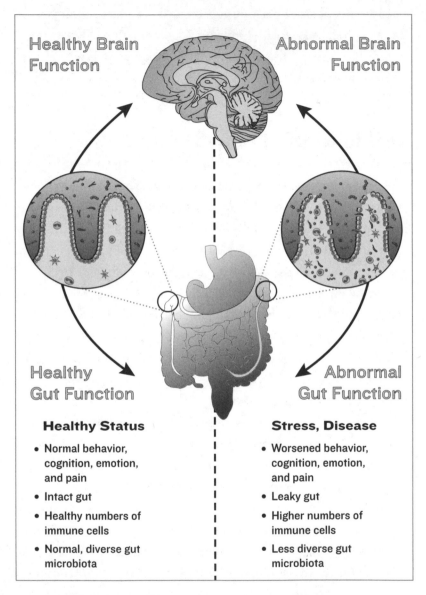

Healthy Brain Function

Abnormal Brain Function

Healthy Gut Function

Abnormal Gut Function

Healthy Status

- Normal behavior, cognition, emotion, and pain
- Intact gut
- Healthy numbers of immune cells
- Normal, diverse gut microbiota

Stress, Disease

- Worsened behavior, cognition, emotion, and pain
- Leaky gut
- Higher numbers of immune cells
- Less diverse gut microbiota

A healthy gut (left) maintains homeostasis; a dysbiotic gut (right) lets pathogens through, sparking an inflammation in the brain as well as the gut.

problematic HPA axis. Fixing problems with this axis, we now understand, can be a way to relieve depression and anxiety.

THE QUEST FOR HOMEOSTASIS

The nervous, the immune, and the endocrine systems all have one thing in common: They are in a rut, and they like it that way. Or, to put it more scientifically, they all seek a state of *homeostasis*. This aspect of living systems was first established by Claude Bernard, a French physiologist in the 1800s who realized that an animal adjusts its biology to its environment, compensating for external changes by using tools including heart rate, hormones, blood pressure, and immune responses, as well as dozens of other biological systems.

The biological imperative to stabilize the internal environment is called homeostasis, and it's fundamental to all living creatures—including bacteria. Homeostasis controls every aspect of your biological life. Your heart rate and breathing rate, for instance, are your body's ways to guarantee that your oxygen levels stay within a healthy range, no matter where you are or what you are doing. You may think it's boring to be in a rut, but when it comes to breathing and pumping blood, you don't want drama.

A classic homeostatic system is temperature regulation. It works like your home thermostat: When the room gets a couple of degrees lower than the set point, the thermostat turns on the heat. If the room gets a couple of degrees hotter than the set point, it turns on the air conditioner. Similarly, your body temperature wants to stay between about 97°F and 100°F. Too cold, and you shiver, generating heat. Too hot, and you sweat, dissipating heat. This is how homeostasis maintains equilibrium and keeps you—and your associated microbiota—alive.

Homeostasis is life pushing back, but it's a moment-by-moment adjustment not designed for long-term engagements. The ultimate goal is to return to an optimal set point, which is done with negative feedback: When a signal is detected, the feedback quickly dampens it. Mother Nature has evolved several different methods of negative feedback. One of the easiest is this: Make the end product turn off the starting switch. This is like the "useless machine" that you may have seen at novelty stores: When you click the switch on the box, a door opens and a hand comes out to turn the switch off. It's a goofy toy, but a great illustration of simple negative feedback. All organic systems include negative feedback of one form or another so that reactions will extinguish themselves, bringing everything back to a homeostatic ideal.

Most of the time, your body maintains homeostasis with ease. But at times things fall out of balance and there are no automatic ways to maintain homeostasis. When that happens, your brain is alerted. It may be a nudge or it may be a Klaxon call, depending on the problem. Sometimes these signals come from your gut, desperately trying to get your attention, but unfortunately, microbes mumble, and all you get is a vague sense of anxiety. If this process goes on for a long time, it can manifest as depression. And when you don't know what the problem is, it's hard to fix it.

Your microbiota is also trying to maintain homeostasis. It works hard to preserve a steady core group of microbes, and it's hard to change when it gets into a groove. Depending on what you eat, you encourage blooms of different bacterial species, but between meals your core microbiota will reassert itself. You have to do a lot of damage to upset this balance, but it can happen over time with a poor diet—or at a much faster pace with a course of antibiotics.

Negative feedback loops in living systems prevent runaway reactions that can be lethal. In the endocrine system, for example, a gland produces a hormone that has a built-in side effect that stops production at a certain point, so only a small spurt is allowed before the loop automatically throttles back. In a stress-free environment, these hormonal systems oscillate during the day, following circadian rhythms and sleep patterns. But a stress-free life is not the norm, and circumstances inside and out can disrupt the cycle. The more effectively you can find ways to help your brain, gut, and body maintain homeostasis, the longer, healthier, and happier your life will be.

A CASE STUDY

To appreciate how all these gut-brain systems coordinate with each other, let's go back to the example of Walkerton, Ontario, the town mentioned earlier (page 43), where an infection struck the entire population of 5,000 people. Many suffered severely and remain affected to this day. It's a dramatic example, but it's not unusual. Infections like this lead to IBS and depression in more than 10 million Americans each year. It was a watershed case in the field of psychobiotics, providing clear evidence of how long-term exposure to pathogens can induce depression and anxiety. It can help us track the operations and interconnections of the three main communication channels in the gut-brain axis: the nervous, immune, and endocrine systems.

When the flood hit Walkerton in 2000, bacteria-ridden farm effluent contaminated the town's water supply with *Campylobacter jejuni,* a well-known pathogen that we will shorten to simply *Campy.* Thousands fell sick with bacterial gastroenteritis, and many of those people later came down with chronic depression and anxiety. Something like this, or a milder version of it, may be a part of your story, too. To really appreciate what these people went through, let's imagine you are living in Walkerton as this catastrophe occurs.

It all starts innocently enough with a sip of water. *Campy* is sensitive to stomach acids, so when you drink the tap water containing it, some will be quickly killed. (If you happen to take antacids regularly, though, more *Campy* will make it through. And if you're on proton pump inhibitors, you double your risk of getting really sick.[5]) Although their numbers will be diminished on the way down, many of these pathogens will still make it to your small intestine and colon. These bacteria have recently come from inside a cow or a chicken, so they are pretty much at home in that environment. For most cows and chickens, *Campy* is a commensal. Not for humans! Why it goes berserk in the human gut is unknown, but *Campy* is potent: It is the number one cause of diarrhea in the United States, ahead of *Salmonella* and *E. coli*.[6]

Your Nervous System Is Notified

Within hours after your first drink of tainted water, you may feel a little queasy and anxious. This is a nervous system reaction—the first system of the gut-brain axis to be triggered by the pathogen. In response to the *Campy,* special cells lining your intestines secrete serotonin, which acts as a warning signal. The vagus nerve collects these complaints from your gut and relays them to your brain within seconds.

You may be about to become very sick, but for now what you feel is vague and hard to pin down. *Campy* and the gut commensals that rally to fight it can cause anxiety even without a full-blown infection. At this point your nervous system alone is detecting the pathogen. So far, your immune and endocrine systems are none the wiser, but your microbiota recognizes the threat and mounts a serious battle against the *Campy,* knocking its numbers down considerably. You may start to feel a little anxious and antisocial, but with no real clue of what is about to occur. This is an early shot over the bow, but your brain now knows something is up down below.

Ironically, if by chance you have taken antibiotics recently for some other reason, you will not have your front line of defense and you will be harder hit by the *Campy*. Some heroic microbes— including *Bifido* and *Lacto* species, both psychobiotics—may emerge from your microbiota to face down the *Campy*.[7] If you're healthy, at this point they can probably outcompete and crowd out the *Campy*, preventing them from sticking to your cell walls. However, if you keep drinking the contaminated water, you will soon overwhelm your microbial defenses, and the pathogens will start to colonize your gut.

Campy can "taste" mucus and when it does, it moves toward it. Once there, it eats through your mucus lining, leaving your gut cells exposed. It attaches to cells and makes a toxin that stops your gut cells from dividing. Without division, your cells cannot renew themselves and instead they die. With an impaired lining, your gut starts leaking. By 24 hours after your first drink of infected water, *Campy* has seeped through your gut lining and is starting to move into the tissues surrounding your gut. Surprisingly, *Campy* has so far escaped the scrutiny of your immune system. Many pathogens have the ability to appear innocent to your immune system, but *Campy* is a master of the technique. Pathogen-induced leaky gut underlies dozens of diseases that are strongly associated with depression and anxiety. The worst is yet to come.

Your Immune System Wakes Up

After 48 hours you begin to sense real trouble. You start to get serious cramping and diarrhea. Your immune system has finally taken notice, and it becomes the second system of the gut-brain connection to go on alert. More serotonin is released, causing strong pulses of peristalsis. Your immune system gets busy releasing cytokines, which act like sirens alerting the local immune community and summoning help. More immune cells are recruited, more cytokines are released, and the effect starts to cascade.

The immune system lacks subtlety and when it gets triggered, it can go crazy. In its zeal to track down and kill the *Campy,* your immune system sends out killer cells that may lay waste to your own gut lining, increasing inflammation and leakiness. Now headaches and fever may go along with your diarrhea as the cytokines make their way up to your hypothalamus via the bloodstream.

Your HPA Axis Is Turned On

Your hypothalamus is always alert to stress signals coming either from the outside or the inside environment. Cytokines trigger your HPA axis. Your hypothalamus responds to the cytokines that it senses in your blood by sending a message to your adrenal glands via the pituitary to secrete hormones designed to keep your infection from burning you up. The end product is the stress hormone cortisol. Now your endocrine system has entered the fray, the third channel of the gut-brain connection.

Cortisol can cause you to become anxious, but its main job here is to temper your immune reaction, which right now is continuing to heat up.[8] During an infection, your HPA axis acts as a pathogen monitor: The more pathogens, the more cortisol manufactured, and the greater your anxiety. Cortisol also exerts negative feedback on itself, dampening the whole HPA cascade— at least until cytokines are detected again, whereupon it again produces stress hormones.

Thus, chronic inflammation produces stress hormones indefinitely, leading to a surprising number of mental issues, including bipolar disorder, post-traumatic stress disorder, attention deficit disorder, depression, and anxiety. Our story here is about *Campy*, but a similar process is initiated by hundreds of other infectious agents. A simple contagion can lead to long-term dysbiosis and consequent mental distress. Antidepressants are often prescribed for these maladies, but if your own psychobiotic microbes can reduce the inflammation, your HPA axis can return to homeostatic normalcy and you may be able to treat some of these conditions without drugs.

If you stop drinking the water, 30 days later you will start to feel better. Your commensal microbes have done their job and returned your microbiota to the homeostasis it craves. You have a low pathogen count, and you're feeling okay. But that's not going to be the case for everyone.

The Aftermath

Three to six months later, one in five of the people in Walkerton who was infected with *Campy* had come down with IBS and was still experiencing its psychological fellow travelers, depression and anxiety.[9] This delay is why many people don't make the connection, but the Walkerton example made it clear that inflammation lies behind many psychiatric issues. Thank goodness, most of the citizens of Walkerton are now fully recovered. The people who came down with IBS and depression have been treated with antidepressants and cognitive behavioral therapy. Some of them are using psychobiotics.

The Walkerton case is extreme, but this scenario represents a fairly typical course of inflammation. First the nervous system is alerted and your gut signals your brain through the vagus nerve. Then your immune system kicks in, battling the pathogens, but not without collateral damage. Finally your endocrine system is called upon to moderate your raging immune system. These three systems represent fast, medium, and slow rates of communication, respectively—and each is capable of inducing anxiety and depression.

It's not known exactly how many cases of depression are related to infections like this one with *Campy*. But postinfectious dysbiosis is not uncommon. If you are depressed, think back. Have you suffered from a gastric insult? Bacterial gastroenteritis is very common: About 180 million cases occur each year in the United States. That's about half of us, each and every year. And gastroenteritis often does bring with it depression and anxiety, both acute and chronic. Learn to defend against this sort of bacterial dysbiosis, and you can improve your mood. A healthy microbiota is your first defense, and keeping it in working order is therefore the key to a good mood.

OTHER GUT-BRAIN CONNECTIONS

Gut microbes can talk to your brain in other ways, each one presenting an opportunity to intercede on behalf of a good mood. Every psychobiotic has its own habits and proclivities, and the more we know about them, the better we can treat them when they are unbalanced. Here are some of those other back channels.

Circulatory Systems

An important route from the gut to the brain is the circulatory system. Your blood regularly ferries microbes and their secretions throughout your body, including to the thousands of miles of capillaries in your brain. Generally speaking, microbes should stay in your gut, not your blood, where they can infect other bodily systems. The job of the blood-brain barrier is to keep invading microbes (and other things) outside the brain, but you can do your part by keeping your gut lining healthy and intact to prevent systemic infections spread by your circulatory system.

Your lymphatic system transports lymph fluid throughout your body. It bathes and cleanses the tissues as it goes. It loads up with bacteria, both alive and dead, that need to be removed from your body. The brain was long thought to lack a lymphatic system, but we now know that it does indeed have one, and it may prove to play an important role in the gut-brain axis. There is no equivalent of a heart to pump the lymph. The circulation of lymph is entirely driven by body motion, so exercise is essential to lymphatic health.

Bacteria to the Rescue

Sometimes your gut bacteria get into the action and set up defenses against pathogens. *Lactobacillus reuteri,* for example, can directly excite sensory neurons in the gut and influence peristalsis, typically to slow it down. *L. reuteri* can also dampen pain, with signals to the brain through the vagus that things are okay in the gut.

Sometimes we can capitalize on long-standing family feuds between bacteria in your gut. Nurturing the proper microbes can subdue pathogens with very little collateral damage, so this is an important new research direction. The probiotic Nissle 1917, for instance, chases down and rids the body of closely related pathogenic *E. coli.* Once pathogens are selectively banished, an all-clear signal is sent to the brain, helping to allay depression and anxiety. This example stands as a possible direction for probiotics in the future. Because they can kill pathogens while leaving commensals alone, probiotics like this might replace antibiotics in some cases, all the more important as bacteria are becoming increasingly resistant to our best antibiotics.

Short-Chain Fatty Acids

Your microbes can also communicate with your brain through small molecules called *short-chain fatty acids* (SCFAs), which some bacteria produce as they consume fiber. SCFAs can essentially melt through cell membranes. They are directly detected by your second brain, which has receptors for them all along the gut that are connected through the vagus nerve to your brain.

Not all SCFAs have the same impact on your gut health and mood, however. Some have been shown to reduce depression and sadness. In one study, people showed an improved mood within minutes of receiving a dose of lauric acid, a fatty acid component of coconut oil.[10] Butyrate is another SCFA with a lot of benefits. It's the preferred energy source for the cells lining your gut. It can also enter the brain, where it encourages brain growth factors and acts as an antidepressant.

Butyrate, along with other fermentation-derived SCFAs, shows promising effects in various diseases including obesity, diabetes, and inflammatory diseases as well as neurological disorders. Indeed, it is clear that host energy metabolism and immune functions critically depend on butyrate as a potent regulator, highlighting butyrate as a key mediator of host-microbe crosstalk. We hypothesize that butyrate and other volatile SCFAs produced by microbes may be involved in regulating the impact of the microbiota on behavior, including social communication.

In higher doses, some SCFAs are detrimental. Propionic acid, another bacterial secretion, has been shown to induce autistic-like behavior in rats.[11] Propionic and acetic acids are also associated with elevated anxiety in patients with IBS.[12] Depleting bacteria that produce these SCFAs is important for balancing your microbiota.

Fatty acids, as the name implies, are energy rich, and too many of them may lead to weight gain, so this approach to psychobiotic therapy might need to be modified for people who are overweight. Nevertheless, SCFAs play an important role in psychobiotics. Later in the book we will come back to them, showing how to increase the butyrate-producing bacteria in your gut to improve your health and mood.[13]

THE GUT EFFECTS OF STRESS

The nervous system uses neurotransmitters to communicate while the endocrine system uses hormones. They have different names, but in reality these two classes of molecules are close relatives, and in fact some hormones can act as neurotransmitters and vice versa.[14] Some double-duty neurotransmitter/hormones, including norepinephrine and dopamine, have a curious effect on gut pathogens such as *Salmonella* and *E. coli*: They cause them to bloom, dramatically increasing their numbers.[15] Different species of bacteria each have a preference for specific hormones, but norepinephrine is a clear favorite of many.

These molecules are stress hormones, called upon as part of the fight-or-flight response. Their job is to make you anxious and alert. They act throughout your body as stimulants, increasing your heart rate and blood pressure. Fight-or-flight reaction takes precedence over all other bodily functions. It subdues the gut and the immune system, which lowers your guard throughout your entire GI tract, potentially allowing pathogens to thrive.

When you combine reduced gut scrutiny with hormones that encourage the growth of pathogens, you have a perfect storm. That means that when you're stressed and your defenses are down, the odds become better for pathogens to attack.[16] People who are stressed become more susceptible to infection and inflammation. That in turn can lead to greater stress, a vicious spiral that can leave people deeply anxious and depressed.

Stress can cause other physical and chemical changes in your gut. It can alter the levels of acids, mucus, and other intestinal secretions, disturbing the cozy environment your microbes have grown accustomed to. These responses to stress can, perversely, favor increased levels of pathogens such as *Clostridia,* further aggravating your stress. One study compared fecal samples donated by students at the beginning of classes to samples donated during finals. The end-of-semester stress significantly lowered their levels of healthy *Lactobacilli.*[17] Stress hormones and neurohormones reduce your good microbes at the same time that they increase your pathogen load. Strategies to dampen these vicious cycles are central to psychobiotic therapies under development.

The evidence is clear: Microbes play a big role in managing your mood. Rather than a simple wad of bacteria, your microbiota acts much more like a bona fide organ, a bulwark against a world of ever-evolving predators. And in the process, it exerts a remarkable amount of control over your frame of mind. We've actually known about this state of affairs for centuries, but that knowledge has gone in and out of fashion repeatedly. In the next chapter, we'll take a closer look at that mottled history.

CHAPTER 6

DISCOVERING PSYCHOBIOTICS

"So, early as Hippocrates, the abdominal viscera
were regarded as the principal seats of disease in mania
and melancholia. This doctrine has been, at various times,
forgotten and revived from that period to the present moment,
according as circumstances have occurred to influence
the minds of the medical practitioners and as the opinions
of the metaphysical or physical pathologists have prevailed."

—David Uwins, M.D., physician to the City of London Dispensary, 1818

HAVE YOU HEARD? THERE IS AN EPIDEMIC OF DEPRESSION! WE hear that pithy declaration a lot these days, but is it correct? How would we know? If you want to know the history of heart attacks, you've got data going back centuries. We even know about the arteries of a 3,000-year-old mummy, because we've examined them. Depression, however, doesn't leave marks. It is invisible to archaeology.

How do you even measure depression or anxiety? Most therapists will ask you questions and review your medical history. If they find an obvious medical problem, you'll be referred elsewhere. So, in a sense, you're not depressed unless you're in otherwise good shape, making historical analysis very tricky. Furthermore, the questions that doctors use have changed over the years, so it's hard to relate them back through history. The question with the longest history is simply, "Do you often feel sad or depressed?" It has been the basic self-report for decades, maybe even longer.

When you get down to it, what is depression? Stripped to its essentials, it is almost indistinguishable from sickness behavior. Whether you ate some bad clams or are just clammy from the flu, you want to lie down, pull the covers over your head, and be alone. Depression behavior likely has a long primal history of survival value by keeping you at home when you are sick. It may also conserve energy so that you can fight infection. In the modern world, however, where inflammatory triggers may be more prevalent—coming from stress, high-fat and high-sugar diets, and sedentary lifestyles—depression may no longer be a useful adaptation.

Ironically, although the survival value of depression has diminished, its prevalence—and the overwhelming use of psychiatric pharmaceuticals to treat it—has recently skyrocketed. Using the simple measure of self-reporting, depression actually does seem to be increasing at a rapid rate, with almost 10 times as many people afflicted since the 1930s. It cuts across all demographics, including high schoolers, college students, and older adults.[1] Measured similarly, anxiety shows the same rate of growth. That's not surprising: Some three-quarters of people with depression also suffer from anxiety. The WHO (World Health Organization) estimates that depression and anxiety will be the top cause of disability for the coming decades. That the rates are increasing, even in the face of escalating usage of psych meds, indicates that we don't yet have a good solution in hand. That's where psychobiotics come in.

EARLY INKLINGS OF PSYCHOBIOTICS

Sometimes you can learn by reviewing history—so let's look back through the history of medicine to see the evolving awareness of psychobiotics, the gut-brain axis, and their role in mental health.

The ancient Greeks had a theory of mental and physical health involving *humors,* or bodily fluids. Four humors were identified, including blood, phlegm, and two styles of bile, yellow and black. "Melancholy" is the Greek word for "black bile," and it was an excess of this humor that they felt caused depression. The theory was wildly popular, spreading from Greece to become a part of Roman, Indian, and Middle Eastern philosophies for centuries.

In 400 B.C., Hippocrates recommended willow bark to relieve the pain of headaches, demonstrating that something you ate could affect your mood and relieve mental pain. Hippocrates was the one who said: "Let food be thy medicine and medicine be thy food."

He was also one of the first people to describe hepatic encephalopathy, a disease that accompanies acute liver injury and causes profound personality changes and anxiety. He was well aware that psychological states accompanied disorders of the humors: "Those who are mad on account of phlegm are quiet, but those on account of bile are vociferous, vicious, and do not keep quiet." It would not be for another 1,500 years that we would find that we could extinguish those personality changes with a round of antibiotics, killing the microbes that caused the anxiety. Hippocrates felt that the supposedly ineffable psyche was at least somewhat grounded in ordinary matter and therefore a legitimate subject of scientific scrutiny.

Hippocrates is often seen as the father of medicine, and he was an early champion of the scientific method. He monitored his patients to see what went in and what went on. He made hypotheses and then tested them. Among other things, he noticed that mental illness was sometimes cured by a fever. Some practitioners took advantage of this finding, inducing fevers to cure mental illness. Called pyrotherapy, it seemed to pit one disease against another.

Today we would say that introducing a new disease kicks the immune system into high gear, making it more sensitive to any other diseases that are present but laying low. By the 1800s, it was realized that microbes were the culprits behind these feverish counter-diseases. In that light, pyrotherapy represents the earliest glimmering that mental illnesses were somehow related to microbes.

In 1860, the French pathologist Charles Bouchard, writing about gut bacteria and disease, called the colon a "laboratory of poisons." He posited that your food was putrefying in your gut, producing toxins that could make you sick and crazy. You were, essentially, being poisoned by your own body, and probably by pathogenic bacteria in your gut. It was called "autointoxication"— literally self-poisoning. That is not far from the truth as we know it today.

An 1893 report in the French journal *Semaine médicale (Medical Week)* discussed the role of autointoxication in mental diseases. Researchers injected urine from hospital patients into lab animals. Urine from "maniacal" patients caused excitement and convulsions in the animals, whereas urine from "melancholic" patients caused depression, restlessness, and stupor. These results proved, the authors wrote, that autointoxication was the cause of the mental state.

BENEFICIAL *BACILLUS*

The studies of Élie Metchnikoff, the Russian Nobel Prize winner who discovered **macrophages**, would posit a solution: Treat these poisonous microbes in the form of beneficial microbes. Metchnikoff had been introduced to yogurt produced by some very healthy Bulgarians, and he decided that their longevity was due to the bacteria they used to curdle the milk. "The dependence of the intestinal microbes on the food," Metchnikoff said, "makes it possible to adopt measures to modify the flora in our bodies and to replace the harmful microbes by useful microbes."[2]

In 1909, Dr. Hubert Norman reported on the value of "soured milk" in the treatment of melancholia. His description of his patient is wonderful: "Like Job, he cursed his stars," wrote Norman. "He was weary of the sun, and yet afraid to die . . . He had the jaundiced eye, the sallow complexion, a more than ordinary constipation." After treatment with soured milk, his constipation cleared, his weight increased, and he started reading, conversing, and taking greater interest in his surroundings. Dr. Norman realized that his anecdote wasn't scientific, but he thought it deserved further study.[3]

In 1910, "The Treatment of Melancholia by the Lactic Acid *Bacillus*" was published in the *British Journal of Psychiatry*. In the article, Dr. George Porter Phillips discussed fermentations that affected mood. He found that simple powdered *Lactobacillus* didn't work, but a formula with prebiotic whey in it worked to reduce depression. He wrote, "Melancholia, with its attendant constipation and faulty alimentation, lends itself at once to a dietetic form of treatment . . . The lactic acid bacillus has a decided beneficial effect on cases of true melancholia with disturbance of the alimentary canal: (a) By diminishing the amount of toxins absorbed from the intestinal tract; (b) by promoting a rapid and easy assimilation of food material."

His treatment was basically a kind of kefir, or fermented milk product, which he manufactured on-site at Bethlem Royal Hospital, the psychiatric hospital where he did his studies. According to Phillips, his patients gradually lost their depression, gained energy, and lost rigidity in their joints. He claimed a success rate of close to two-thirds. Thus *L. bulgaricus* became the first psychobiotic.

Phillips wasn't the only one finding that the gut seemed to be instrumental in mental health. In 1914, Dr. Bond Stow, a New York pathologist, expanded on the idea of "intestinal intoxication": "Man from the beginning has been and ever will be subject to the attacks of these hostile putrefactive bacteria, and the innumerable examples of autointoxication . . . are a proof thereof. They are the cases that present the sallow, bloodless, or ashy-gray, muddy complexion, foul fecal odorous breath, cold, clammy, moist hands and feet, headaches, malaise, total lack of ambition so that every effort in life is a burden, mental depression often bordering upon melancholia, frequent attacks of indefinite abdominal pains due to flatulency, sudden attacks of acute diarrhea alternating with periods of constipation. The degrees of these cases of intestinal intoxication vary over a wide range but in all intestinal states an excessive accumulation of . . . putrefactive bacteria in the bowel . . . is the underlying etiological factor . . . [One must] strike at the root of the trouble by dispelling a malevolent intestinal flora with a beneficent one. This problem requires an organic force equal and even greater in power than this evil organic one so strongly entrenched in the intestinal tract of every human being."

Stow was thus a proponent of probiotics and psychobiotics, although these terms hadn't yet been invented. He also realized that probiotics weren't a cure, but an ongoing therapy. He called it "a battle royal," and knew that after the first successful treatment, the helpful bacteria "must be kept on the field of battle forever at guard, for the germs of putrefaction are ubiquitous and swallowed with every mouthful of food and drink." He summarized colorfully: "Malevolent microorganisms are ubiquitous and unavoidable, hence this battle never ceases."

Stow also understood the importance of conditioning the gut by stopping bad dietary habits and discontinuing drugs that had an antibiotic effect. "Just as a field must be cleared and ploughed before planting the seed so must the intestinal tract be made ready for the proper receptions of the *Bulgarian bacillus,*" he wrote. "One must constantly bear in mind he is dealing with a viable microorganism which drug medication may destroy or attenuate."

Cut Out the Colon

By 1923, acidophilus milk was being touted for the treatment of psychosis. It was a promising start that quickly went sour. It was a bad time to be a mental patient. A New Jersey doctor named Henry Cotton became a big booster of colectomies—the complete excision of the colon—in an effort to eliminate the germs of his mental patients. He also advocated pulling their teeth to expunge the last of their bacterial poisoning. He called it "surgical bacteriology." He claimed a remission rate of 80 percent, which would have sounded pretty good had his mortality rate not been over 30 percent. It was truly a nightmarish scenario at the New Jersey State Lunatic Asylum where he worked. We now know that periodontal disease is indeed associated with inflammation and heart disease, as well as premature birth—but we also know that pulling teeth and using dentures are associated with depression.

The theory of autointoxication was inspired, but just too vague to be prescriptive, and these horrible cures turned out to be far deadlier than the disease. Pharmacists, however, spotted a true opportunity, and before long magazines and newspapers were carrying ads for probiotic treatments. They far outpaced the science. New York-based Berlin Labs produced something called the Intesti-Fermin tablet that "promotes physical and mental health and provides a truly scientific aid to high efficiency in every-day life." By 1917, there were 30 different probiotics on the market.

This is reminiscent of today's proliferation of commercial probiotic products (which are, by the way, supported by scant human studies). The bubble burst, and the demise of products like Intesti-Fermin, along with the vagueness of the theory of autointoxication, spelled doom for this first phase of psychobiotics. Then something happened that swept the therapeutic world by storm and would eclipse psychobiotic treatments for a century.

FREUD AND TALK THERAPY

Sigmund Freud started his psychiatric practice in Vienna in the late 1800s. His theories so saturated psychiatric thinking that they now seem commonplace even to the general public. Psychoanalysis, id, ego, superego, libido, Oedipus complex, penis envy, sex drive, dream interpretation, anal personality, defense mechanisms, projection, sublimation denial, catharsis, neurosis, Freudian slips—these concepts and many others flew out of his fertile mind and captivated the world.

Freud placed sex at the center of the psychoanalytic universe, pinpointing early sexual abuse as the root cause of most pathologies. Patients, he felt, repressed memories, and talking about them could cure the patients. Recovered memory theory has been debunked many times. It's not that people don't repress memories; they do. It's just that it is extremely easy for therapists to insert phony memories. Often, neither the patients nor the therapists are exactly aware that this is happening, which can lead to poor outcomes. Anxiety became a cornerstone of Freud's analysis, bringing it out of simple malaise and branding it as a unique and possibly treatable syndrome. Freud said that anxiety was "a riddle whose solution would be bound to throw a flood of light on our whole mental existence." Freud felt anxiety was a consequence of repressed desires, and knew it might take years of therapy to dig up your buried treasures.

Given the primitive conditions in asylums and the beatings that passed for psychotherapy in his day, Freud was a blast of fresh air. What made Freud so groundbreaking was the idea that you could help people just by talking with them and engaging their minds. Why does talk help? It is still not clear, but as we learn more about the gut-brain axis, we realize that it's a two-way street. Gut issues can affect the brain, but the brain can also affect the gut. So one might say that talk therapy ultimately is a conversation between the therapist and the gut microbiota.

We cannot revisit Freud's patients—most of whom suffered from hysteria—but we can theorize that they were similar to patients undergoing therapy today. And as with current patients, many of them may have had dysbiotic guts. Because the microbiota doesn't send clear signals about its distress, it can seem confounding to patients. It is not inconceivable that gut problems are even the roots of Freudian repression. The secret hiding at the core of a patient's problems might not be an abusive parent but rather an abusive microbiota.

FEVER THERAPY RETURNS

In the 1920s, a psychiatrist named Julius Wagner-Jauregg reinvigorated Hippocrates's notion that inducing a fever could cure mental illnesses. In fact, Wagner-Jauregg found that infecting mental

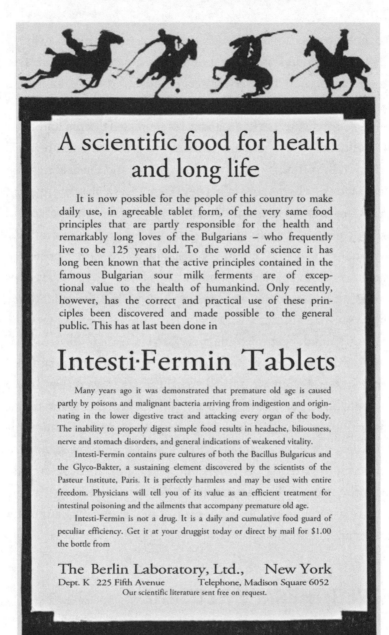

A scientific food for health and long life

It is now possible for the people of this country to make daily use, in agreeable tablet form, of the very same food principles that are partly responsible for the health and remarkably long loves of the Bulgarians – who frequently live to be 125 years old. To the world of science it has long been known that the active principles contained in the famous Bulgarian sour milk ferments are of exceptional value to the health of humankind. Only recently, however, has the correct and practical use of these principles been discovered and made possible to the general public. This has at last been done in

Intesti·Fermin Tablets

Many years ago it was demonstrated that premature old age is caused partly by poisons and malignant bacteria arriving from indigestion and originating in the lower digestive tract and attacking every organ of the body. The inability to properly digest simple food results in headache, biliousness, nerve and stomach disorders, and general indications of weakened vitality.

Intesti-Fermin contains pure cultures of both the Bacillus Bulgaricus and the Glyco-Bakter, a sustaining element discovered by the scientists of the Pasteur Institute, Paris. It is perfectly harmless and may be used with entire freedom. Physicians will tell you of its value as an efficient treatment for intestinal poisoning and the ailments that accompany premature old age.

Intesti-Fermin is not a drug. It is a daily and cumulative food guard of peculiar efficiency. Get it at your druggist today or direct by mail for $1.00 the bottle from

The Berlin Laboratory, Ltd.,   New York
Dept. K   225 Fifth Avenue   Telephone, Madison Square 6052
Our scientific literature sent free on request.

This 1915 advertisement promoted Intesti-Fermin, an early probiotic product said to contain the ingredient that helped Bulgarians live to the age of 125.

patients with malaria could sometimes cure them.[4] It was particularly effective for patients with syphilis, and it also helped people with schizophrenia—but, unfortunately, many of these patients also died. Some accepted this turn of events, as patients with syphilis represented a large fraction of the asylum population and they were likely doomed anyway.[5] To others, injecting patients with malaria was pretty much a direct repudiation of the Hippocratic Oath to "First, do no harm." Despite the controversy, Wagner-Jauregg received the Nobel Prize for his work. Malaria therapy is still used experimentally for various diseases—including AIDS—but most of this work occurs in places like China that are considerably more relaxed in their regulations about research on humans.

It is still not clear why malarial therapy works, but the idea that aversive events could help with psychosis and depression took on a life of its own. A theory made the rounds suggesting that epilepsy and mental illness were antithetical to each other. Perhaps seizures prevented mental illness? The push was on to bring patients to the brink of death with a wide array of known dangerous techniques.

In the 1930s, sulfa drugs made a dramatic entrance and actually started curing infections. Soon after, the discovery of penicillin led to a cure for syphilis. No one really noticed it, but killing pathogens was improving mental health, as well as physical ailments. It would take years, though, for scientists to pay attention to the connection between microbes and mood.

TALK THERAPY YIELDS TO CHEMISTRY

When Santiago Ramón y Cajal mapped out brain cells at the turn of the 20th century, it was already understood that electricity stimulated neurons. But when Ramón y Cajal looked closely, he saw that the nerve cells never actually touched each other. The electric pulse must have a way to jump the gaps from one cell to the next. A few years later, in 1897, Charles Scott Sherrington gave the gaps a name: *synapses*. Finally, in 1921, Otto Loewi showed that a chemical bridged the gap. Because it allowed neurons to send signals, it was called a neurotransmitter. Loewi had discovered the first one: acetylcholine. To affirm its effects on the body, Loewi injected acetylcholine into frog hearts: It slowed their beating.

Once a chemical basis was discovered for nerve transmission, the rush was on to find other neurotransmitters. Soon a new picture of the nervous system started to develop. Certain neurotransmitters excited neurons and others, like acetylcholine, inhibited them. We now know that is a little simplistic, but the basic idea is sound.

The first antidepressant was discovered accidentally in 1951 when a new antibiotic, iproniazid, was trialed to treat tuberculosis. Iproniazid did help patients with TB, but it also caused some of them to become quite happy and even rambunctious. Where patients had been lethargic and moping the day before, they now were laughing and dancing in the halls. It was an astonishing turnaround.

Researchers discovered that drugs like iproniazid seemed to increase levels of the neurotransmitter serotonin in the brain, explaining why the drug lifted patient spirits. Due to this unexpected success, scientists started to look for more drugs that could boost serotonin levels. In quick succession, Prozac, Paxil, and Zoloft hit the market. Other drugs, including monoamine oxidase inhibitors (MAOIs) and tricyclic antidepressants (TCAs), also worked to affect levels of serotonin and another neurotransmitter called norepinephrine.

This wasn't always straightforward. It turns out that most of these neurotransmitters cannot cross the blood-brain barrier. Simply eating these drugs won't work. You could inject them into the brain, but that is certainly inconvenient. The solution was to find chemicals that could pass through the BBB that could enhance the production or reduce the absorption of various neurotransmitters. Soon the race was on to address every neurotransmitter possible. As soon as a new chemical messenger was found in the brain, pharmacologists would seek ways to manipulate its levels. They developed drugs to modify levels of dopamine, GABA, and others. There was a feeling that science could address every brain malady by just finding the right neurotransmitter and then manipulating its levels. A little down? Try some norepinephrine or dopamine. A little agitated? Try some GABA. It was a very seductive model.

Unfortunately, recent research has shown that not all of these neurotransmitter enhancers are particularly effective. Some only show an effect in people with severe depression. People with mild depression may find a placebo to be just as helpful. Many of these drugs have severe side effects, affecting weight, sleep, and libido. The fact that these drugs aren't universally effective points to the complexity of the brain, as if that were ever in doubt.

Several researchers are quite skeptical of the notion that drugs can "top off" a low level of neurotransmitters. To them, saying that depression is caused by low levels of serotonin is akin to saying that headaches are caused by a lack of aspirin. There may be a connection, but an organ as complex as the brain probably cannot be measured by a simple dipstick. At least we know from the studies of psychoactive drugs that neurotransmitters are involved. The drug ketamine, for instance, seems to work by mimicking neurotransmitters, but it is only for severe depression and has numerous side effects, including hallucinations and addiction. Any new approach to depression is therefore quite welcome.

What may have been lost in the neurotransmitter revolution is one interesting fact: Iproniazid was invented to fight bacteria, not lift moods. Could this bacterial connection be important? Could the change in attitude be down to an improved microbiota? If so, can psychobiotics help?

PSYCHOBIOTICS TAKE THE STAGE

Over and over, through this long and often dreadful history of mental health treatments, the suggestion arises that your microbiota has a major impact on your mood. Unfortunately, we have discovered this connection multiple times throughout history and have failed to take proper advantage of it.

Modern research and some serendipity have led to new psychiatric drugs, to be sure. We now have antipsychotics, for example, that act on psychosis brought on by other drugs like phencyclidine, also known as PCP or angel dust. In these cases, people who took angel dust to get high instead became psychotic, complete with delusions, self-mutilation, and paranoia. Sometimes the psychosis can last for months.[6] Antipsychotics like lorazepam can help these people—but amazingly, so can microbes. Butyrate, the fatty acid created by certain gut bacteria, can quickly clear up this drug-induced psychosis, hinting at a possible connection between gut bacteria and all kinds of psychoses, not just depression or anxiety.

Pharmaceutical manufacturing has become one of the biggest businesses in the world. The number of drugs that you can choose from is staggering. They are not, however, without problems of their own. Your medications for acne, insomnia, asthma, malaria, birth control, smoking cessation, and blood pressure may come with a side effect of depression. Ironically, even some anxiety meds can cause depression.

Since the accidental discovery of iproniazid as an antidepressant in the 1950s, scientists have invented an astounding variety of psychotropic medicines. This has led to a revolution in psychiatry. These drugs are miraculous for some patients, but often little better than a placebo for others. That doesn't mean they aren't powerful: If you stop taking some of these drugs, you may be asking for a world of hurt. The downsides of going cold turkey are real, including headaches, dizziness, thoughts of suicide, and a return of your original symptoms. Don't discontinue these medications without the help of your doctor.

We have made much progress with these drugs, but we have hardly solved all the mysteries of mental problems like depression and anxiety. The rates of depression and anxiety are rising, not falling. Clearly, the final answer is not at hand. If you're prone to depression or anxiety, you need to be aware that your microbiota may affect not only your mood but also even the absorption of your meds, adding another level of complexity. Depending on your gut microbes, you may have to adjust or change your meds.[7] This is new territory for medicine, but one day it may help you to personalize your therapy.

Today, psychobiotics are poised to become a valuable tool for treating anxiety and depression. This time around, the science is lined up, and the future is bright. It couldn't have come at a better time, as depression is afflicting a rapidly increasing percentage of the world's people. For decades, we have been doing something wrong with our microbiota, and it has been ruining our mood. Now is an auspicious time to fix it.

CHAPTER 7

YOUR PERSONAL PSYCHOBIOTIC JOURNEY

"Every path but your own is the path of fate.

Keep on your own track, then."

—Henry David Thoreau, *Walden*

JUST LIKE YOUR MICROBIOTA, YOUR DEPRESSION AND ANXIETY are as unique as you are—which makes it impossible to declare a singular fix for everyone. But most of us can follow a number of general rules and ways to unravel our special situation and take charge of our destiny.

Your microbiota is an ecosystem in miniature. Just as in the natural world that you can observe, species coexist, feed and eat each other, and depend on each other for survival. In the savanna, for example, lions eat zebras and gazelles. Lions also eat hyenas, which also eat zebras and gazelles. The ungulates eat grasses, and the grasses thrive on animal dung for fertilizer. When any of these animals die, they are eaten by vultures, which are in turn eaten by lions and hyenas. It is not a food chain so much as a food web, with arrows of digestion pointing in all directions. Finding no gazelles, the predators will hunt zebras for dinner. There is enough redundancy in the system that it has some resilience. But take away certain important players, like the lions at the top, and the system can go out of whack. Prey populations will explode to the point that the savanna becomes overgrazed and massive die-offs can ensue. In the savanna, the lion is a keystone species. Like the architectural unit at the top of an archway, the keystone species itself is under no strain, but without it, the arch will collapse.

A parallel universe exists in your gut microbiota. Like the omnivorous animals in the savanna, bacteria eat fiber, yeasts, protozoa, and each other. Like dung beetles carting away fecal prizes, bacteria excrete chemicals that are consumed by other microbes. Viruses act as bacterial go-betweens, passing genes from one microbe to another. And within this intestinal ecosystem are keystone species: The *Bifido* species, typically the first bacteria to move in to your gut, represent one of them. Only 2 percent of your bacteria are *Bifidos,* but they exert a disproportionate influence. *Bifido* microbes may be the lions of your gut.

If you are a generally healthy person already, the guidelines in this chapter will help you maintain your health and mood by keeping a balanced ecosystem in your gut. But many of us experience distress that can be addressed by rebuilding the gut, even though you may not have associated the way you feel with the health of your microbiota. If that is the case, your first act on your psychobiotic journey is to rebuild your gut, taking steps to heal any lesions or permeability—so-called leaky gut. There are a number of possible causes for such distress, including:

- Infections
- Inflammation

- Chronic stress
- Overuse of painkillers
- Continuing or repeated rounds of antibiotics
- Excessive alcohol consumption
- Autoimmune disorders like lupus
- IBD and IBS
- Gluten sensitivity or food allergies
- Radiation or chemotherapy
- Overeating
- Lack of exercise

Some of these, like alcohol or painkiller overuse, are under your control to some extent, and doing all you can to minimize the damage you are doing to yourself is an excellent start to fixing things. Problems may be lurking that you are not even aware of—in these cases, depression or anxiety can be signals of disease that may need further medical attention, and by caring for your microbiota, you can participate in that treatment. In some cases, you may have received a physical diagnosis such as rheumatoid disease or type 2 diabetes, but have never understood how that condition could affect your mood and mental health. In all these cases, you can do things that hold the promise of mitigating physical and psychological distress. The rest of this chapter offers suggestions for embarking on your own psychobiotic journey and taking better care of your microbiota.

PSYCHOBIOTIC SUPPLEMENTS
· ·

Say "gut health" these days, and the first thing that comes to mind for many people is probiotic supplements. It's a tendency of our times: Take a pill to cure your ills. The bad news: It's not that easy. But there is plenty of good news, too: We are learning which bacteria work best to promote a healthy gut and a happy mood; probiotic formulations containing these ingredients are commercially available and scientifically validated; and, most important, you can boost your health and improve your mood in ways beyond supplements. But first, let's consider supplements.

Today an abundance of probiotic products are on the market. Not all have been proven to be effective, and not all are psychobiotics—a term coined by Ted Dinan to identify probiotics that improve your mood. This is a new field, and key research is under way at this very moment, as mentioned in earlier chapters.

The only effective pharmacological therapies developed so far for the treatment of common psychiatric disorders target simple neurotransmitter systems within the brain. The paradigm giving rise to such therapies dates back to the 1950s, and efforts by the pharmaceutical industry to develop therapies based on alternative paradigms have proved relatively fruitless. Over the past decade another paradigm has begun to emerge, the gut-brain axis. This bidirectional communication between the digestive tract and the brain plays a key role in maintaining brain health and the stress response.

More recently, the gut microbiota has emerged as a master regulator of this axis. Indeed, preclinical studies have shown that the microbiota is key to normal neurodevelopment and behavior, raising the potential of targeting this microbiota-gut-brain axis in the development of novel psychotropics. This approach offers a promising new avenue for treating psychiatric conditions such as major depression or anxiety disorders.

The hope is that psychobiotics could eventually be used as easily as we now use Prozac (fluoxetine) to treat depression or Valium (diazepam) to treat anxiety, but with fewer side effects. But finding the correct dosage, combination, and method of delivery presents an unusually knotty problem. There are thousands of species of bacteria and other microbes to choose from, and they have to somehow settle in and interact beneficially with your existing microbiota, which is unique to your own history and genetic makeup. Even seemingly simple lifestyle differences, such as whether you drink or smoke or eat a Western diet, can make your psychobiotic needs different from the next person's.

Many of the probiotics now being confirmed as effective in research exist in ferments, usually yogurt, but most of them do not dwell naturally in our guts. A few *Lacto* species might camp out temporarily in your small intestine, and a few other species (in particular *Bifido longum*—one of the first microbes you encountered as a baby) are called persisters and have proven capable of lasting at least six months in the gut.[1] But most of them are transients, so whatever effect they have is while they are passing through. For them to work, you need to keep eating them.

Some of the probiotics available as supplements are popular because they are easy to manufacture, not necessarily because they are efficacious. Sadly, in the United States the Food and Drug Administration (FDA) isn't authorized to review dietary supplements for safety or efficacy before they are marketed, so caveat emptor. To help you become an educated consumer of probiotic products, here are some guidelines to follow.

Anatomy of a Probiotic Label

The label on your probiotic supplements can tell you a lot, if you know what to look for. Here are the main features.

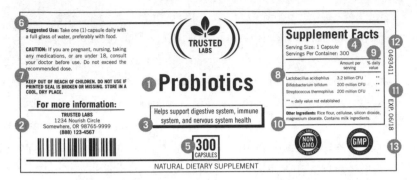

1	Product name	7	Warnings
2	Manufacturer's name and contact information	8	Supplement facts
		9	% daily value
3	Claims	10	Other ingredients
4	Dosage	11	Expiration date
5	Format	12	Lot number
6	Suggested use	13	Quality seals

A typical probiotic supplement label will have these elements.

1. Product name

The product name may be informative, or it may simply be a marketing tool. Sometimes the name will identify a single probiotic; sometimes the product will identify itself with the number of bacterial strains contained in the formulation. A surprising number of products are simply named "Probiotic." Read on!

2. Manufacturer's name and contact information

The manufacturer's name must be on the label for you to contact them should you have questions or experience side effects. Manufacturers are required to report any serious effects to the FDA, so if you have problems, report them. You may be able to save other people from experiencing the same thing.

3. Claims

The United States imposes few rules on supplement manufacturers, but it does restrict their claims. In fact, many labels actually state, "These statements have not been evaluated by the Food and Drug Administration" and "This product is not intended to diagnose, treat, cure, or prevent any disease." (If they did make that kind of claim, the product would be classified as a drug and be subject to FDA scrutiny and testing.) Despite this incredibly low regulatory bar, many manufacturers do test their products, making them more reliable. Look for studies (some in this book), and beware of any product that seems to claim too much.

4. Dosage

Microbes are tiny, and it takes billions of them to have an effect. Most of them need to be alive to work. Being alive means each one has the capacity to split in two and eventually form a new bacterial colony, so the typical dosage unit for probiotics is the CFU, which means colony-forming unit. However, fewer than a third of them will survive the torture chambers of your gut, so the numbers involved here run sky-high. Typically, a probiotic mix will have tens of billions of CFUs.[2] Unlike approved drugs for which dose-response studies are required, however, there are very few probiotics for which the ideal dosage has been established.

5. Format

Probiotics come in many forms, from pills to capsules to powder. The idea is to get as many of the probiotics into your lower gut as possible, and that means the best delivery systems are those that protect the bacteria from stomach acids on the way down. Capsules are by far the most common, and those that resist digestion by stomach acids are preferred. Often the material of the capsule is listed on a label as well, and enteric coatings tend to best provide safe passage into the intestines.

Pills may be smaller and easier to swallow than an equivalent capsule, but unless they are coated, they may be subject to more digestion than capsules.

Prebiotics are often formulated as powders, as they require larger amounts per serving, up to a tablespoon or more, generally mixed into water, juice, or a smoothie. Because you have to mix them, they are less convenient but typically cheaper than the other options. (Don't put these into your carry-on luggage, however. Powders send off alarms these days, and you will likely be tested. Capsules or pills are more convenient for travel.)

Probiotics are rarely sold in powder form, because manufacturers are aiming for a more calibrated dosage. Sometimes you might want probiotics in a powder, say for making yogurt or a smoothie. The easiest way to do that is to open a capsule and pour out the contents.

6. **Suggested use**

This section tells you the manufacturer's suggested usage, such as how much to take each day, how to distribute dosages through a day, how to mix the product, and so on. This information is also conveyed as "serving size" and may be helpful when comparing products.

7. **Warnings**

This section, if it exists at all, will list contraindications, such as "not for children" or "not for pregnant women." There may be more you need to know than can be written on a small label, however. Throughout this chapter, you will find more information on contraindications, to keep you from taking the wrong supplement or from taking the right supplement but at the wrong time.

8. Supplement facts

This section of the label details the ingredients as a list of microbial species and, often, the proportion of each in the formulation. To read this list—the heart of any probiotic label—you need to know about various types of bacteria. Later in this chapter we will offer an overview of the most common psychobiotics. This section of the label may also include prebiotics, typically sugars or fiber.

9. % daily value

This is another reminder that probiotic supplements are in unmarked territory. There is no established daily value for probiotics, so this column is blank.

If there are prebiotics in the product, they may be listed by % daily value, where the percentages are usually based on a 2,000-calorie diet.

10. Other ingredients

Supplements may contain other nonactive ingredients, for instance, fillers, binders, flow agents, the capsule itself, and other specialty items. You should pay attention to this part, if you are concerned about allergies, dietary restrictions, or religious preferences.

11. Expiration date

Probiotics are living organisms, and so for the most part,

they will die over time and lose their effectiveness. The number of CFUs on the label is guaranteed up to the listed expiration date. After that, the effectiveness can fall quickly, so keep an eye on this and be aware. Also, many probiotics require refrigeration. The expiration date only applies to a properly refrigerated product, so follow storage instructions carefully.

12. Lot number

If you have a problem with a product, you will need to provide the manufacturer with the lot number, so they can track down the constituent components of that lot and pinpoint the source of a problem.

13. Quality seals

You may see many different quality seals on a probiotic label, but the most important is GMP—Good Manufacturing Practice—which means that the manufacturer has invited FDA representatives to visit the premises and approve company protocols for cleanliness, proper management of source materials, and employee training. This doesn't guarantee a quality probiotic, but if a manufacturer doesn't observe GMP, then they aren't even clearing this low bar. A related seal is cGMP, which means current GMP, and applies to maintaining up-to-date processes.

There are dozens of other quality seals, indicating compliance with organic rules, GMO-free products, allergen-free products, and more. However, if you're buying a simple probiotic with no added prebiotics, you shouldn't pay more for these extra promises, because bacteria are by nature non-GMO, gluten free, nut free, soy free, corn free, and vegan.

KNOW YOUR PSYCHOBIOTICS

The following list includes psychobiotics that have been well studied over the past few years and found to be effective. These bacteria should be compatible with one another in a combined psychobiotic formula. It's useful to note that most are *Bifido* and *Lacto* species. This is not a finite or final list. The field is new and important work is ongoing, and so new psychobiotics are certain to be identified as this research gathers steam. After most of the psychobiotic names, in parentheses, is a number that identifies the specific strain used in the studies. These numbers are usually trademarked by the manufacturers, who typically have isolated each strain for large-scale fermentation.

Bifidobacterium longum (RO175 & 1714) or *Bifidobacterium infantis* (35624)

B. longum inhibits pathogens in the large intestine, reducing inflammation and helping to prevent diarrhea. It also helps mitigate lactose intolerance and food allergies. Some research has shown that it can lower cholesterol and can act as an antioxidant. Via the neuroendocrine system and the vagus nerve, *B. longum* reduces anxiety and cortisol levels.[3] Through its effects on hippocampal growth factors, it can reduce depression as well. It can also improve cognition, and so might be useful for healthy people who want to improve performance.[4] Under stress, it can improve your coping skills. It has been tested on humans[5] and the results track those found in mice and rats.

> *In a clinical study, we tested whether psychobiotic consumption could affect the stress response and cognition in healthy volunteers. Our results indicate that consumption of* B. longum *1714 reduces the perception of stress, reduces morning cortisol levels, and improves memory.*[6]

B. longum boosts the amount of available tryptophan, a precursor to serotonin, which can have an antidepressant effect. This is the same neurotransmitter involved with SSRIs. *B. longum* is now considered to be technically the same as *B. infantis,* and the strain numbered 35624 is known to be a potent anti-inflammatory. You may see it listed as either *longum* or *infantis* on an ingredient list.[7] Along with *L. helveticus,* it is naturally found in yogurt, kefir, and sauerkraut.

> CASE STUDY: *Jenny (not her real name) is a 36-year-old mother of two who had recently started a stressful job. She went to her doctor complaining about diarrhea and discomfort. The doctor put her on a high-roughage diet and a drug to lower her bowel frequency, but it didn't work. After a colonoscopy, it was determined that she had IBS. A psychiatric visit showed that she suffered from depression.*
>
> *Jenny was sent to a dietitian who recommended a FODMAP diet (see pages 181–82), which is highly restrictive; she could only maintain it for five weeks. She started to take* B. longum *daily, which she felt to be a natural alternative to medicines. After one week, her diarrhea improved, and shortly thereafter she reported feeling less anxious. In another two weeks, her depressive symptoms cleared entirely.*
>
> *This case illustrates the capacity of a psychobiotic to improve mood as well as alleviate the symptoms of IBS. Jenny is determined to continue with the treatment for the foreseeable future.*

Bifidobacterium breve (1205)

B. breve has shown results similar to *B. longum,* but with slight differences. It seems to have a greater influence on anxiety than depression.[8] It prevents the growth of *E. coli,* as well as *Candida albicans,* the fungus behind yeast infections. Its strong antipathogen effect may explain why it helps in the fight against diarrhea, IBS, and allergies. It improves gut health in both premature babies[9] and those born by cesarean delivery,[10] often with a lifelong impact. In addition, *B. breve* has long been known to alleviate problems associated with antibiotics.[11]

> *In our laboratory, we found that both* B. longum *and* B. breve *helped to lower anxiety in a mouse bred to be anxious. Whereas* B. longum *acted as an antidepressant,* B. breve *lowered anxiety. Both species compared well against the antidepressant escitalopram (marketed as Lexapro or Cipralex) to reduce anxiety and depression. In our lab* B. longum *reduces perception of stress and morning cortisol levels in healthy volunteers.*
>
> *These results also suggest that each bacterial strain has intrinsic effects and may be beneficially specific for a given disorder. These findings strengthen the role of gut microbiota supplementation as psychobiotic-based strategies for stress-related brain-gut axis disorders.*[12]

Bifidobacterium animalis (DN 173 010, BB-12, Bi-07) or *Bifidobacterium animalis lactis* (HN019, DR10)

B. animalis, another member of the *Bifido* genera that includes the subspecies *B. animalis lactis,* has proven a benefit to people with ulcerative colitis.[13] It has been shown to improve both constipation and diarrhea associated with irritable bowel syndrome (IBS).[14] *B. animalis* is friendly with other psychobiotics, including various *Bifido* and *Lacto* species. It causes their numbers to increase, giving you extra bang for the buck.[15] *B. lactis* has been shown to improve mood when used in combination with *L. bulgaricus, S. thermophilus,* and *L. lactis.*[16]

Bifidobacterium bifidum

If you were born vaginally, *B. bifidum* will be one of your oldest bacterial friends. Newborns typically pick it up as they pass through the birth canal. It competes with pathogens including *E. coli* and yeasts such as *Candida* and helps prevent diarrhea. *B. bifidum* in combination with *L. acidophilus* and *L. casei* (in capsule form) for eight weeks has been shown to help people with major depressive disorder.[17]

Lactobacillus acidophilus (ATCC 4356)

L. acidophilus is the most popular bacteria in probiotic and psychobiotic formulations. It has a long history of safety and is found in fermented foods such as yogurt, sauerkraut, and kefir. It helps to prevent diarrhea and is useful in treating small intestinal bacterial overgrowth (SIBO). It not only lowers inflammation but also increases opioid and cannabinoid receptors, acting as an analgesic and mitigating gut pain.[18]

    L. acidophilus is a potent fighter against *Campylobacter jejuni*, a pathogen that causes gastroenteritis and anxiety. *L. acidophilus* outcompetes *jejuni* and prevents it from sticking to and infecting the cells lining your gut.[19] This antipathogenic behavior is a major contributor to its antianxiety effect.

Lactobacillus delbrueckii (bulgaricus) or Lactobacillus helveticus (R0052 & NS8)

L. bulgaricus is found in yogurt and kefir and is often found with other *Lacto* and *Bifido* species in these products. It has been shown to improve mood when used in a mix with other milk fermenters. Because it ferments lactose, it can help with lactose intolerance. Human studies have shown it to improve immune function and to moderate the response to emotional stimuli. Recently, *L. delbrueckii* has been reclassified as *L. helveticus*.

L. helveticus is a popular addition to cheese cultures, as it inhibits bitter flavors. It has been shown to reduce blood pressure as well as depression and anxiety. Recent studies report that increasing the level of *Lacto* in the gut lowers the blood pressure of people with hypertension.[20] Its main mode of action is to lower inflammation and enhance serotonin signaling. In animal models of liver disease, *L. helveticus* helps prevent anxiety and cognitive impairment.[21] Studies have shown that *L. helveticus* can mitigate the inflammation and anxiety involved with eating a Western diet.[22] Although most of these studies have been done in mice, human studies have shown that *L. helveticus* enhances nutrient absorption, removes allergens, and fights pathogens.[23] Its use in cheesemaking ensures that it is safe for human consumption.

Lactobacillus rhamnosus (IMC 50I, JB-I, GG)

L. rhamnosus has been found to be useful for treating peanut allergies, diarrhea, dermatitis, and obesity. It has been shown in animal studies to reduce both depression and anxiety, possibly by increasing levels of the neurotransmitter GABA. The effects depend on the vagus nerve, and if it is severed, the effects disappear.[24] *L. rhamnosus* can alleviate obsessive-compulsive disorder (OCD) in mice. It lowers levels of corticosteroids, which reduces levels of stress, and it produces short-chain fatty acids, including butyrate, that both feed and heal the gut. Butyrate can also penetrate the BBB, where it acts as an antidepressant.

In our laboratory, we showed that regular treatment with L. rhamnosus *induced region-dependent alterations in GABA throughout the brain in comparison with controls. Alterations in GABA expression are implicated in the pathogenesis of anxiety and depression, which are highly comorbid with functional bowel disorders.*

Importantly, L. rhamnosus *reduced stress-induced corticoste-rone and anxiety- and depression-related behavior. Moreover, the neurochemical and behavioral effects were not found when the vagus was severed, identifying the vagus as a major modulatory communication pathway between the gut bacteria and the brain.*[25]

L. rhamnosus is found in yogurt, Parmigiano-Reggiano cheese, kefir, fermented sausage, and fermented soy cheese. *Note:* Use caution with this psychobiotic if you have an impaired immune system, such as what accompanies HIV or lupus, as it could trigger sepsis.

L. rhamnosus GG (LGG) is contained in products, including Culturelle, Nutramigen, LGG, and others. It is one of the best studied strains of *L. rhamnosus* and has been shown to be effective in treating IBS,[26] a disease associated with depression and anxiety. However, in tests with healthy volunteers, it was not shown to reduce stress or improve cognitive performance.[27]

Lactobacillus reuteri

L. reuteri is one of the most ubiquitous species of gut bacteria, present across a wide spectrum of animals and always with a positive effect on health. In mice, it has been found to correct problems in pups born to mothers on a high-fat diet, including problems socializing.[28]

L. reuteri produces antibiotics against pathogenic bacteria, yeasts, and protozoans, making it a potent probiotic and an anti-inflammatory. It colonizes in the gut quickly. It improves skin tone, along with reproductive fitness, lowers inflammation, and increases oxytocin levels in both mice and humans.[29] It increases levels of leptin (the satiety hormone) and decreases levels of ghrelin (the hunger hormone), potentially decreasing your caloric intake.

L. reuteri has been shown to reduce visceral pain, which can reduce pain-related anxiety. Interestingly, this deadening effect is similar whether the *L. reuteri* is killed or alive.[30] *L. reuteri* can also lower levels of LDL (bad cholesterol) and inflammation, helping to prevent heart disease.[31]

Lactobacillus plantarum (299v, PS128)

L. plantarum is found in many fermented foods, including pickles, kimchi, brined olives, and sauerkraut—all great ways to consume this psychobiotic. It has been shown in humans to attenuate soy allergies and reduce inflammation. In animal studies it has been shown to enhance memory, even reducing age-related memory loss.[32] Some popular products for bowel support contain only this species of bacteria.

L. plantarum strain PS128 competes with *Clostridia* and *Enterococcus* species, so it not only boosts *Bifido* levels, it also knocks down those potential pathogens.[33] *L. plantarum* inhibits inflammation and has been shown to reduce gut pain in patients with IBS.[34]

Lactobacillus casei (Shirota, DN-114001, Immunita)

L. casei, like other *Lacto* species, is used in cheese- and yogurt-making and enjoys the company of *L. acidophilus*. It has been found to be useful in preventing antibiotic-induced diarrhea and *C. diff* infections, both of which are strongly associated with anxiety. When patients are on antibiotics, many doctors today will prescribe yogurt to help mitigate the inevitable damage of these drugs on the microbiota, and it's thanks to the *L. casei* in the yogurt that it has beneficial effects. Studies in humans with depression showed an improvement in mood after 10 days of consuming yogurt containing *L. casei*.[35]

Patients with chronic fatigue syndrome had less anxiety and better gut health after eating *L. casei*.[36] Interestingly, *L. casei* caused numbers of *Bifido* to increase, which likely contributed to the effect—an example of how many of the psychobiotics listed here can work as a team.

Lactobacillus paracasei (IMC 502)

L. paracasei is commonly found in fermented milk products and is common in probiotic mixes. It has been shown to lower levels of pain and intestinal distress caused by antibiotics and is a good adjunct when taking those drugs. In combination with *L. rhamnosus,* it has been shown to minimize the oxidative stress associated with intense physical activity.[37] *L. paracasei* has also been shown to reduce the liver damage resulting from chronic alcohol consumption.[38]

Streptococcus thermophilus

S. thermophilus may not sound like a psychobiotic—after all, strep throat is caused by its cousin, *S. pyogenes*—but this species is a good gut citizen and has been used in fermented foods for centuries. *S. thermophilus* is a bacteria found in yogurt and kefir, and is often a fellow traveler with *L. delbrueckii.* They are synergistic: The *S. thermophilus* provides folic acid to *Lactobacillus bulgaricus,* thus improving the numbers of that psychobiotic. Women who consumed *S. thermophilus* in a yogurt formula showed less response to negative emotional stimulation, which is used as a rough determinant of anxiety.

Saccharomyces boulardii

Saccharomyces boulardii is the only psychobiotic on this list that isn't a bacterium. It is instead a yeast and as such is not recommended for anyone with a compromised immune system or sensitivity to yeast. For others, however, this fungus has a long history of treating diarrhea. Given with antibiotics, it helps to reduce the chances of *C. diff* infection. Some studies have shown it to be effective with IBS and its attendant anxiety. It has also been shown to be effective in treating the two manifestations of IBD: ulcerative colitis and Crohn's.[39]

TESTED BRANDS OF PROBIOTICS

Not all probiotics are reliable. One sobering study showed that out of 13 commonly available probiotics, only four contained what was claimed on the label. Some fell short on CFU count, some didn't have the claimed microbe species, and some had microbe species *not* listed on the label—including, in some cases, potential pathogens.[40]

Ideally, a psychobiotic formulation is a blend of several species that enjoy each other's company. Mixtures have been shown to be more potent than a solitary species.[41] That doesn't mean any old mixture will do. Specific strains, especially close relatives, are competitive with each other, and if combined could cancel out any benefit. Formulating probiotics at this point is more of an art than a science.

The following list contains brands that have been tested in independent research laboratories and shown to match the information on their label, their constituent probiotics tested for safety and efficacy as well.

Probio'Stick

One of the early studies touting the value of probiotics for treating stress came from the French in 2008. Probio'Stick, a probiotic from the French company Lallemand SAS, contains *L. acidophilus* (R-52) and *B. longum* (R-175). One study found that Probio'Stick reduced anxiety in rats and alleviated psychological distress in humans, making it a psychobiotic.[42] Another study found it could reduce abdominal pain, nausea, and vomiting in people affected by chronic stress.[43] The study also showed that you can benefit from psychobiotics even if you're already healthy. It might not seem too amazing that cognition improves as depression and anxiety recede. After all, these mood conditions are distracting and your motivation can be seriously reduced. Still, it's nice to think that if you can reduce your mood problems, you might get smarter, too.

This was a randomized, double-blind placebo-controlled study—the gold standard for research—but at least one of the authors works for Lallemand, the product's manufacturer. Nevertheless, this study and other animal studies[44] were enough to convince the Canadian federal health authorities in 2016 to approve Probio'Stick for the relief of stress and anxiety as well as to balance mood, making it possibly the first government-approved psychobiotic. This formulation, which comes in a sachet, contains three billion CFUs per dose.

VSL#3

VSL#3, a probiotic from Sigma-Tau Pharmaceuticals, Inc., of Maryland, contains four *Lacto* strains, (*acidophilus, casei, helveticus,* and *plantarum*) and two *Bifido* strains (*longum* and *breve*) as well as *S. salivarius thermophilus*. It has been studied in several randomized controlled studies and found to be effective for treating pouchitis (an inflammation of the ileal pouch created surgically in the treatment of colitis[45]) as well as IBS[46] and ulcerative colitis[47]—all conditions associated with depression. It is administered in large doses of 200 to 900 billion CFUs.[48]

Mutaflor

Mutaflor, a probiotic from the German company Ardeypharm GmBH, has a surprisingly long history. It contains a version of *E. coli* (O6:K5:H1), also known as Nissle 1917. Named for its discoverer and the year of its discovery, the beneficial effects of this bacterial species have been known for 100 years. It was first isolated from the feces of a German WWI soldier who happened to be the only one unaffected by an outbreak of dysentery. It was able to be cultured on a manufacturing scale and has been available ever since. In WWII, it was used to treat Hitler's flatulence. It is still a frontline probiotic for treating Crohn's disease,[49] ulcerative colitis,[50] constipation,[51] and IBS. It is provided in a dose of 10 billion CFUs per capsule. It does have psychobiotic properties: It lowers inflammation and enhances serotonin production.[52] Recently researchers have created strains of Nissle 1917 that produce GABA, a neurotransmitter that can reduce anxiety, but this version is not yet on the market. The FDA decided to block the sale of Mutaflor, and so for now neither version is available in the United States.

Align

Align is a single-strain probiotic containing *B. infantis* 35624, available from Procter and Gamble. In a randomized placebo-controlled study, it was shown to relieve the symptoms often associated with depression for both the diarrhea and constipation forms of IBS.[53] It comes in a capsule with one billion CFUs to be taken once a day.

Culturelle

Culturelle is a single-strain probiotic containing *L. rhamnosus* GG (LGG) from Amerifit. It comes in a capsule with 10 billion CFUs to be taken once a day. This product is popular for treating IBS and diarrhea, especially antibiotic-induced diarrhea, along with comorbid depression and anxiety. LGG is one of best tested probiotics, having shown good results in studies of IBS and asthma.[54]

Florastor

Florastor is a single-strain probiotic containing *S. boulardii* from Laboratories Biocodex, a French company that has been producing it since 1953. The dose is 250 milligrams, containing about a billion cells per daily capsule. It is available for both children and adults and has been tested for both product integrity and efficacy.[55]

Yakult

A 2009 study looked at a probiotic treatment of patients suffering from chronic fatigue syndrome (CFS). The researchers split the 39 patients into a probiotic and a placebo group. The probiotic they used was *L. casei* strain Shirota, with a dose of 24 billion CFUs. This bacterium was isolated in the 1930s by Minoru Shirota, who used it to produce a fermented milk product called Yakult. After two months, the patients with CFS taking the high-dose probiotics had a significant decrease in anxiety symptoms. It was notable that even though they only used a single strain of *Lacto,* they also noted an increase in levels of *Bifido.* Apparently, the two microbes work as a team, and introducing extra *Lacto* creates an environment friendly to *Bifido.*[56]

In another study with the Shirota strain, researchers followed 47 Japanese medical students as they prepared for and took exams. The half taking Shirota had lower levels of cortisol and other measures of anxiety than the placebo group, showing it to be a psychobiotic. They also suffered fewer abdominal problems.[57] These studies were paid for by Yakult's manufacturer.

Activia

Activia is a line of yogurt products from Danone (the French parent company of the U.S. Dannon brands) that are designed to improve gut health. In 2013, Kirsten Tillisch and Emeran Mayer conducted an intriguing study using fMRI imaging to look at the brains of healthy women to visualize the mental changes brought about by eating yogurt. The yogurt they used contained a standard mix of probiotics, including *B. lactis, S. thermophilus,* and *L. bulgaricus,* a combination similar to the formula in Activia, which adds other *Bifido* species to the mix. They found that after four weeks, the women had enhanced activity in the parts of the brain processing emotion and sensation— changes that corresponded to an improvement in mood.[58] This was one of the first human studies to directly visualize the gut-brain connection, clearly demonstrating that consumption of a probiotic can modulate brain activity. It also demonstrated, once again, that even healthy people can benefit from psychobiotics. Funded by Danone, the French yogurtmaker, it also represented the first time fMRI had been used as a tool for visualizing psychobiotic activity.

Research continues today and into the future on the possibilities for psychobiotic products, not only evaluating given commercial probiotics but also observing the effect of single bacterial strains and combinations of bacteria on the gut-brain axis activity, on mood, and on any number of diseases that have been found to be accompanied by depression or anxiety. By learning to recognize the types of psychobiotics pertinent to your situation and by reading labels carefully, to evaluate the legitimacy of a manufacturer, you can find your way through the growing number of probiotics on store shelves and select the ones most appropriate to your needs. This next section and the chapter that follows offer some guidelines in selecting the right psychobiotic supplements for your particular situation.

CHOOSING PSYCHOBIOTICS TO TARGET YOUR AFFLICTIONS

Although psychobiotics have wide-ranging effects, most of them act by healing the gut, which reduces inflammation and thereby improves mood. But remember that each bacterial species has a preferred location in your GI tract, so some of these microbes will work on a given gut issue better than others. Although anxiety and depression are often fellow travelers with a number of persistent health problems, some conditions are best addressed by specific psychobiotics. The following list can serve as a rough guide, based on the current published literature.

Anxiety
Probio'Stick, *L. helveticus, L. plantarum, B. breve, B. longum*

Depression
B. bifidum, B. breve, B. longum + *L. helveticus, L. acidophilus, L. brevis, L. casei, L. delbrueckii, L. plantarum, L. rhamnosus, L. salivarius, L. lactis, S. thermophilus*

IBS
B. bifidum, B. infantis, B. animalis, B. lactis, L. plantarum, Mutaflor

Ulcerative colitis
F. prausnitzii, B. breve + galacto-oligosaccharide (GOS), VSL#3, *L. plantarum, L. rhamnosus, L. reuteri* ATCC 55730, *L. delbrueckii* + *L. fermentum,* Mutaflor

Crohn's disease
S. boulardii, Mutaflor

Diarrhea
B. bifidum, B. infantis, B. longum, L. rhamnosus, S. thermophilus

Antibiotic-induced diarrhea
B. lactis, S. boulardii, L. rhamnosus, L. plantarum, L. casei

An expanded version of this short list is found in Chapter 8, with further information on the psychobiotic aspects of some of today's most troublesome diseases.

FOOD: THE BEST PSYCHOBIOTIC

Eating the right kinds of foods has always been and still is the best way to achieve and maintain a healthy gut. Our modern inclination is to take the easy route and reach for a bottle of pills, but even that approach must be bolstered by adjusting your everyday diet not only to ingest the healthy microbes but also to make dietary choices that provide the best food to sustain your gut microbiota. Many studies, both quantitative and anecdotal, confirm the age-old adage attributed to Hippocrates: "Let food by thy medicine and medicine be thy food." In particular, you should be eating more vegetables and fruit and less meat. Among other good things, fruits and veggies contain substances called *polyphenols* that are important to your health. Polyphenols act as antioxidants, protecting you against pathogens as well as diabetes, heart disease, and neurological problems. They are, however, largely useless unless your microbiota is healthy and can properly break them down.[59]

Here are basic guidelines for a diet rich in psychobiotics and the prebiotics they crave—a diet most likely to help you balance your mood and ward off depression and anxiety.

Eat More Fiber, Nature's Original Prebiotic

We all eat fiber every day, in fruits and vegetables and often in the grain products we consume. The human digestive system is not capable of directly digesting fiber, but that doesn't make it any less important to your health. Some of your friendly gut bacteria really like fiber. *Bifido,* for example, consume the fiber moving through your intestines and produce butyric acid as a by-product. Butyric acid turns out to be a superfuel for the cells lining your gut, helping to rebuild your lining on a continuous basis. Butyric acid can also affect your brain, encouraging the production of feel-good neurotransmitters.

Since the late 1800s, food manufacturers have sought ways to reduce the fiber in our everyday foods. Consider wheat, for example: Industrial mills were designed to remove the husk and bran from the grain and grind the grain ever finer. Snow-white flour was a big hit, and for good reason. Refined white flour baked into beautiful, fluffy loaves of bread that were easily twice the size of their whole wheat counterparts. Or consider fruit juice: Manufacturers pressed the fruit and separated the juice from the skins or pulp of grapes, apples, and oranges. Consumers ate (or drank) it up.

The problem with refined food is that it takes no account of your gut bacteria. What we gave up was manna for our microbes. Today, we recognize the fiber processed out of refined foods as **prebiotic—** food for gut bacteria. In short, modern processing removes the prebiotics from your food. This is but one of the many insults perpetrated on the Western gut over the past century. It usually starts with good intentions (white bread and orange juice!), but once you establish a market, inertia can take over. At that point, neither the manufacturers nor consumers want to change their habits. Unfortunately, along with that inertia come longer belts and antidepressants.

We, the consumers, bear the largest measure of blame by remaining ignorant of our own dietary needs. We don't even seem to know when we are killing ourselves, even as we double up in pain from IBS, ulcerative colitis, Crohn's disease, and many other modern inflammations of the gut. Manufacturers cannot force us to eat healthy food. They are in the business of selling what people will buy. The more we demand our missing fiber, the sooner new products will show up on our store shelves.

Including prebiotic fiber in your plan to feed your microbiota solves a lot of the problems that ingesting only probiotics will pose. Prebiotic fiber can survive the bacteria-killing acids and enzymes of the stomach and small intestine, so it can make it intact to the colon where the action is. If you get fiber from foods, the recommended route, you will get several different prebiotics that will ensure that you're feeding a varied pool of microbes. Finally, with fiber-containing veggies, you will also get vitamins and antioxidants. And all this proves your mother was right all along: You should eat your vegetables!

Fiber comes in soluble and insoluble forms. Insoluble fiber doesn't dissolve in water and mostly passes through your gut quickly and with little ceremony. Soluble fiber, on the other hand, is the real gold. Millions of years ago, when animals first struck a deal with bacteria to share the colon, the terms were all about fiber. We couldn't digest it, they could, deal done. So it shouldn't come as a shock that our bacteria are rebelling over our recent distaste for fiber. We've broken our end of the bargain.

The short of it is: Eat more fiber. Choose whole grain baked products over refined. Experiment with other whole grain dishes such as quinoa, brown rice, and bulgur. Eat whole fruit rather than drinking fruit juice. Add more vegetables, raw or cooked, to your meals. Every choice you make in favor of increased fiber in your diet will amplify the health of your gut—and improve your mood.

Important Warning: Some people with IBS may react poorly to a high-fiber diet and will require what dietitians call a low-FODMAP diet. FODMAP is an acronym for "Fermentable, Oligo-, Di-, Mono-saccharides And Polyols"—a mouthful that simply refers to various sugar chains that can cause trouble in the small intestine of some people. A low-FODMAP diet eliminates a number of excellent foods. Although it may be essential for some people, it is not something to undertake lightly. If you think you may be a candidate for a low-FODMAP diet, ask your health care provider—and follow instructions carefully. The only good thing about this diet is that it typically doesn't last forever. Most people only stay on it until their guts heal, and then they can return to a normal diet.

Meet the Complex Sugars Your Gut Microbes Love

There is a lot of confusion about fiber. Many people immediately think of tree bark. But fiber is merely a chain of sugar molecules that are too complex to be digested by any of the acids and enzymes in your digestive system. They sail on through to your colon, where they can feed your microbiota. These molecular chains are called oligosaccharides, Greek for "a few sugars."

To most of us, sugar refers to the white crystals we spoon out of the sugar bowl—table sugar. But to chemists, table sugar is actually two simple sugars joined together: glucose and fructose. Because it has two sugars, it's called a *di*saccharide. Those two, along with galactose and a handful of others, are the basic links of complex sugars.

The oligosaccharide chains that feed your microbiota have at least three sugar molecules and rarely more than ten. Typically a chain is made by adding identical links of a single sugar, which determines the first part of that complex sugar's name. Fructo-oligosaccharide (FOS) is a chain of fructose, whereas galacto-oligosaccharide (GOS) is a chain of galactose, and both are proving to have psychobiotic possibilities.

We are particularly excited about the potential of prebiotics for dealing with stress-related responses. In recent unpublished work with mice we have shown that the prebiotics FOS and GOS reduce anxiety, enhance cognition, and dampen the stress response. More-over, this prebiotic combination can counter the immune and behavioral changes found in mice that are chronically stressed by housing them with bully mice. This is a mouse study, but it mirrors what we see in other unpublished human studies.

All of these sugar chains are assembled by enzymes. GOS, for example, is produced by enzymes that use lactose (milk sugar) as a starting material. Lactose is yet another disaccharide, composed of galactose and glucose. The enzymes add extra galactose sugars to the original disaccharide, building it up into an oligosaccharide. These enzymes are made by, among other creatures, bacteria. In fact, commercial production of oligosaccharides is typically done in big steel tanks by bacterial fermentation. That means that these prebiotics are created by probiotics, and bacteria both consume and produce oligosaccharides.

GOS is sometimes consumed by *Lacto* bacteria, and it is avidly gobbled up by *Bifido* species, which shows it to be a beneficial pre-biotic. You can buy GOS products now, but it can be a chain of three to eight sugar links, so which is best? A 2008 British study with 59 healthy people found that GOS made with enzymes produced by living *Bifido* species, as opposed to commercial enzymes, worked better to increase levels of *Bifido* in the gut. In other words, *Bifido* might be the best producer of GOS for other *Bifido*.[60]

Other researchers are coming up with similar results for FOS and GOS. A 2013 study from Michigan State University with 45 overweight adults found that GOS improved the gut microbiota and reduced inflammation.[61] In 2015, an Oxford study with 45 healthy volunteers compared FOS, GOS, and a placebo. They found indications that only GOS was able to reduce stress, but that all showed a reduction of anxiety similar to that produced by SSRIs or diazepam (Valium).[62] Their results suggest that these prebiotic oligosaccharides, and GOS in particular, offer a psychobiotic treatment comparable to drugs, but with fewer side effects.

Interestingly, although people with IBS may not react well to some prebiotics (see warning on page 188), a British study of 44 patients with IBS in 2009 found that consuming GOS significantly enhanced *Bifido* species, improved measures of gut discomfort, and improved depression and anxiety scores.[63]

If that reminds you of your own situation, you might want to try some GOS—whether or not you are depressed. It may help you keep your cool. Although these fiber supplements can work wonders for some people, be careful not to overdo it. All bacterial fermentations produce gas, but GOS leads to the least flatulence. If you feel bloated or gaseous after increasing your intake of psychobiotic oligosaccharides, scale back. With prebiotics, there can definitely be too much of a good thing.[64]

Choose Foods Naturally Rich in Prebiotics

High-fiber foods are natural prebiotics, especially foods that are naturally rich in the complex sugars that psychobiotics love. The advantage of eating prebiotic-rich foods over taking prebiotic supplements is that you are less likely to overdo it. Inulin is a kind of FOS found in many plants and a major natural source of fiber. A number of common foods contain inulin, and adding them to your menus will make your microbiota happy. Here is a list, roughly in order of most inulin to least:

- Sunchokes (Jerusalem artichokes)
- Artichokes
- Chicory, endive
- Lentils

- Asparagus
- Beans, especially limas
- Onions
- Garlic
- Leeks
- Bananas
- Beets
- Broccoli
- Fennel root

What about meat? Meat, like all animal flesh, is completely devoid of fiber. Animals use glycogen, not oligosaccharides, to store energy. You have to turn to plants to find edible fiber. For this reason, many a study of gut-healthy diets recommends a Mediterranean diet, but other studies have found more species of gut bacteria, lowered anxiety, and improved cognition on a diet that includes lean beef.[65] This is likely because the greater the diversity in your diet, the greater the diversity in your microbiota. It pays to mix it up. Still, the preponderance of evidence suggests that we should consume a lot less red meat and a little more fish.

This is one of the major takeaways of all the research on gut health and diet: Narrowing your food choices will reduce the variety of microbes in your gut, which can lead to dysbiosis. Elimination diets are not recommended. Instead, balanced meals with plenty of variety (and lots of vegetables) will give you the best results.

Research continues apace on prebiotics and their probiotic and psychobiotic targets. Studies are demonstrating roles for some common foods. Garlic and black peppercorns, for example, appear to enhance *L. reuteri* and inhibit pathogenic *E. coli*. Bananas, apples, and oranges enhance *L. reuteri*, *L. rhamnosus,* and *B. lactis*. Ginger inhibits pathogenic *E. coli*.[66]

Researchers have been documenting the loss of gut microbes for years, watching as species have been starved out, generation by generation. Even reintroducing fiber may sometimes be insufficient to rebuild a normal microbiota. These microbes are actually becoming extinct, and we may not be able to get them back. The sooner you, as an individual, and we, as a species, rebuild our life-giving relationship with the myriad bacteria dwelling inside us, the healthier and happier we will be.

Eat Fermented Foods

Fermentation has been used to preserve food for at least 5,000 years. Fermenting vegetables was a key survival technique that allowed people to move farther away from the ever-verdant tropics into regions of the world where they could only grow vegetables for part of the year—but, through fermentation, preserve the harvest for months thereafter. Because fermentation kills pathogens, it has been a lifesaver—and a continuing source of nourishment for the microbiota. Refrigeration may be a marvel of technology, but it has also displaced fermented foods from our diets, with unfortunate consequences. Thankfully, fermented foods are still abundantly available.

Almost any food can be fermented or pickled, just by encouraging the growth of probiotics already residing on its surface. Pickling is fermentation by another name, in which salt and lack of oxygen discourage unwanted pathogens for bacteria, usually *Lactobacillus* species, to grow unimpeded. Pickles can be made of fruit as well as vegetables, including mangoes, cucumbers, lemons, and watermelon. People pickle fish and even whale blubber. Other fermented products include kombucha, fu-tsai, and many other exotic fermentations. Every culture has its own cultures, all of which have probiotic and, sometimes, psychobiotic effects.

Traditional Japanese bean-based ferments such as tempeh, miso, natto, soy sauce, and dozens more belong in your psychobiotic pantry. Other bean ferments that may surprise you include coffee and chocolate. Certainly a lot of people will swear to the psychobiotic effects of chocolate and coffee!

Cabbage can be fermented into sauerkraut and kimchi. The bacterial enzymes in kraut release vitamins C, B, and K as well as other nutrients, making it more nutritious than the original cabbage, with a probiotic kick to boot. A single cup of sauerkraut can contain 10 million CFUs of *Lacto* and another species, *Leuconostoc*—enough to qualify sauerkraut as a true probiotic.[67]

Historically, fermentation was understood to be a simple chemical process, and the signs of fermentation, like bubbling foam, were mistaken for a kind of boiling. The word "yeast," in fact, comes from the Greek word for boiling, and in earlier times the idea was that during fermentation, sulfurous particles were being given off by decaying matter.

It took Louis Pasteur, in the 19th century, to realize that living microbes were the overlords of fermentation. For as long as humans have pounded grain into flour, some 30,000 years ago, there have been bakers. The first bread was a flattened dough ball, crisped over the fire, like a tortilla or matzo. But leavened bread, with bubbles provided by yeast, was light and chewy, a definite gustatory improvement over flatbread. Bakers coveted the starter that created a great batch of bread and tossed the starters that went flat, tasted bad, or made them sick. In this way, yeast for fermentation evolved to its current robust form. So closely related is brewing to baking that over the millennia, the same yeast, *Saccharomyces cerevisiae,* has come to dominate both.

Winemaking takes advantage of yeast organisms naturally found on grapes, and this is what Pasteur discovered. He also discovered that the wrong kinds of microbes could spoil wine. He determined the conditions, including temperature and oxygen, that affected the proper fermentation of grapes. Pasteur's work saved the French wine industry, and for that alone we owe him a great debt of gratitude.

Using what he learned about microbes in wine, Pasteur went on to explore the role of microbes in disease. He figured out how to kill the pathogens lurking in milk and other liquids—the process now named after him, pasteurization. But Pasteur was not a germophobe. He understood that microbes were essential to the healthy growth of animals and humans.

Important Warning: Before we continue with the discussion of fermented foods: If you have a compromised immune system, probiotics and fermented foods may be problematic. If you suffer from severe IBD, you will want to proceed carefully. If you have either of these two problems, talk to your doctor before you try probiotic supplements or add fermented foods to your diet.

Up Your Intake of Yogurt, the Best Known Psychobiotic

Milk can be made into yogurt, cheese, kefir, lassi, airag, kumis, and many more. Traditional buttermakers added a little old milk to the mix before churning—that's what cultured butter is all about. Throughout history, milk has gone bad, and desperate people drank it anyway. When they not only survived but also felt better, every family and tribe repeated and refined the experiment, thereby developing the world's many fermented milk products.

Yogurt has been recognized as a healthy food for thousands of years, but it took Élie Metchnikoff, who was one of Pasteur's colleagues, to really study the matter. Metchnikoff's Nobel Prize for work on the immune system, his study of the relationship between aging and bacteria, was inspired by Bulgarian peasants whose longevity he attributed to the yogurt in their diets. An enthusiastic scientist who acted on his discoveries, Metchnikoff ended up eating yogurt for the rest of his life.

Yogurt and other fermented milk products are made by introducing bacteria, including psychobiotics such as the *Lacto* and *Bifido* species, into the milk and providing the best possible circumstances for them to multiply. *Lacto* species eat lactose, which is milk sugar. Once fed, they produce lactic acid, which sours (or ferments) the milk. If you are lactose intolerant, you may find that you can eat yogurt because the *Lacto* species have eaten most of the lactose for you.

That makes fermented milk an excellent first choice for your personal psychobiotic journey. Some yogurts are pasteurized, which means that you aren't ingesting live bacteria when you eat them. But other yogurts have more than 10 billion CFUs per serving—plenty to make a difference. In the United States, look for the Live & Active Cultures seal to ensure that the product has living probiotics in it. If you are trying yogurt for the first time as a psychobiotic, give yourself four weeks of a daily serving to see if it works for you. If you get bloating or diarrhea, back off the serving size. One caveat: Many yogurts are packed with sugar, which pretty much negates their probiotic benefit. Read the label and choose yogurt with no added sugar.

Research also indicates that vitamin D enhances the psychobiotic effect of the active microbes in yogurt.[68] Although most milk products are fortified with vitamin D, many yogurts are not. Check the label: If the yogurt you like doesn't have it, you might consider taking a supplement with your yogurt meal.

Another point to ponder: We have all been told to lower our fat intake, and that is reasonable. After all, there are more calories in fat than any other type of food. But when you take the fat out of milk products, you concentrate the milk sugars, changing the relative proportions of *Lacto* bacteria and the sugars they like to eat and making the product less effective as a psychobiotic. In a large Spanish study of 14,500 university graduates, only whole-fat, not low-fat, yogurt lowered depression risk.[69] So go for full fat if you can find it, or reduced fat—but stay away from fat-free yogurt products.

Probiotic Pickles Everywhere

For almost any given food, someone somewhere has tried to pickle it. Would you eat raw fermented meat? If you've ever eaten pepperoni, salami, or prosciutto, the answer is yes. Americans eat some 250 million pounds of pepperoni each year, mostly on pizza. Few of those pizza eaters realize they are eating fermented meat. In fact, pizza might be the perfect fermented food, with its yeasty crust, tangy microbial cheese, and fermented meat. (Except that cooking it pretty much kills its probiotic punch.)

Depending on the microbe and the nutrients you feed it, fermentation can produce some wonderful things. Feed sugar to yeast cells and they will produce alcohol, which kills pathogens. Take that alcohol and feed it to acetic bacteria and they will produce vinegar, an acid that also kills pathogens. Take complex carbs and feed that food to gut bacteria, and they will produce short-chain fatty acids, a potent energy source. A side benefit of gut fermentation is the liberation of B vitamins that are otherwise difficult to obtain from fresh food. Fermentation is nature's basic chemistry set, and humans benefit enormously by harnessing it.

Due to their invisibility and generally good nature, beneficial microbes have insinuated themselves into our world without anyone realizing it. The microbes used in fermenting foods—from milk to soy to cabbage to grains and grapes—are the same microbes being sold as probiotic products today. Many of these fermentation microbes are also potentially psychobiotics. Indeed, eating fermented foods has been shown to improve social anxiety in susceptible people.[70] By killing the bad microbes and thereby lowering inflammation, these microbes are keeping you healthy and happy.

It makes sense that fermentative microbes are the same as probiotics, because they both fit the same niche, namely fighting pathogens. There are parallels. If fermentation doesn't function properly, you get spoilage. If your microbiota doesn't function properly, you get infection and inflammation. We have coevolved with these probiotics, bringing them into our houses, our kitchens, our restaurants, wineries, breweries, and bakeries. As a counterbalance to the deadly world of pathogens, probiotics save the day.

It has taken a couple hundred years, but bacteria—at least in the form of probiotics—are getting a better reputation. Unfortunately, our shunning them for the last century may already have taken a toll. Our newfound fascination with the microbiota may be just in time.

THE PSYCHOBIOTIC PYRAMID

Perhaps you have seen the Food Guide Pyramid used by the U.S. Department of Agriculture (USDA) to represent a balanced diet. Here's a variation on that model, a psychobiotic pyramid, that conveys how to get the proper proportions of good mood food, including probiotics.

The main message of this graphic is that by far the biggest psychobiotic contributor to your diet should be leafy greens and vegetables. Fruits, nuts, and berries are important, as are fish and fermented foods. You should consider probiotic supplements an important but a relatively small player in the mix of what you eat for gut health and good mood.

PSYCHOBIOTIC RULES TO LIVE BY

Adjusting your menu and including psychobiotic supplements in your daily routine are two essential steps toward gut health and, with it, a better mood. Here are more changes you can make in your daily routine to enhance the process. Nothing is an instant fix. Your microbiota changes constantly, but big-picture population shifts, and the mood changes that can come with them, take time. A lot of variables are involved with psychobiotic balance, including diet, exercise, genetics, immunity, and hormones. It's an exquisitely complex system, and your success will depend on keeping all of these factors in top shape. The odds are good that you will start to feel better after just two weeks of this healthy, anti-inflammatory diet.[71] For good measure, you may even lower your blood pressure[72] and lose weight.[73] Reshape your habits in these directions, and you will be doing yourself—and the microbes inside you—a service.

Stop Eating Junk Food

You can help yourself by adding new foods to the menu, but first, you need to stop eating the bad ones. That, in fact, may be all it takes to make you feel better. What do we mean by junk food? Think processed meats (hot dogs, sausage), refined grains (white bread, cake, pancakes, cookies), sweets (cola, sweetened fruit juice, ice cream, candy bars, ice pops, jam), and salty snacks (cheese puffs, potato chips). In other words, a delicious all-American diet.

Junk food affects your mood—and your microbiota. Studies have shown that foods with added sugar can induce depression, possibly by boosting pathogenic bacteria.[74] Prebiotics have been shown to moderate this effect. A large Norwegian study with 23,000 women and their children found that a junk food diet predicted depression and anxiety in the children. It wasn't just the kids' diets; children born to

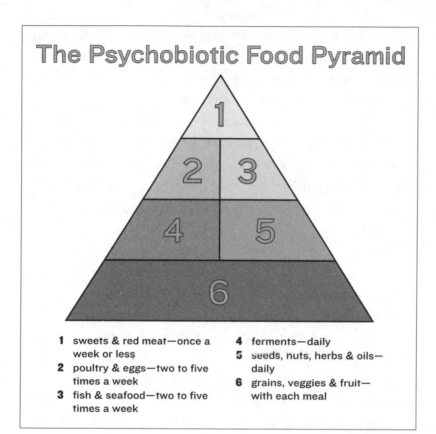

The Psychobiotic Food Pyramid

1 sweets & red meat—once a week or less
2 poultry & eggs—two to five times a week
3 fish & seafood—two to five times a week
4 ferments—daily
5 seeds, nuts, herbs & oils—daily
6 grains, veggies & fruit—with each meal

Like the traditional dietary pyramid, this one visualizes the foods that will nourish a healthy microbiota. Eat plenty of those at the base— these foods represent the foundation of a psychobiotic diet— and proportionally less of those in the smaller sections at the top.

mothers who ate a junk food diet when they were pregnant had more psychological problems.[75] Another Norwegian study of 5,700 people showed a direct connection between a poor diet and depression and anxiety.[76] These are big, significant studies that are hard to ignore.

Just to get you off on the right footing, a healthy diet consists of vegetables, fruit, fish, high-fiber grains, nuts, eggs, and quality vegetable oil. These are elements of both the Nordic and Mediterranean diets, known to add healthy years to your life. These diets are also, fortunately, very tasty. So put down the corn puffs and pick up some nuts. Yes, it can start that simply.

Another good diet that encourages *Bifido* and *Lacto* species is the Japanese diet, with fermented foods, veggies, and fish. The Japanese, especially those in rural areas, have a lot of fiber in their diet, and their guts show a lot of diversity.[77] As far as a healthy diverse microbiota is concerned, diet turns out to trump environment and geography both.[78]

Fiber is potent and essential to gut health, even on a high-fat diet. A 2007 Belgian study on participants who began with a diverse microbiota, with high levels of *Bifido,* found that when they ate a high-fat diet, that gut biodiversity was destroyed. But when they added fiber into the diet, it helped to normalize the gut microbe population.[79]

All signs point to the conclusion that the typical American diet can actually be toxic. Studies have shown that a high-fat, low-fiber diet increases inflammation and endotoxins—illness-inducing chemicals released by certain injured or killed bacteria—by some 70 percent. Fortunately, adding fiber or switching to a Mediterranean-style diet for 30 days reverses these poisonous changes.[80] High-fat and high-sugar diets increase inflammation, the source of much disease and discomfort, and can actually degrade your blood-brain barrier (BBB), allowing dangerous toxins to access your brain.[81]

The research indicates that for many, depression and anxiety may simply come down to a lousy diet. This is easy to fix, in principle, and so this should be your number one goal. In practice, it might be hard to break the bad habits you've spent years cultivating—and that your family and culture encourage! But unfortunately, the big payoff from the tasty Western diet is depression and anxiety. The solution lies in substitutions. Here are some simple ones with which to start.

For this food	Try this healthy replacement
White bread	Whole wheat or rye bread
White rice	Brown rice
Pasta	Whole wheat pasta
Ice cream	Yogurt
Candy	Fruit
Processed meat	Fish
Chips	Vegetables

Every tip in the rest of this chapter will mean less if you don't stop eating junk. Eating yogurt can't fully compensate for eating candy bars. The psychobiotic bacteria in your gut—the good microbes, the ones that will help you get beyond depression and anxiety—need good food to live on. Fast food simply doesn't qualify.

Minimize Sugar

Food is processed in many ways and for many reasons, including shelf life, but mostly it's to make the food taste better. This is why, when you look at all the packaged food in the store, you will find it hard to find anything that doesn't have added sugar. Sugar tastes good to us because our bodies recognize it as a rich source of instant energy. It is absorbed directly by your small intestine and can be used immediately by your body for energy. That explains the big rush sugar can give you, within minutes of eating it.

Stress makes people crave sugar as well. It is part of the fight-or-flight response that wants to prepare you for running from or fighting a lion. Certain bacteria in your small intestine love it as well, but many of those that love sugar are pathogenic. Sugar, of course, can actually make you happier, but the effect is temporary. Long-term sugar use can make you sick, inflamed, and depressed. Fructose, a common sugar, can increase circulatory bacterial toxins and lead to liver damage as that poor organ tries valiantly to eliminate those toxins.[82] It's not just an American phenomenon—a large multinational study has found a significant and strong correlation between sugar consumption and depression around the globe.[83]

You can probably make no single change to your diet that will be as good for your health and well-being as cutting down on sugar. Fortunately, we have some sugar substitutes that may actually be good for you. Real maple syrup contains some fiber in the form of oligosaccharides, suggesting it may be a prebiotic.[84] Make sure it's real, though. Cheap fake maple syrup is just fructose with maple flavoring. Honey also contains oligosaccharides, and so it may be considered a prebiotic.[85] Humans have been eating it since the Stone Age, and it is associated with decreased anxiety and improved memory.[86] Honey has also been shown to decrease edema and lower inflammation.[87]

The bottom line for sugar is to ditch it as much as you can. If you are buying prepared foods, it can be hard to avoid. So until manufacturers stop topping off with delicious, meretricious sugar, you're better off cooking your own food.

Get Plenty of Omega-3s

Although oils are fats, and fats can be inflammatory, different types of fat have different effects on your microbiota and your health. Saturated fats—think those that are solid at room temperature, like butter or meat fat—are the ones that can cause inflammation and gut distress. Omega-3 oils are the opposite. They are polyunsaturated as are olive or nut oils and the oils naturally occurring in fish. A diet deficient in omega-3s leads to microbial overgrowth in the small intestine—related to IBS—and inflammation,[88] whereas a diet rich in omega-3s dampens inflammation and improves the diversity of your microbiota—boosting numbers of *Bifido* species.[89] These oils are also essential for creating new nerves and synapses, which can improve cognition and memory.

> *In our lab, we found that polyunsaturated fatty acids such as ome-ga-3s reverse the impact of early-life stress on the gut microbiota. Rats that are separated from their mothers are stressed, leading to gut-brain dysfunction and a long-lasting dysbiotic microbiota. These rats show signs of depression and anxiety. Supplementing their diet with omega-3s, however, restores their microbiota and reduces levels of cortisol.*[90]

Many foods are high in omega-3s, including nuts, olives, soybeans, and the oils made from them. Fish oil is generally considered to be superior, and eating fish—especially salmon, trout, tuna, sardines, and cod—is a good way to increase this essential element in your diet.

Beware: Some fish may contain mercury, decidedly unhealthy. The worst offenders include shark, swordfish, king mackerel, and tilefish. A healthy microbiota can actually help you excrete mercury, but a dysbiotic microbiota allows the mercury to concentrate in your body, especially your brain.[91] The fish with the least mercury include salmon, trout, tuna, sardines, and cod.

Drink Less Alcohol

Like sugar, alcohol in excess can diminish the health and diversity of your microbiota, actually suppressing your psychobiotics. This is an important factor, because there are those, especially men, who tend to self-medicate their depression with alcohol—a habit that can mask and often worsen their condition. Although people may laugh and dance while drinking alcohol, technically it's a depressant.

That isn't what you should be taking if you already have depression. Alcohol also disturbs a good sleep pattern, and proper sleep is a key factor in mental health.

> *We recently conducted a study where we exposed mice to alcohol vapors and measured the impact on their gut microbiota. After four weeks, we collected fecal matter and analyzed it to show that the diversity of the microbiota was notably decreased and pathogen levels were increased. These results are in line with other studies that show a similar alteration in the microbiota during alcoholic hepatitis and psychological stress.*[92]

Elsewhere in this chapter we discuss the health of a glass of red wine. But even that may be too much for people taking antidepressant drugs, especially monoamine oxidase inhibitors (MAOIs). Remember that the poison is in the dosage. A little may be beneficial; a lot may be lethal.

Get Antioxidants From Food

We hear about antioxidants a lot these days, including on the labels of various commercially available supplements. Antioxidants are your body's way of fighting off the damage brought about by ordinary metabolic processes. If you imagine your body as a slow-burning fire, then antioxidants act as a chimney flue, moderating the flame.

The science of antioxidants is full of reversals, but as far as depression is concerned, antioxidants are beneficial. Certain antioxidant foods—such as coffee, cocoa, green tea, turmeric, strawberries, and blueberries—have been shown to lower the risks of depression and cognitive decline.[93] Just adding berries to your diet can delay mental decline by two and a half years or more. Curry spices, especially turmeric, have been shown to improve cognitive function.[94]

All of this does involve your microbiota, as you might imagine. Antioxidants can increase levels of healthy *Bifido* and *Lacto* species, generally strengthening anyone's gut health and especially improving outcomes in people with inflammatory bowel diseases.[95] Even red wine gets into this act, as it contains resveratrol, a compound in some plants (including grape skins) that also improves gut microbe diversity. As Benjamin Franklin said, "Wine is proof that God loves us and wants us to be happy." As you get into it, you'll find that the psychobiotic path is not so bumpy after all.

Avoid Emulsifiers

Emulsifiers are the diplomats of the food world, bringing together oil and water and getting them to work together. The natural world is full of emulsions—oil-water combinations—foremost of which is milk, a collection of fat droplets suspended in a watery base. So emulsions are not in themselves a bad thing, but industrial food processors sometimes use certain emulsifiers with negative effects on your gut. Two commercially important emulsifiers, carboxymethylcellulose (CMC) and polysorbate 80 (P80), have been shown to negatively affect both the thickness of your gut mucus and the diversity of your microbiota.[96]

A thinning mucus layer can lead to a leaky gut. Your microbes start to press in against the cells lining your intestines. At that proximity, they can pry open the junctions between the cells, which can then leak bacteria and cause inflammation. Tiny amounts of emulsifier can cause this kind of immune reaction—less than the amounts typically found in certain foods. Unfortunately, those foods include delicious things like ice cream and cake. I feel your pain.

In mouse studies, CMC and P80 promoted obesity and colitis. Human studies are under way. Although emulsifiers seemed primarily to affect the mucus layer, when the gut microbiota impacted by emulsifiers was transferred to another mouse, many of the same symptoms occurred. That indicates that the changes are happening to the microbiota, not just the mucus.

Ironically, one of the big uses for these two problematic emulsifiers is in gluten-free foods, where they are used to make up for a lack of the gluey gluten molecule. That means people with celiac, who must avoid gluten, may be exposed to substances that could be giving them other intestinal problems. If you suffer from celiac, do all you can to avoid processed foods containing these two emulsifiers. And if you don't strictly need to avoid gluten, this is a good reason to abandon the gluten-free foods that contain them.

Not all emulsifiers are equally bad. Lecithin, originally isolated from egg yolk and now also derived from soybeans, is a good substitute, because it doesn't induce the same dysbiotic effect as CMC and P80. The hopeful takeaway here is that you can quit eating foods containing these emulsifiers and your gut can recover as your microbiota settles down.

Unlike studies in which superdoses are used, these commercial emulsifier studies looked at doses that were less than a tenth of an equivalent human dose. So how do chemicals like this make it past the regulatory hurdles for food additives? The answer is simple: The FDA doesn't test for potential microbial dysbiosis.[97] As we learn more about how these drugs interact with our microbiota, we will probably insist on better testing for additives. Until then, it's up to you to read your labels carefully.

Minimize Your Use of Proton Pump Inhibitors (PPIs) and H2 Blockers

If you are afflicted by heartburn, you may find yourself popping antacids for some quick relief. Proton pump inhibitors (PPIs), in particular, are often prescribed for gastroesophageal reflux disease

(GERD) and heartburn. But new research indicates that you shouldn't make that a long-term habit. Studies have shown that PPIs (omeprazole, lansoprazole) and to a lesser extent H2 blockers (ranitidine, cimetidine) are related to small intestinal bacterial overgrowth (SIBO),[98] one possible cause of IBS, which can result in depression and anxiety. Interestingly, people suffering from depression or anxiety in addition to their GI problems get less relief from PPIs than people without depression do, suggesting that preexisting dysbiosis can mitigate the effects of PPIs.[99] PPIs—even in low doses—have also been shown to reduce the diversity of your microbiota to levels similar to patients with *C. diff* infections.[100] These reductions remain, even after one month of quitting PPIs.[101]

Stomach acids are important, helping you to absorb vitamin B_{12}[102] and triggering important digestive enzymes. A simple pill to quell stomach problems by lowering gastric acidity can thus cause problems all the way to the colon. This has led the FDA to mandate that labels for PPIs contain a warning that PPIs can increase the risk of *C. diff* infections, which can cause anxiety and depression.

Although PPIs have a long track record of safety, these new studies revealing changes to the microbiota are making doctors reevaluate their usage. In particular, long-term PPI use (more than 14 days) should be discouraged in favor of other treatments for GERD and acid stomach. Talk to your doctor about chronic stomach problems, especially if yours are mild. You might be able to rid yourself completely of these issues without starting trouble in a different part of your gut. Some simple techniques include eating smaller portions and less fat, as well as avoiding late-night snacks.

Exercise for the Sake of Your Psychobiotics

Ah, the relief of swaying in a hammock. Or binge-watching TV in your comfy recliner. Or baking on the beach blanket. Is this not what we work so hard to achieve? It's actually okay to kick back. That's our well-earned reward for toiling away. Unfortunately, a lot of us work really hard while also sitting on our butts. We might be "kicking back" from the moment we get out of bed in the morning to the moment we slide back in at night. Most of us are not athletes by any measure. That may make us more likely to be depressed.

So, get some exercise! That's what everyone tells us. Of course, that is one of the last things you want to do if you have depression or anxiety. But I've got another reason why exercise helps with every aspect of your physical and mental health: It makes your microbiota happy. Even Hippocrates knew it, more than two thousand years ago: "If you are in a bad mood go for a walk. If you are still in a bad mood go for another walk." If you can walk, do it. If you can run, even better.

When you exercise, you contract your muscles, which in turn release anti-inflammatory chemicals that can cool down your immune system and quickly improve your mood. You can get a little bit of that "runner's high" with almost any exercise, including yoga, tai chi, and nature walks.

New research is showing that exercise can improve cognition in older people,[103] treat diabetes,[104] reduce IBS,[105] and improve depression,[106] all by improving your microbiota.[107] It's actually difficult to overstate the benefit of low to medium levels of exercise (aerobics), which improves every system in your body. If you've been sedentary for a long time, talk to your doctor about exercise and make sure not to overdo it. Start slow, and then keep increasing your exercise regimen over time. You'll know when you hit peak exercise, because that is when you will start to feel better.

Lose Weight

Weight control is an important example of homeostasis: You need to match the calories you bring in against the calories you expend to maintain your weight. Depending on how much energy you expend, your body must finely control your appetite. That job falls to a hormone named ghrelin, sometimes called the hunger hormone. The stomach secretes ghrelin when it's empty to tell you to eat. Secretions stop when the stomach is stretched, a simple negative feedback loop.

Balancing the hunger hormone ghrelin is the satiety hormone leptin, which tells you when to stop eating. The word "hangry" sums up the emotion that often accompanies hunger, and excess ghrelin or lack of leptin is typically behind that feeling. In fact, leptin treatment has been shown to reverse the anxious behavior of stressed-out animals.[108] Your microbiota plays a part in these signals to your brain that you are full: *E. coli* bacteria in your gut produce chemicals to suppress hunger.[109] This molecular signal comes about 20 minutes after eating, and it may be a way for your gut bacteria to maintain population stability—a microbial homeostatic mechanism. But sometimes the signals get mixed up, which is one reason why depression can affect a person's appetite, for better or worse. Research is showing how much your microbiota and the HPA axis—the communication channels between your gut and your brain—play a role in eating and overeating.

People under chronic stress often change their eating habits, and many of them overeat. Psychological stress elevates circulating ghrelin, which stimulates a preference for calorie-rich "comfort" foods. These foods activate reward circuits, increasing dopamine and reducing stress-induced anxiety and depression.

In our laboratory, we found that a high-fat diet protects against the deleterious effects of chronic stress. This blunting effect of a high-fat diet on stress is likely mediated by the HPA axis. At some point this can move behavior from impulsive to compulsive. Like an addiction, you can become tolerant to comfort food, and no longer get the same dopamine reward. That can increase your anxiety and depression, which can lead to additional overeating. This in turn can lead to obesity, which further contributes to anxiety and depression.[110]

People who are overweight or obese have varying degrees of dysbiosis, leading to chronic inflammation. Losing weight will bring your microbiota into balance, lower your levels of inflammation, and improve your mood. Accumulating evidence shows this can go both ways: Balancing your gut bacteria can help you lose weight. That should provide extra impetus to keep your microbiota in top shape, especially by adding fiber and lowering fat consumption.[111]

The Value of Intermittent Fasting

You and your microbiota need to be fed, but a little fasting can actually strengthen your cells. Diets with very low calorie counts are one of the few ways we know of to lengthen the life of animals. We would not recommend these diets, as they are miserable for the long haul. But a day or two of fasting every once in a while may have the same effect, with a lot less stomach gurgling.

Fasting seems to tell your body to shape up. There can be an increase in acuity, presumably to help you hunt down or dig up some food. But your body also undergoes something called autophagy (eating yourself), during which some of your sick cells kill themselves and are reabsorbed by your body. This is a fascinating theory that earned its discoverer, Yoshinori Ohsumi, a Nobel Prize in 2016.

A popular intermittent fasting program is called 5:2, where you eat normally for five days of the week and then eat a 500-calorie diet the other two days. But there is an even simpler way to take advantage of your body's attempts to clean house on a fast. All you need to do is stop eating at night and then wait at least 12 hours before you eat again. You might quit eating after eight at night and then wait until eight the next morning before you eat breakfast. As a bonus, by not eating after eight at night, you can minimize your chance of getting gastroesophageal reflux disease (GERD), reducing the need for PPIs and their associated dysbiosis.

Fasting changes your microbiota, increasing levels of *Akkermansia*, a microbe known to encourage your gut to produce more mucus, providing greater protection from pathogens.[112] *Akkermansia* is associated with a healthy gut and improved insulin sensitivity. Intermittent fasting and calorie restriction also increase levels of *Lacto* species with psychobiotic properties.[113]

Temper Your Use of Antibiotics

Antibiotics could easily be the most important breakthrough in medical health of all time. Countless lives have been saved by them. Before antibiotics, people could die from an infected splinter. Those were not the good old days. But today we overuse them. People think there is no downside to using them, so they will beg their doctors for a prescription, even if they have a virus—which antibiotics cannot help.

But taking antibiotics is like dropping a bomb into your guts. It doesn't just take out the pathogens that are creating the illness you want to treat; it can destroy everything, commensals included. Small pockets of microbes—your first line of defense—may survive, but the neighborhood they need for thriving is wiped out. By indiscriminately killing all your intestinal flora, you leave yourself vulnerable to all kinds of new problems.

CASE STUDY: Sarah (not her real name) is a 70-year-old successful businesswoman who has suffered from bipolar illness since her 20s.

She has suffered far more episodes of depression than elation over the years.

Over the past three years she has had four urinary tract infections that required antibiotic treatment. On each occasion the antibiotic treatment resulted in an episode of depression that lasted in excess of eight weeks. For the last episode of depression she took a Bifidobacteria longum *supplement and the episode of depression was attenuated to about two weeks. B. longum seems to be able to reverse some of the deficit incurred by the antibiotic treatment.*

The most extreme result of antibiotic abuse is a *Clostridium difficile* infection, which can involve severe symptoms of gut pain, diarrhea, nausea, and fever, with other extremely painful repercussions. Because this bacterium can form spores that are extremely difficult to eradicate, *C. diff* is often the last bug standing. It is typically a hospital-acquired disease, and it can kill you. Right now, one of the best therapies for *C. diff* is a fecal transplant: in essence, borrowing a healthy and biodiverse population of bacteria from someone else and inserting it into your ailing intestines. This unorthodox treatment is showing a success rate claimed to be over 90 percent. As gross as it sounds, when your choice is between a painful disease and death or a fecal transplant, the decision is easy.

You don't have to contract *C. diff* to feel the pain associated with antibiotic overuse. Different types of these drugs will have different side effects,[114] but many people suffer from diarrhea and nausea at the end of antibiotic treatments. For some, these symptoms last for months or even years as their guts try to reestablish a normal microbiota.

All the advice given in this chapter and elsewhere in this book also applies to the situation of gut dysbiosis caused by antibiotics.

Eat well and use prebiotic/probiotic supplements regularly, and especially at the same time you are taking antibiotics. Probiotics have been shown to help to restore gut flora that have been depleted by antibiotics.[115] *Lactobacillus* GG—found in cultured yogurt—will often build back microbe diversity and gut health as well.

Scientists are working on better antibiotics that target specific pathogens, not just bacteria in general. If you need antibiotics, talk to your doctor about using a narrow-spectrum antibiotic if possible. If not, be sure to repopulate your gut when the therapy is completed. Start slowly, though. Your gut will thank you.

Vilified for their collateral damage, antibiotics may soon play a more positive role in depression and anxiety. Researchers are at work singling out specific pathogenic bacteria that contribute to depression, sometimes conditions that have lasted for years. Candidate culprits include *Clostridium, Alistipes, E. coli, Shigella, Salmonella, Vibrio, Campylobacter, Yersinia enterocolitica, Aeromonas,* and *Listeria*. By selectively targeting and eliminating these pathogenic species, researchers may find ways that antibiotics could be a part of future treatments for depression and anxiety. Obviously these techniques will have to be designed to spare your beneficial bacteria, but they may represent the future, a welcome breakthrough in the world of antibiotics.

WHERE DO YOU FALL ON THE PSYCHOBIOTIC HEALTH SCALE?

All people can benefit from tending to their microbiota's health, but maybe you are wondering where you fall on the psychobiotic spectrum. You cannot really take a survey of your intestinal population, and you may not even be sure if you're grappling with unnecessary depression or anxiety. The answer is that we all have to be scientists and subject ourselves to testing.

Poll Your Microbes

There are businesses that offer swab tests to analyze your microbiota, including uBiome and Second Genome. You establish an account with them, and they send you the equipment and instructions to sample your feces—and, if you wish, other moist body areas such as your mouth or your armpits. It's really quite easy, and not all that gross. You send your samples in and shortly receive a readout of the population of bacteria that showed up. Both companies give you guidance in how to read the results they provide. Remember that your microbiota population is changing constantly, so a single swab may not track exactly what is living in your mucus lining,[116] but it's a start.

Then—especially if you want to track the effects of making some of the changes discussed in this chapter—you can sign up for a series of such samplings to look for changes. Of course, you hope to find you've boosted the numbers of probiotics and psychobiotics while at the same time reduced the number of pathogenic microbes. In general, you are looking to increase *Lacto* and *Bifido* species and to reduce bacteria in the Proteobacteria genera, which contains a lot of pathogens. (See chart on page 52 to review the names of various species.)

Keep a Mood Diary

Biome tests are one way of gauging the success of your efforts to boost your psychobiotic level, but you may also want to track your progress by keeping a mood diary. Psychobiotic therapies can take a week or more to kick in, and a diary will help you see changes through time. It doesn't need to be a complicated journal; a scratch pad might suffice. Or, if you are a nerd like me (the author), you might use a spreadsheet to track progress.

Try to monitor three or more things in your life that contribute to your health and mood the best. Here are some of the factors that you might want to track. Psychiatrists have used many of these for years to determine how depressed or anxious their patients are:

- Feelings of sadness or despair
- Feelings of nervousness or fear
- Sleep patterns
- Daily cycles of alertness
- Clarity of thought
- Ability to concentrate
- Changes in bowel movements
- Changes in appetite or cravings

Choose three or more items in this list and begin by jotting down where you find yourself now, as you start this process. This will be your baseline.

Update your diary every week or so, and compare your current status to your baseline. If you aren't seeing a change or improvement after a couple of weeks, it might be time to try a different psychobiotic approach. If your changes are in the positive direction, you're doing something right.

HEALTHY GUT, HAPPY LIFE

The basic principles outlined in this chapter are intended to help you keep your gut and mood in top shape. Developing and maintaining a healthy mix of gut microbes will keep you on an even keel.

The steps are simple: Eat more leafy greens, fermented foods, and fiber. Think spinach, pickles, and almonds, and expand from there. Quit eating junk, and get used to vegetables. If you need a boost, try supplements that include some of the psychobiotics listed earlier in the chapter, and include some prebiotics to feed them in the mix. Above all, stick with it. Our bad habits can be hard to break, but once you find a better groove, it will be easy to maintain because it will feel good.

You now have the knowledge and tools to repair your gut, soothe your mind, and lift your mood. You only have your microbes to outwit. You can do it.

CHAPTER 8

PSYCHOBIOTICS AND TODAY'S MAJOR DISEASES

"A crust eaten in peace is better than

a banquet partaken in anxiety."

—Aesop

ALL PEOPLE WILL FACE SOME DEGREE OF DEPRESSION AND ANXIETY at some point in their life. It is an inescapable and often appropriate response to the vagaries of the world. Depression serves to keep you at arm's length from life's brutishness, and anxiety prepares you to deal with stress by heightening your senses. In other words, it's not always bad.

Life is full of surprises. Alas, not all of them are parties. Grief over loss is normal; this is called situational depression. But when your depression doesn't resolve after a time, something else may be at work. If you feel blue most of the time, you may have persistent or major depression—a kind of depression caused by your brain chemistry, not the world outside. At least 5 percent of the population is clinically depressed at any point in time, and 10 percent of the population will suffer a depressive episode at some time in their lives. It is often accompanied by weight fluctuations and sleep problems. Gut problems are often involved, either as cause or effect. If this is you, psychobiotics may help.

Stand-alone depression is familiar to most people, but there is another kind: depression as a comorbidity—a fellow traveler—of other diseases. This is remarkably common. Almost every disease you can think of will increase your odds of having either depression or anxiety. What is surprising is that it goes both ways: Depression is often noticed first, before the accompanying disease is even diagnosed. When this happens, depression is acting as a message from your gut of an impending microbial upset.

This chapter explores these connections ailment by ailment, and brings you some of the latest advice about balancing your gut and mitigating the effects of dysbiosis as part of a larger, and perhaps more familiar, illness or condition. In each case, after describing the role your gut health plays in each condition, we look at the promise of psychobiotics in treatment. What you will find, surprisingly, is that gut dysbiosis is proving central to many of the most serious diseases we face today—which goes far to explain the mental distress, especially depression and anxiety, that often accompanies these conditions. Furthermore, you will learn how essential boosting the health of your microbiota is to treatment—and to your mood as you progress toward better health.

IRRITABLE BOWEL SYNDROME

"Irritable bowel syndrome (IBS)" is a term used to describe a cluster of lower intestinal and colon problems, all of which, as the name implies, cause abdominal pain. It is also responsible for bloating, cramping, and either constipation or diarrhea. In some unlucky cases, patients suffer from both diarrhea and constipation. IBS is quite common; indeed, it is the most common disorder gastroen-terologists see, afflicting some 10 to 25 percent of adults in the United States. Up to 90 percent of people with IBS also experience depression or anxiety, making it clear that IBS is a disorder of the gut-brain axis.

> *Patients with IBS were painfully aware of the kind of signals the gut can send to the brain long before the concept of a dysregulated gut-brain axis emerged as the favored explanation for their travails.*[1]
>
> *Clinical studies of IBS confirm alterations in the stability and diversity of the gut microbiota. Manipulation of the microbiota can influence the key symptoms of IBS, including abdominal pain and bowel problems. In our laboratory, we have shown with mice that early life stress results in an altered brain-gut axis and therefore can serve as an important model for investigating IBS.[2] In human studies, we have also shown that visuospatial memory, which is related to cortisol levels, is impaired in many IBS patients.[3]*

Stress can increase the odds of getting IBS. Survivors of Nazi concentration camps came away with persistent cases of IBS, as well as post-traumatic stress disorder (PTSD).[4] Early childhood exposure to war also increases the incidence of IBS.[5] There seems to be a genetic component to IBS as well, but twin studies are somewhat equivocal, and there is good reason to think that the syndrome has epigenetic components—that is, individual experi-ence can change the expression of genes affecting this disorder. There is evidence that a gene involved in the HPA axis may be affected, leading to an extended overreaction to stress. An epigenetic effect could explain how the syndrome persists, even long after the initial childhood trauma.[6]

Some people with IBS may have food allergies, so some of their inflammation is related to diet. Diets can have epigenetic effects, and this might be a straightforward way to affect IBS. Researchers compared two diets, one rich in rye and the other rich in wheat. Both of these diets are high in fiber and have a low glycemic index, meaning they don't jack up sugar levels, although the rye diet had a lower insulin response. Why rye beats wheat is not clear, but some researchers speculate that the physical structure of rye is responsible.[7] For whatever reason, these two diets leave different epigenetic marks in your gut, and they may be long-lasting.[8] Because metabolic swings are associated with inflammation—so-called metaflammation—there might be reason to try foods with a low insulin response to treat IBS.[9]

Possible Directions

Probiotics, especially *B. longum,* have been shown to work to calm the distress and normalize the inflammation experienced as part of IBS.[10] This effect may have an epigenetic basis. Studies have also found good results from other *Bifido* species, including *B. bifidum, B. infantis, B. animalis*, and *B. lactis*. There have been years of successful trials with Mutaflor, which contains Nissle 1917, a subspecies of *E. coli*. Unfortunately, the FDA has blocked the sale of Mutaflor in America, even though it has an astonishing 100 years of safety studies behind it, but you can get it everywhere else in the world.

Studies with prebiotics have demonstrated efficacy as well. Galacto-oligosaccharide (GOS) at a rate of 3.5 grams/day has been shown to improve stool consistency, flatulence, bloating, and anxiety in those suffering from IBS.[11] Because GOS is a food for *Bifido* species, it might make some sense to mix GOS in with your probiotics to boost the utility of both. IBS is still difficult to treat, and you should talk to your doctor before you try these potential remedies, but research with prebiotics and probiotics is starting to sound hopeful for both the gut and the brain aspects of this widespread syndrome.

INFLAMMATORY BOWEL DISEASE: CROHN'S DISEASE AND ULCERATIVE COLITIS

Crohn's disease (CD) and ulcerative colitis (UC) are lumped together as types of inflammatory bowel disease (IBD), because they both involve gut inflammation. They may both result in abdominal pain and diarrhea. If the disease is bad enough, a person can have internal bleeding that may lead to general inflammation and anemia. Crohn's can affect any segment of the GI tract, whereas ulcerative colitis is limited to the colon. Young sufferers may experience stunted growth, as the disease can adversely affect nutrient absorption. Up to one in five sufferers has headaches and depression, and up to one in three has anxiety.

There is a genetic component to the disease, and some 70 genes have been found to be associated. As with many of the genetic diseases discussed here, these mutations mainly affect the immune system, and each individual mutation adds to the risk and degree of inflammation, but there is also a large environmental contribution as well, with smokers being twice as likely to develop these diseases as nonsmokers. So, as a first step to feeling better, stop smoking.

As yet, there is no cure for Crohn's, but a small study has shown some promise for fecal transplants.[12] For some people, steroids and a specific tuberculosis antibiotic may provide some relief. Other antibiotics can sometimes make things worse. Ulcerative colitis is sometimes treated surgically, with removal of the affected parts of the colon.

The microbiota is the number one culprit in these inflammatory diseases. Recent research has identified a problematic biofilm composed of a yeast, *Candida tropicalis,* and two bacteria, *Serratia marcescens* and *E. coli,* that may be a key to understanding IBD. This biofilm represents a hardy cross-kingdom community, with yeast and bacteria forming a lichen-like partnership. Biofilms are notorious for their tenacity; they are difficult to dislodge because they can protect their denizens from acids, dehydration, and antibiotic attacks. The biofilm formed in CD is especially thick and robust.[13]

Both UC and CD have been characterized by a reduction in *Bifido* and *Lacto* species, and treatment with probiotics has had encouraging results—but only in the quiescent stage, before the symptoms become virulent. When the disease becomes active, that situation reverses and there is an overgrowth of these species, so adding more only exacerbates the problem.[14] For most people, these are the good bacteria, but if you are having a flare-up of UC or CD, you should probably stay away from these commonly available probiotics. These patients also have a sharp decrease in *Faecalibacterium prausnitzii,* from a healthy 14 percent to almost 0.3 percent. Future therapies will likely target these bacteria to help rebalance the gut.

Other than quitting smoking, the possible treatments for IBD and related inflammations are still rudimentary. But knowing that biofilms are involved will likely advance the field and lead to new treatments and possible cures. Certain peptides have been shown to help break up biofilms and keep them from reestablishing, but more human research is needed.[15]

Ever since studies in the 1960s showed that Bedouin Arabs developed colitis upon resettlement, there has been a growing emphasis on the connection between stress and depression with IBD.[16] In a study of more than 700 people in Manitoba, researchers examined the factors leading to flare-ups in IBD and found that stress was the most important influence.[17] Interestingly, patients with Crohn's who get cognitive behavioral therapy spend fewer days in the hospital, a sign that the disease not only drives depression, but that depression might also drive the disease.[18] Although psychobiotics may not be appropriate for those with severe IBD, addressing external conditions causing stress and depression may be.

Possible Directions

For now, *S. boulardii,* a probiotic yeast, can help to fight the *Candida* often found in CD. Mutaflor, if you can find it, has also been shown to provide relief. For UC, there are more probiotic possibilities, including *F. prausnitzii, L. plantarum, L. rhamnosus, L. reuteri* ATCC 55730, and Mutaflor. A few combination biotics have also shown promise, including *L. delbrueckii* and *L. fermentum;* VSL#3; and a probiotic-prebiotic mix containing *B. breve* and GOS.

Be sure you talk to your doctor first. If you are currently inflamed, your gut may be leaky and even the best probiotics might not be safe.

CELIAC AND GLUTEN SENSITIVITY

Imagine how exciting the first loaf of leavened bread must have been. Some 10,000 years ago, some unsung baker tossed a lump of fermenting wheat onto some dying embers, only to have it rise into a delightfully chewy bread. That chewiness came from the gluten, a protein that makes bread elastic enough to contain the yeasty gases in bready bubbles. It elevated a hardtack chunk of unleavened bread into a light, easily digested loaf of heaven. Easy to digest— except for the one percent of Stone Agers who felt just awful after eating it.

Celiac is a disease with a genetic component that predisposes sufferers to sometimes intense gastrointestinal problems in response to eating gluten. The villi along their intestines may become damaged, affecting the absorption of food and sometimes leading to malnutrition and stunted growth. It can also involve bloating, which is likely due to ongoing fermentation, meaning that typical applications of prebiotics and probiotics could exacerbate the situation. Celiac can cause your gut lining to become more permeable— so-called leaky gut, a condition that may affect brain function by leaking antigens into the circulation. Celiac can result in poor absorption of nutrients, which can also lead to depression. In fact, people who suffer from celiac disease are almost twice as likely to have depression or anxiety as those without the disease.

Celiac has an immune component as well, with white blood cells building up in the pits between the villi. It is associated with various autoimmune diseases, including diabetes and psoriasis. Celiac patients have antibodies against gluten and gliadin, another protein found in grains. Besides wheat, plants that contain gluten include barley, rye, spelt, durum, and other related species. For some sufferers, the list goes on. Shopping can be an exercise in frustration.

A fifth of celiac patients develop psychiatric problems, from depression to ADHD, neuropathy, multiple sclerosis (MS), and schizophrenia. It has been known since the 1950s that people with schizophrenia are at a higher than normal risk of having celiac. When these patients are given a gluten-free diet, their guts feel better and their behavior often improves. One study showed that patients with schizophrenia on a gluten-free diet were discharged at twice the rate as the controls.[19] There have even been anecdotal reports of people cured of their schizophrenia with a gluten-free diet.[20] That doesn't mean you can cure any case of schizophrenia with a gluten-free diet, but it does imply that some cases of celiac are bad enough to cause schizophrenic symptoms.

Autism is sometimes associated with celiac, and a gluten-free diet may help these people, not only with their gut, but with their behavior as well.[21] (See the section on autism spectrum disorder, page 233.)

Although celiac occurs in only one percent of the population, gluten sensitivity (GS) may affect six times as many people. GS is related to, but distinct from celiac. People with GS don't have as much intestinal damage but may have higher rates of psychological problems. Severe GS can lead your immune system to attack your brain and spinal cord, causing problems with walking and coordination. The resultant chronic inflammation can trigger bouts of anxiety or depression on top of these other woes. Patients with celiac and GS can feel better by eliminating gluten, which also, unfortunately, is associated with beneficial fiber, making it all the more important for these people to eat more vegetables! Typically, psychiatric issues disappear within a year of maintaining a gluten-free diet.

Patients with celiac disease often have cross-reactions with foods other than wheat, including casein from dairy.[22] Other problematic foods include oats, yeast, millet, corn,[23] quinoa,[24] rice, and other grains.[25] This is because the antibody to one type of gliadin can also cross-react with other similar-looking proteins, responding to these as if they were gluten. In fact, people with celiac can have cross-reactions with other proteins, and so some sufferers have to steer clear of a lot more than just wheat and gluten.

Possible Directions

Some nutritionists recommend a kind of paleo diet for patients who don't respond to a gluten-free diet. Others recommend a more balanced diet with plenty of fruits and veggies, meat, fish, eggs, beans, and nuts. Yogurt and cheese are generally acceptable, and their probiotic effects may help with depression. Fortunately for us, plenty of good fiber sources don't come from grains. These include chicory root, artichokes, sunchokes, leeks, and other veggies that are recommended in this book. In addition, psychobiotic fiber in the form of resistant potato starch and banana starch may be helpful to feed the good bacteria. Celiac reactions can be dangerous, so be sure to consult with your doctor before you fill up on any of these plant-based fibers.

A tip for new moms: Mothers who breast-feed their children until they start to eat gluten cut the risk of celiac by 50 percent. That's evidence of a pretty large environmental contribution. If you can breast-feed, you may save your child—and yourself—a good deal of grief.

EATING DISORDERS
· ·

You have a set of hormones that are designed to tell you when you're hungry and when you're full. But you also have bacteria that can mimic these same hormones, allowing your microbes to game the system. Anorexia and other eating disorders (EDs) like bulimia are the most deadly of psychiatric syndromes. People with eating disorders have deficient nutrition, stressing every organ in their body, including—intensely—the gut and the microbiota it contains. They are literally starving to death.

Most cases of anorexia begin in the teenage years and arise from deliberate dieting. It is usually seen in high-achieving obsessional people who develop a distorted body image. Anorexia has multiple causes, including genetics and the environment. Many people mistakenly believe it is simply psychosomatic—people should just eat right—but there is a real biological problem behind EDs. Anorexia is often associated with inflammatory or autoimmune disorders, like IBD or diabetes. These diseases often show up before depression and anxiety set in. Anorexia and bulimia are both associated with dysbiosis; the numbers of bacteria are seriously depleted in these patients because they aren't consuming enough calories to feed themselves or their microbiota properly. The few microbes that do exist are dysbiotic—skewed toward a few unhealthy species.[26]

The rates of depression and anxiety in these patients are directly correlated to their dysbiosis. Those with both an autoimmune disease and inflammation are two to three times more likely to have an accompanying mood disorder of some type.[27] When patients are hospitalized and brought up to more normal weight, their dysbiosis improves at the same rate as their mood.[28] It's a continuous cycle of cause and effect, and it's heartening to see a normal appetite and more cheerful frame of mind appear when the microbiota comes back into balance.

Possible Directions

Much more research needs to be done in this area, but treating people with EDs and gut dysbiosis with prebiotics and probiotics seems to have promise.[29] In particular, studies have shown that people suffering from anorexia have significantly lower levels of *L. plantarum, B. fragilis, C. leptum,* and *C. coccoides.* Of these, only *L. plantarum* is currently available as a probiotic. Anorexia can be treated by feeding a high-calorie diet, which can be difficult for patients, but has a good prognosis. Yogurt containing 100 million CFUs of *L. bulgaricus* and *S. thermophilus* has been shown to be helpful in treating patients with malnutrition, including anorexia.[30] Supplementation with *L. plantarum* may help improve the outcome, but more research is necessary.

OBESITY

Jolly fat people exist, but they may be a minority. Obesity dramatically raises the risk of depression, anxiety, and dementia. It goes the other way, too: Depression and stress can lead to obesity.[31]

One-third of adults are obese, and two-thirds are overweight. That is more than double what it was in 1990.[32] Why are so many of us overweight? Many factors are involved. One of them in North America is antibiotic use in farm animals raised for meat. These antibiotics are not to help the animals deal with disease so much as to put weight on quickly (an effect discovered in the last century, experienced by humans as well). If you can, avoid antibiotic-treated meats. No matter how small the effect may be, it is yet another contribution to obesity that you just don't need.

Also unhelpful: In the last century, the government decided to recommend high levels of carbohydrates in the diet. A food pyramid was published and widely circulated that placed bread and pasta at the foundation of your diet. That was a bad decision based on bad science, but it has taken far too long to redress the error. Carbs are delicious, but they become deadly when the fiber is refined out.

There are genetic influences on obesity as well, but as we've seen with most of these genetic proclivities, it is possible to overcome them. We are also living a life that requires far less activity than it used to. The only exercise some people get is operating the remote control. Exercise can be difficult if you're overweight, but even if you're bedridden, you can try stretches and movement. Lying or sitting still is damaging to almost every system in your body. Humans are not built for that.

Last in this litany of things that cause obesity are psychiatric drugs. Several types of antidepressants, such as Remeron (mirtazapine) are known to cause swift and significant weight gain. Antipsychotic drugs are sometimes used off-label to treat both depression and anxiety but a few, such as Zyprexa (olanzapine), are notorious for weight gain. Because obesity by itself can lead to depression, this can turn into a downward spiral.

In 2012, we conducted a study with rats receiving a daily dose of olanzapine for three weeks. We found that male rats had a slight increase in adiposity, but female rats gained significant weight. Furthermore, we found that olanzapine induced an altered microbiota profile in both genders.

Obesity is associated with brain pathology, including problems with learning and memory. These changes may lead to an acceleration of age-related psychological problems, including depression and dementia.[33] You can, in effect, look at obesity as an age accelerator. The diseases of old age will hit you sooner as long as you remain obese. Obesity increases your risk of heart disease, further increasing the odds of depression and anxiety. These associations are stronger the greater the obesity. Diseases like dementia are thought to be somewhat inevitable with age, but their onset depends heavily on obesity and heart disease.

Obesity is typically measured by body mass index (BMI), but a better cutoff may just be when the fat you are carrying around begins to cause health issues. These health issues include chronic inflammation, metabolic syndrome, type 2 diabetes, heart disease, and GI issues. BMI is actually difficult to measure, and may be less important than another easy metric: the height-to-belt ratio. A reasonable measure here is 2. If you're five foot six (66 inches), then your belt length should be no longer than 33 inches.

High-fat diets can change your gut microbiota. People with obesity have lower levels of *Akkermansia muciniphila*, bacteria that love mucus. They settle down deep in the mucus lining of your gut, and encourage your gut to produce more mucus. *Akkermansia* is associated with lean people and may someday represent a future treatment for obesity. Although *Akkermansia* is a mucus lover, other bacteria are involved in obesity that crave fat and refined carbs. The microbiota of people with obesity is perversely efficient, squeezing the last bit of energy out of each morsel. That's why your skinny friends don't gain weight: Their bacteria are inefficient.

People with obesity appear to have excess quantities of *Bilophila*, a family of bacteria that loves bile. Bile is necessary to digest meat and fats, two common mainstays of a weight-enhancing diet. But *Bilophila* also appears to secrete toxins that may, in turn, lead to chronic inflammation that can affect your mood. In short, the effects of obesity on the microbiota may be contributing to depression, but probiotics and changes in diet can address these psychological deficits.[34]

Possible Directions

One study has shown that consuming *L. rhamnosus* GG and *B. lactis* at 10 billion CFUs per day plus dieting lowered the risk of weight gain in pregnant women.[35] Another study showed that consumption of *L. gasseri* LG2055 at 100 billion CFUs a day for 12 weeks helped to decrease abdominal adiposity (fat deposits) and body weight.[36] Prebiotics, including FOS, have been shown to improve glucose regulation and promote weight loss.[37] Despite these positive results, many other studies have not shown any effect of prebiotics or probiotics on obesity, but more studies are needed.

Clearly there are no shortcuts as yet, but you may find that if you do lose weight, you also shed your depression and anxiety. Diet is hard to maintain in the face of so much delicious junk food, but the benefits of exercise and good diet are so significant that it's hard to overstate them. They can work miracles. Don't do it just to look marvelous. Do it so that you can feel better, think better, and act younger. If exercise and a proper diet were to be packaged into a pill, people would pay millions for it—yet you can get it all at no extra charge.

DIABETES

Some 16 million Americans have diabetes (type 1 or type 2), and these people have between two and four times the risk of developing depression.[38] Worse yet, people with depression have an increased risk of developing diabetes; in fact, some 80 percent of people with diabetes have a previous history of depression. Diabetes alters your blood sugar, which has an adverse effect on your brain that may lead to depression. That, however, doesn't explain why people with depression are at greater risk of developing diabetes. The dual nature of the connection might be due to a third as yet unknown complication underlying both conditions. The link between depression and diabetes is greater among women.

Depression can elevate your levels of cortisol, a stress hormone, which affects your metabolism and can increase insulin resistance. Antidepressants may help alleviate depression, but can lead to weight gain. This, in turn, can increase your odds of getting diabetes. It can be a vicious cycle.

Depression can influence the behavior of diabetics as well, leading to a worse health outcome. Depression may prevent people with diabetes from properly monitoring their blood sugars. Unmanaged blood sugars, in turn, can lead to anxiety, adding yet another psychological insult to the mix. Unfortunately, people with both problems—diabetes and depression—are 50 percent more likely to have strokes and heart attacks.

Obesity is a common factor leading to both diabetes and depression—and it's linked to a dysbiotic gut, as outlined previously (pages 222–225). Because obesity is often considered a lifestyle choice, many practitioners blame the patients. But exhortations to diet don't lead to long-term success, likely because the complex system of hunger and satiety has been somehow compromised. Depression can alter your diet and your exercise regimens, both of which have a known impact on your microbiota and your weight. Many people with depression start to crave carbs, especially sweets, and this doesn't help weight control—or diabetes.

Type 2 diabetes is somewhat tractable with changes in diet and exercise. In fact, exercise, is something of a panacea. As a bonus, exercise causes an increase in endorphins—"happiness hormones"—which can increase blood and brain levels of the so-called neurotrophic factors that support mood and cognition. Exercise pumps your lymph around through your body, increasing the effectiveness of your immune system. Exercise also lowers inflammation throughout your body, which can affect all manner of psychological symptoms. It helps you to lose weight and has a beneficial effect on your gut microbiota. Exercise leads to a better heart rate, better circulation, and an increase in stamina.

Depression exerts a strongly negative influence on maintaining diabetes. Anything that decreases depression can therefore improve diabetic outcomes, so to the extent that psychobiotics improve mood, diabetes can be better controlled, and type 2 diabetes may be ameliorated or even banished.

Tying it all together, research has shown a correlation between the gut microbiota, obesity, and diabetes.[39] As we've learned, the microbiota of people with obesity is highly efficient, helping them to easily absorb fats and sugars. This same phenomenon is seen in people with type 2 diabetes. Solutions to solve one of these issues may also solve the other.

Sometimes solutions seem to pop out of the blue. For example, people who suffer from intractable *C. diff* infections (see page 206) may choose a fecal transplant as treatment. These transplants completely change the patients' microbiota and have a remarkable curative property. They can also have an unexpected benefit: Poop from lean donors can help people with diabetes by improving their insulin sensitivity. This is correlated with an increase in microbial diversity, especially those microbes that produce butyrate.

Fiber in the diet has long been advocated for treating diabetes, as it exerts a powerful effect on steadying blood sugar levels, but fiber also feeds the beneficial bacteria that produce butyrate, making it a prebiotic. That gives fiber a double punch in the fight against diabetes. If you can get 25 grams of fiber in your diet each day, you will see a remarkable improvement in your general health.

Stock up on grains and vegetables, which are full of fiber. Fruit, especially berries, is also fiber-rich, but if you are especially sensitive to sugar, you might want to watch your consumption. Beans, lentils, and peas are fantastic sources of fiber as well—a cup of these legumes can provide more than 10 grams of fiber alone. Fair notice: When you eat fiber, you grow beneficial bacteria that produce gas. That can lead to flatulence, but bear with it; it gets better as you go. Farts are humorous; diabetes is not.

Possible Directions

On the probiotic front, at least one study has shown that you can reduce glucose in your blood and raise the good cholesterol (HDLs) with a shake containing 100 million CFUs of *L. acidophilus* and *B. bifidum* and two grams of FOS.[40] This is good news, but more studies are definitely needed.

PARKINSON'S DISEASE AND LEWY BODY DEMENTIA

Parkinson's disease (PD) and Lewy body dementia have several things in common. Both of them have a devastating impact on the brain, leading to a drastic decline in motor control, and neither of them is currently curable. They both involve the accumulation of certain proteins in the brain. Importantly, both of these diseases are associated with an increase in depression.

PD is an illness that is centralized in a part of the midbrain called the substantia nigra (Latin for "black substance"), a dark-colored chunk of tissue that is largely ruled by dopamine. Although it mostly affects the motor system of the brain, over a third of patients with PD also suffer from depression. The cause of PD is still poorly understood, but there may be a genetic component because it can sometimes run in families. (Keep in mind that a microbiota can also run in families.[41]) PD involves a buildup of proteins in neurons that, like uncollected trash, gets in the way of normal cell function and ultimately kills the cells.

Lewy body dementia, much rarer, involves a similar malfunction of particular types of protein deposits, called Lewy bodies after their discoverer, Frederic H. Lewy, a colleague of Alois Alzheimer. Lewy body dementia is less understood than PD, although one famous sufferer was Robin Williams, whose death put a spotlight on this horrible progressive disease. Much less is known about the connection between Lewy body dementia and the microbiota, but the similarities in the initiation and progression of the disease hint that the microbiota plays a role here as well.

For PD and Lewy body dementia, a clue to the protein detritus lies in gut problems that can start up to a decade before the brain and motor symptoms kick in. There, in the second brain, the tiny masses of protein called Lewy bodies start to aggregate. They reside inside nerve cells and grow by accretion with a protein called alpha-synuclein. Lewy bodies interfere with normal cell function and can lead to constipation when they are active in the gut.

PD seems to migrate from the gut to the brain via the vagus nerve. In 2015, Scandinavian researchers found the perfect experimental setup to test this hypothesis. From 1970 through 1995—before *Helicobacter pylori* was identified as the culprit behind ulcers—thousands of Danes underwent surgery to stop their ulcers. Almost 15,000 people had their vagus nerve partially or totally severed. In those patients, the rate of PD was cut in half, indicating that the vagus is an important conduit for the transmission of PD from the second brain to the first.[42]

Sarkis Mazmanian and Rob Knight researched a strain of mice that produce excess alpha-synuclein and can be used to research PD. These mice have motor deficits (poor muscle control)—but only when they have an active microbiota. In the study, germ-free mice remained healthy, demonstrating that a microbiota is required for motor impairment. Remarkably, transplanting a microbiota from a human patient with PD caused motor impairment and inflammation, whereas transplanting a microbiota from a healthy donor did not.[43]

The gut microbiota of patients with PD is distinctive. In particular, the level of *Prevotella* species is greatly reduced in those with PD,[44] while levels of another microbe, *Enterobacteria,* are elevated in patients with the worst motor control. These two types of microbes may someday offer a way to diagnose PD before symptoms show up, and some researchers are hopeful that probiotics might mitigate or even forestall the disease altogether.

Possible Directions

PD is so far incurable, but a drug called levodopa has been helping for more than 50 years. Levodopa helps to increase the amount of dopamine available in the substantia nigra. It is very helpful, but not without quirks. Whereas PD generally leads to a kind of paralysis, levodopa leads to dyskinesia—a kind of writhing, twitching motion. Right now, much of the medical attention given to patients with PD is involved with tweaking levodopa dosages without increasing dyskinesia. It's a tricky balancing act, and very uncomfortable for patients.

Some experts feel that priming the gut is key to successful levodopa treatment. Some experts recommend a Mediterranean diet before prescribing levodopa. Others, to reduce interactions between levodopa and protein, recommend a low-protein diet. The evidence for a low-protein diet is thin, but there is somewhat better evidence to support moving your protein consumption to the evening.[45] Exercise, on the other hand, has demonstrably beneficial effects, lowering the risk of PD in the first place and improving cognition in those who already have the disease.

There is also evidence that probiotics can help. In one study, patients with PD were given approximately two ounces of a kind of kefir containing six billion CFUs of *L. casei* Shirota daily for six weeks. This regimen improved stool consistency and bowel habits, improving quality of life and potentially slowing the progression of the disease.[46]

HEART DISEASE

Heart disease is the number one killer of Americans—and, as it turns out, it is intimately entwined with depression. People with heart disease experience depression more than others—and people with depression tend to suffer more from heart disease. People who survive heart attacks are six times more likely to have depression than the general population. Having heart disease *and* depression more than doubles your yearly mortality rate. The more severe your depression, the worse your odds are.[47] Worse yet, for as long as you have both symptoms, your risk keeps increasing over time.[48]

If you already have heart disease, your friends and family might feel your depression is inevitable, just a normal part of being sick. Depression may, however, be amplifying the underlying heart disease. Because of this tight coupling, if you can lift your depression, you might just improve your cardiac odds. If you have heart disease, don't ignore your depression: It can exacerbate your condition.

One thing to do immediately is to quit smoking. People associate smoking with lung cancer, but one-fifth of deaths from heart disease are due to smoking. Interestingly, smoking has a bacterial connection, because it affects your oral microbiota. Puffing on a cigarette creates an environment in your mouth similar to a backyard smoker, which kills bacteria. Unfortunately, smoke kills the good bacteria along with the bad.[49] Killing beneficial oral bacteria can lead to overgrowth of more pathogenic species like *Streptococcus,* which is known to lead to tooth and gum decay. And the effects don't stop at your mouth: Recent studies have determined that smoking affects your gut and its microbiota as well as your mouth.[50]

Your gut microbes play a role in the health of your heart. A chemical called trimethylamine N-oxide (TMAO) is known to contribute to atherosclerosis.[51] When the gut microbiota processes meat, it may produce excess TMAO and thus increase your odds of getting heart disease.[52] There are good reasons to eat meat, because it is an excellent source of protein and other nutrients. But Americans probably eat too much meat, and if you have depression or heart disease, you may benefit from cutting back and substituting in veggies.

On the positive side, the resveratrol in red wine (see page 199) may come to your rescue. By changing the relative abundance of various gut bacteria, this plant compound may lower TMAO and thus the odds of heart disease.[53] Specifically, resveratrol inhibits the growth of *Prevotella* and increases the population of our friends *Bifido* and *Lacto*. If you're a fan of red wine, that might sound like great news. Just keep in mind that the dosage makes the poison. Depending on your weight, a glass or two of wine may be fine, but that third one can lead to other problems.

Possible Directions

Clinical depression can triple your odds for ischemic heart disease. If you're at risk, you should pay close attention to the psychobiotic advice in the previous chapter. When you lift your mood, you may also improve the health of your heart in a virtuous cycle. Probiotics can counter the bacteria that increase levels of TMAO and LDL (the bad cholesterol) in your body, ultimately reducing your risk for heart disease. In particular, the psychobiotic *L. reuteri* can lower LDL levels and decrease inflammation.[54] *L. acidophilus*—along with fiber like GOS or FOS—can also reduce cholesterol and inflammation.

AUTISM SPECTRUM DISORDER

Autism is a controversial mental syndrome. Some of the people affected are completely disabled whereas others can have high-functioning daily lives. Autism has such a wide range of symptoms that researchers and clinicians now call it autism spectrum disorder, or ASD. Like many other mental syndromes, autism is on the upswing, with a tenfold increase in diagnosis over the last 40 years. The generally recognized symptoms of autism include difficulty socializing and repetitive behavior, but many people with ASD excel at math, music, or art. The spectrum includes people with barely noticeable social issues, many of whom aren't even aware that they have ASD.

Early researchers distinguished autism from schizophrenia and characterized it as extreme aloneness. It is interesting to note that this extreme aloneness is something like sickness behavior—the desire to just be left alone while recovering from an illness. It also looks like depression and may well involve its attendant GI symptoms.

Germ-free (GF) mice have proven to be invaluable for assessing the role of the microbiota in stress response, anxiety, and social behavior. Mice, like humans, are social animals, but GF mice have a reduced preference for socializing. As with autism, this antisocial behavior predominantly affects males.

In our laboratory, we found that colonizing these male mice with beneficial bacteria after weaning made them more social but didn't affect their disinterest in meeting new mice. This demonstrated that some, but not all, social behaviors seem to be permanently established in the preweaning period. It also showed that other social behaviors can be improved simply by the addition of a normal microbiota. [55]

There is a large genetic component to autism. A hundred genes have been identified as involved, but most of them are weak predictors of autism. Somewhat confusingly, only 15 percent of genetic autism cases can be directly attributed to changes in genes. These genetic changes don't have to be inherited: They can happen spontaneously, due to seemingly random alterations, such as deleting, doubling, or reversing a gene. This is why the parents of most children with autism do not have autism themselves.

Although most of the genes implicated with autism affect nerve tissue, at least one of them is linked to gut repair and immunity.[56] This gene is also involved with brain development, and it is tempting to hypothesize that early gut development—involving microbial challenges—is related to brain development as well, shaping the gut-brain connection differently, perhaps even in utero. Because the altered genes that are found in those with autism are also found widely in the general population, it is likely that a particular combination of them is required to produce the syndrome.

Most genetic mutations merely indicate a propensity to disease, not necessarily a slam dunk. It may take a genetic change in combination with an environmental change to produce autism. Genes change slowly, so the rapid increase in incidence of autism recently is unlikely to be solely due to genes. The increase is thus likely due to the environment. And because symptoms show up early, the trigger is likely to occur around the time of birth or before.

Parental age is a factor, as is prematurity. There is some evidence that air pollution and pesticides can contribute as well. People with autism are more likely to have had antibiotics as an infant. Others have vexing GI problems—including an unusual microbiota—and they often have weird cravings. Many kids with autism love carbs, sugar, and salt—the pillars of the Western diet.[57]

Some 40 to 80 percent of people with autism suffer from depression and anxiety, a rate that is two to four times greater than that of the general population.[58] And some 50 to 80 percent of people with ASD suffer from gut dysbiosis. Is there a gut-brain connection with ASD? Many researchers say yes, and new animal studies are supporting that hypothesis. An Italian study in 2010 showed that not only do people with autism have a high level of troublesome GI symptoms, so do their close relatives, whose GI problems run four times higher than normal. The authors of that study conclude that hereditary factors related to gut permeability may be to blame.[59]

These findings suggest that psychobiotics may make a difference in the lives of children with autism. Many kids with autism can handle supplements in pill or chewable forms. There have been good results with augmenting the diet with vitamins, especially the B vitamins. These nutrients are produced naturally by bacteria in the gut, but in people with autism, these helpful bacteria may be depleted or absent. Probiotic or prebiotic powders may be easy to add to food without changing the flavor or texture of a meal. Remember that probiotics must not be cooked, but added just before serving. Psychobiotics, especially *L. reuteri,* also increase levels of oxytocin, the so-called cuddle chemical that is both a hormone and a neurotransmitter that makes people more social. It also seems to tamp down inflammation, potentially lifting mood. Oxytocin can reduce repetitive behavior in people with ASD, and has been shown to improve the recognition of emotion in children with ASD.[60]

Possible Directions

The development of an ASD mouse model has had a huge impact on the field. But how do you make an ASD mouse? The clues come from human studies, where it has been observed that viral infections of a pregnant mother are associated with ASD. Based on that observation, researchers used a molecule that simulates a viral infection in pregnant mice. The resulting mice pups had all the hallmarks of autism, including less sociability, repetitive behavior, and leaky guts. Studies done with these ASD mouse models revealed a deficit in microbiota and, specifically, a relatively low number of the microbial species *Bacteroides fragilis*.[61] Amazingly, simply adding *B. fragilis* to the mouse chow can greatly mitigate most of these behaviors.

That would seem to make *B. fragilis* a psychobiotic. There's only one problem: In humans, *B. fragilis* is generally considered to be a pathogen. This may be another case in which the dose makes the poison. *B. fragilis* is a normal commensal as long as it stays in the gut, but it is a troublemaker in the bloodstream—or any other organ, for that matter. This microbe is not ready to be declared a probiotic until researchers determine the safety and proper dosage in humans. For now, it remains a tantalizing target.

Another determinant of autism is the weight of the mother when pregnant. Mothers with obesity are 50 percent more likely to have children with autism than mothers of normal weight. To investigate the connection, a study in 2016 looked at mice whose mothers were made obese by feeding them high levels of fat.[62] More than half of the resulting pups had a tendency toward autistic behavior, shunning other mice in favor of inanimate objects.

When the researchers looked at the gut microbiota of these mice, they found less diversity and a distinct deficit of *Lactobacillus reuteri*. When they added this single microbe back to the pups' diet, their antisocial behavior disappeared, although anxiety was not affected. Still, this is an exciting development, even if we're not sure yet that it tells us anything about the human experience of autism.

L. reuteri is found in yogurt, which is a known safe probiotic. Many children with autism are very picky eaters, so it might not work, but there is little to prevent people from trying a safe, natural food, even if it only addresses dysbiosis. Improving GI pain and dysfunction can mitigate a lot of disruptive behavior.

Beyond bacteria, there are the bacterial metabolites: the effluvia produced by microbes as they metabolize. One metabolite in particular, called 4EPS, comes from the hairlike projections called fimbria of certain bacteria. In some kids with autism, 4EPS levels are some 50 times higher than in nonautistic populations. The metabolite 4EPS is a bad actor, and provokes a swift and powerful immune reaction. If you inject 4EPS into normal mice, they turn into extremely anxious animals, complete with autistic-type behaviors.

Another chemical that can induce autism-like behaviors is propionic acid, a short-chain fatty acid produced by many bacteria. *Clostridia* species produce propionic acid, which is not damaging in small quantities but may affect behavior in larger doses. Antibiotics knock out a lot of bacteria, but *Clostridia* are usually the last bugs standing. This can lead to an excessive amount of propionic acid in the system. As with 4EPS, if you inject propionic acid directly into their brains, rats will exhibit abnormal movement, repetitive behavior, and impaired sociality. Propionic acid doesn't need to be shot into the brain to make it dangerous, though. Just increasing its levels in the diet can also lead to autistic behaviors in rats, including GI inflammation. Propionic acid is a simple molecule, and it can make it across the blood-brain barrier, meaning that any excess acid produced by bacteria may make its way directly to the brain.[63]

The probiotic story looks promising. A Finnish study in 2013 took 75 babies and put half on the probiotic *L. rhamnosus* GG and the other half on a placebo for the first six months of their lives.[64] At the age of 13, the kids were assessed for neuropsychiatric disorders. Of the kids who got the placebo, 17 percent exhibited attention deficit/hyperactivity disorder (ADHD) or Asperger's. The children who received *L. rhamnosus* GG supplements had no evidence of either. Intriguingly, their microbiotas were also different. The supplemented kids had a higher level of *Bifido* in their guts.

Other studies have also found significant microbial differences in children with autism. Several unusual *Clostridial* species are found in some children with autism.[65] In particular, *C. histolyticum* levels are higher,[66] which can produce toxins leading to dysbiosis. In general, treating gut dysbiosis will improve the anxiety associated with autism and may improve sociality as well.

CHRONIC FATIGUE SYNDROME

Chronic fatigue syndrome (CFS) is a mysterious illness that leaves its victims constantly exhausted. Some 97 percent of patients with CFS also suffer from psychological disturbances like headaches, difficulty focusing, and sleep problems. Roughly half of them have depression or anxiety.

Those who suffer from CFS often have dysbiotic guts, including IBS. Their levels of *Bifido* are lower than normal. A study in 2009 by Alan Logan and colleagues gave 29 patients with CFS either a placebo or a strain of *Lactobacillus casei*. After two months, there was a significant decrease in anxiety in the group receiving the probiotic.[67] The *Lacto* species in their gut increased, which isn't too surprising, because they were given 24 billion CFUs daily. What was surprising, though, is that their levels of *Bifido* also rose, even though they weren't being supplemented. This isn't the only example of this fellow-traveler effect. Several studies have also shown that supplementing with *Lacto* can increase numbers of *Bifido*.

The practical implication of this research is that persons suffering from chronic fatigue syndrome may find relief by treating their gut microbiota, especially by ingesting *Lactobacillus casei* in a probiotic supplement or food. *L. casei* can be found in yogurt, Sicilian green olives, and cheddar cheese. The strain used in research can also be found in a milk product from Japan called Yakult. Talk to your doctor, and if there are no objections, you might want to try a few of those products to see if you get any relief.

TO SUM IT UP

Many of today's ailments, from simple annoyances to chronic and debilitating disease, involve the microbiota. That isn't news. The new findings, though, show us that because of the dynamic relationship between your gut and your brain, an ailing microbiota often means depression and anxiety. Sometimes these psychological states predate and signal oncoming bodily disease, and often they accompany the physical symptoms, creating a downward spiral in which those debilitating feelings actually exacerbate your physical symptoms. Often physicians do not pay attention to the role the gut-brain axis plays in disease, and we hope that this book will help you learn about these vital connections and do something to break the cycle and regain health and well-being.

What should you do if you sense this interaction between gut and brain health in yourself? First, consult with your health care provider, especially if you suffer from the more serious diseases covered in this chapter. Consider treating your microbiota to a good helping of commensal bacteria by determining the best probiotic supplement formula, using the information in Chapter 7. But don't assume that pills will cure all your ills. Take full responsibility for your own gut-brain health by making lifestyle changes we've outlined here: Reconsider your diet, your drinking and smoking habits, your sleep and exercise levels. On every one of these fronts, shifts in a positive direction can build a healthier microbe population in your gut, reshaping your mood as well as your metabolism.

CHAPTER 9

THE FUTURE OF PSYCHOBIOTICS

"Now, good digestion wait on appetite,

And health on both!"

—William Shakespeare, *Macbeth*

PSYCHOBIOTICS ARE REVOLUTIONIZING PSYCHIATRY, AND THEY have the potential to revolutionize health care as well. Today's research is revealing that gut microbes exert an amazing amount of control over your mental state. Psychobiotics, including many prebiotics and probiotics, can transform your mood and even help you develop a hardy immune system to battle the diseases that are plaguing the modern world.

But there is much more to come. We have just pried the lid off of psychobiotics. As we learn more about the surprisingly intimate relationship between our body, brain, and microbes, we will discover new tools and new philosophies about how to stay healthy. This chapter will look at some of the research that is expected to bear fruit in the next few years—and some old ideas that resonate with the new findings about the power of psychobiotics.

TOMORROW'S MENU

Civilizations around the world have taken thousands of years to develop their traditional cuisines, honed through centuries of trial and error to use the indigenous flora and fauna to put together something tasty and healthy.

The Japanese have a cuisine that makes some of their citizens, like those of Okinawa, among the oldest living people in the world. The Japanese overall have the highest life expectancy in the world, at 83 years. They carefully balance their carbs, fats, and protein, and toss in a hefty serving of fermented food in the form of soy sauce, miso, natto, sake, and pickles galore. They eat a lot of rice, fish, and veggies, including seaweed. More than a thousand years ago, this same diet would have kept a samurai in top fighting shape.

The Italians and Greeks, who are responsible for the Mediterranean diet, are healthy and also enjoy long lives. Their diet has been enjoyed for thousands of years in this part of the world, and it has a good local balance of nutrients, with an emphasis on vegetables. Fermentations include milk products like yogurt and cheese—and, of course, wine. They eat a lot of veggies, fish, olive oil, dairy, fruit, and nuts. Aristotle would have recognized every item on the plate.

The Scandinavians, over many thousands of cold winters, have developed a different diet that emphasizes their own northern flora and fauna. It is heavy in fiber from all kinds of wheat, berries, veggies, dairy, nuts, fish, and fowl. Vikings would be right at home with this diet.

What's absent from these cuisines? Highly processed foods. Each of these diets harks back to basic peasant foods, hearty and inexpensive. The combination of fats, carbs, protein, and fiber has all been worked out for their particular locale. Humans are amazing omnivores, and we can acclimate to any of these cultures. But modern processed foods pose a conundrum. They are cheap and delicious, and millions of people around the world are in agreement: Processed foods are awesome! The only problem is that they aren't good for us.

Modern processed foods were developed, for the most part, in the United States. We have a tradition going back only hundreds of years and resulting in a mixed, poorly vetted, inconsistent cuisine. The quintessential American food is the hot dog, a finely ground sausage of varying animal parts. We eat corn products like they are going out of style (they are not). Americans look at a turnip with bemusement. Our presidents are on record as hating vegetables. Ronald Reagan passed a regulation that pickles and ketchup counted as vegetables. George H. W. Bush banned broccoli from Air Force One, saying, "I'm president of the United States, and I'm not going to eat any more broccoli!" Donald Trump, famous for eating fast food, has let Michelle Obama's vegetable garden go to seed. Disconcertingly, the country with the least experience in healthy cuisine is driving worldwide demand.

As we spread our cheap treats around the world, Western diseases and obesity follow close behind. It's time to look a little more seriously at how ancient cuisines contain important clues about proper nutrition—and not just for physical health, but for mental health as well.

The diets we should strive for all have fiber and probiotics, the items most desirable for a well-balanced microbiota. Western food has lost both. Probiotic foods like sauerkraut have often been abandoned now that refrigeration is ubiquitous. Most store-bought fermented products such as sauerkraut are likely pasteurized, meaning that most of the microbes have been killed (although some new living probiotic krauts are thankfully reaching the market). And fiber has been felt to be coarse and unrefined. It makes you fart.

These bad culinary decisions have left a substantial stain on global health. In the very near future, chefs will become more conversant with the microbiota and will return to fermentations and other methods of improving the psychobiotic environment within. Fiber will be brought back, and along with it all the nutty flavors we lost when these foods were tossed. Already, some forward-looking chefs are bringing back the appealing and wholesome foods of the ages, with an eye toward health.

The evidence suggests that diseases as disparate as Alzheimer's and IBS have microbial roots. We ignore this at our peril. We are about to embark on a new path to feed your microbiota properly, and bring an end to these fairly recent, but totally nefarious, diseases of the Western world. The revolution will be delicious.

BETTER TARGETED ANTIBIOTICS

Antibiotics are true miracle drugs, and have saved the lives of millions. And although this book has warned you many times not to abuse them, some can play a positive role in psychobiotic therapies.

CASE STUDY: John (not his real name) is a chemical engineer who suffered his first episode of depression at 44, concurrent with financial and marital stress. He was becoming short-tempered and had difficulty concentrating. At the recommendation of his doctor, he started taking Prozac, but it didn't improve his condition. In fact, he felt it exacerbated his anxiety. He was switched over to venlafaxine along with cognitive behavioral therapy, but his symptoms increased and he started to experience suicidal thoughts. For the next three months, he was prescribed a range of medications including olanzapine, quetiapine, amitriptyline, and mirtazapine. Nothing helped.

In desperation, he was placed on minocycline, an antibiotic known to have a salutary effect on inflammation and depression. In a week's time, his agitation diminished and he started to sleep better. Ten days later he described himself as "the most normal I have felt in at least a year." Six weeks after starting minocycline, he was back to his normal self. Exactly how minocycline works is unclear, but its psychic effects are likely due to its action on the gut microbiota. A year later, John remains well and is getting on with his work and marriage.

This case study shows that at least some antibiotics can be useful in the treatment of depression and anxiety—for John, this one targeted the pathogens in his microbiota that were triggering mental distress. But other antibiotics are poorly targeted and kill the good bacteria along with the bad. Instead of a sniper, you get an explosion that wipes out everything. It would be great if you could target individual bacterial species and leave the rest alone. Nature may provide us with just such snipers.

Antibiotics weren't invented by man; they are essentially toxins created by microbes, designed to kill their pushy neighbors. They are a major part of the life-and-death struggle of these tiny warriors. The broadest antibiotic toxins are cross-domain, like animal versus yeast or yeast versus bacteria. That is because their biology is so different that whatever poison they make for their enemies is unlikely to affect them. Penicillin, for instance, is from fungi—which are often at war with bacteria. These fungi create toxins that can wipe out whole legions of bacteria quickly and mercilessly—without bothering themselves at all. These are broad-spectrum antibiotics.

For humans, broad-stroke antibiotics are the go-to cures. If you have sepsis, doctors won't wait to find out which specific bacteria are at fault. They will just hit you with the most powerful antibiotic they have on hand. That will likely destroy your microbiota, but it can also save your life. However, researchers are finding ways to torch specific pathogens without burning down the whole house. That comes from studying close relatives: Microbial cousins share similar proclivities for food and shelter, so they are often forced into competition over resources. For instance, one species of *E. coli* produces a toxin called colicin, which kills other *E. coli* species but doesn't seem to bother any other genus of bacteria.

These narrow-spectrum antibiotics are called bacteriocins. They are largely produced by commensal bacteria—the good guys in your gut. Unfortunately, bacteriocins are far less robust than broad-spectrum antibiotics and are easily destroyed by the enzymes and acids they encounter in your digestive system.

And they are more expensive. It costs a kingly amount of money to develop a new drug, mostly due to government requirements for large-scale testing. But now, in response to the looming emergency of antibiotic resistance, the FDA is allowing smaller trials, with subsequent oversight from the Centers for Disease Control and Prevention (CDC). This could encourage pharmaceutical companies to ramp up their studies. There may be some well-targeted bacteriocins in your future.

Another approach is also stolen from the bacteria themselves. A few years ago, scientists were shocked to find out that bacteria have their own kind of adaptive immune system called, with typical biological clarity, "clustered regularly interspaced short palindromic repeats." Thank goodness, the name yields the snappy acronym CRISPR. CRISPR is, in essence, a terrific biological cut, copy, and paste machine that we can replicate in laboratories.

When attacked by a virus, a bacterium chops off a bit of the viral DNA and stores it in a tiny library, allowing it to recognize a repeat invasion and stop it quickly. Scientists realized that the gene clippers the bacteria used could also be used to clip any DNA, anywhere. In fact, the technique allows you to specify exactly where you want to make the cut and even allows you to insert another gene at that spot.

Once in a cell, the CRISPR system, which contains a short DNA sequence matching the one you want to destroy, will attach itself to the DNA at that spot and then cut it. That may be all you need to do to inactivate the gene. If done correctly, using this on a bacterium can kill it. And so, just as with antibiotics, we are poised to steal another technology from microbes and turn it against them. The difference between CRISPR and antibiotics is the specificity. Because CRISPR recognizes particular DNA sequences, researchers should be able to custom-build toxins that only affect specific strains of bacteria, leading to antibiotics that take aim at the pathogens that cause depression and leave your psychobiotics in peace.

RECONSTRUCTING PHAGE THERAPY

There is yet another targeted way to fight bacteria, again stolen from nature. It co-opts viruses that attack and infect bacteria. Viruses are primitive and cannot actually propagate on their own. Instead, a virus injects its DNA into the body of a hapless bacterium and takes over its protein factories. Then it sets about making copies of itself. Viruses are unusually good at this, and the copies start to fill the body of the bacterium. At some point, the bacterium is simply stuffed with viral copies. Unable to hold them all, the bacterium bursts, spilling its insides—and hundreds of freshly manufactured viruses—into a neighborhood filled with similar bacteria.

These tiny viral Davids explode their way out of the comparative Goliath of a bacterium. These viruses are called bacteriophages (bacteria eaters), or simply phages. They are not the human viruses that give you a cold or flu—they only affect bacteria. All phages are exquisitely tuned to a particular bacterium, so they satisfy the criterion for snipers, not bombers.

A typical phage may create 200 "daughter" phages. If each goes on to infect another bacterium, there will quickly be 40,000 new phages in the neighborhood. By the next round, there will be eight million. At that rate, it doesn't take long to wipe out an entire population of bacteria. Contrast this to antibiotics, which are consumed as they do their job, requiring a continuing application. Phages multiply exponentially, as long as they have a target. Remarkably, phages can even mutate along with their targets—a characteristic that suggests this vanguard treatment could overcome today's critical problem of bacterial resistance.

Phages were discovered by multiple researchers at the beginning of the 20th century, and Canadian microbiologist Felix d'Hérelle, professor of protobiology at Yale, pursued them as a treatment for infectious diseases and set up phage therapy centers in the United States, France, and Soviet Georgia. Numerous problems with the science threw the techniques into question, and newly developed antibiotic treatments quickly eclipsed the phage therapy.

It wasn't until the 1980s that phages again surfaced as therapy. First, animal studies showed great success in treating rats, cows, lambs, and chickens with potentially fatal infections and diarrhea. Researchers were impressed that a single inoculation with phages could be superior to continued courses of antibiotics. Work on humans continued in Georgia, though, where even today phages are in common use, especially to treat dysentery. Further human studies have been conducted in Poland, where medical researchers have refined the techniques and now report a success rate of up to 90 percent in treating dysentery. Still, the science is not up to current U.S. and European standards. Thorough controlled, double-blind studies are needed before the West will embrace the science.

But antibiotic drug resistance and the danger of collateral bacterial damage require that we look for new solutions, and phages are primed for a new look. In the not-too-distant future, you could find yourself consuming a viral concoction that could make long-lasting changes to your microbiota. And if the therapeutic formula is created to target microbes known to be involved with depression and anxiety, you might be able to say goodbye to the blues forever.

THE FUTURE OF FECAL TRANSPLANTS

It isn't too surprising that fecal studies started in rodents. Mice and rats are quite fond of eating their own—and other's—fecal pellets. They aren't the only ones. Geese, rabbits, and many other animals like to take a second swipe at last night's partially digested dinner— often they can eke out more nutrition from it. Many young animals also eat fecal matter to kick-start their microbiota. Horses will die without a robust microbiota that allows them to survive on a diet of grass, and newborn foals commonly eat their mother's road apples to get things going.

Believe it or not, coprophagia, or poop eating, has a long history in human medicine as well. The fourth-century Chinese doctor Ge Hong was an enthusiast of a soup made from the fermented feces of healthy people—an unsavory precursor to today's fecal microbial transplant (FMT)—icky, perhaps, but quite successful. It's been a godsend for people with intractable *C. diff* infections, who are often at death's door and therefore find FMT completely acceptable.

The psychobiotic implications of FMT are something new: Animal studies have shown that, along with the microbes, a fecal transplant can also transfer depression and anxiety. Animals given poop from an anxious person became anxious, indicating that psychological distress can not only be transferred, but that it can also be transferred from one species to another.[1] That tells us that certain pathogenic bacteria are amazingly universal.

Anecdotal reports have indicated that something similar can happen in human-to-human FMT. One patient tossed off his depression in just a few hours after a fecal transplant. More studies need to be done, but these examples provide some further evidence for the promise of psychobiotic therapy. Transferring a microbiota from one person to another may cure depression and anxiety. If you sign up for a fecal transplant, you might want to get a psych workup done for your donor first.

Fecal transplants are a somewhat organic, even primitive, way to transfer a microbiota. The Internet even gives you instructions for a DIY FMT. *Don't do it!* Your microbiota is like an organ in your body, so an FMT is like an organ transplant. You wouldn't do that in your kitchen, would you?

In the future, we will probably develop something more like Hong's yellow soup—not soup exactly, but an oral version of the transplant. Already researchers are putting poop in pills (which almost inevitably have been dubbed "crapsules"). But it's still a complicated science; FMTs are hard to control, even in a laboratory. There are too many bacterial species, and questions still remain as to which ones are healthy and which ones are toxic. For people who are critically ill, the risks may be worth it—in a hospital setting. But for others, it is probably better to wait. Soon we will know better which microbes are psychobiotic, and hopefully, we can make a pill with just those species that will go down as easily as yogurt.

THE PROMISE OF microRNA

Almost everything structural in animals is made of proteins. They are the bricks and mortar of life. In the form of enzymes, they also keep the metabolic wheels turning. The instructions for making proteins are coded in your DNA. Each gene in your DNA codes for a specific protein. Cells can start and stop making proteins by simply controlling the expression of these genes. But there is another way to stop the manufacture of proteins, by using micro RNAs: small bits of RNA that act like sand in the gears of the protein-making machinery.

Scientists have known about how cells use microRNA (also called miRNA) to control internal protein production since the early 1990s. But researchers are just now learning how gut cells use this powerful molecule to control your gut microbiota.[2] This is a fascinating breakthrough that once again points to the long relationship animals have had with microbes. MicroRNA is a powerful tool that your gut can use to stop the growth of pathogens and even change the internal biology of beneficial bacteria. That implies that our cells somehow know enough about bacterial genetics to stop bacteria from making specific proteins. If we can replicate this process in a lab, it would represent a significant step toward more precise control over our bacterial comrades.

Gut cells release these miRNA molecules, which were first discovered in feces and thereby earned the name "fecal miRNA"— a somewhat misleading name, because their action takes place in the gut. In animal models where miRNA is deficient, the gut microbiota becomes dysbiotic and starts to ruin the health of the animal. Amazingly, reintroducing miRNA cures the dysbiosis. This was initially done by feeding ailing animals fecal pellets from normal animals, but the science has advanced, so that now the miRNA is simply added to normal chow, with the same positive results.[3]

If these results could be transferred to human health care, miRNA could represent a potential game changer for the health of a microbiota. Doses of the right miRNA could eliminate pathogens and return a dysbiotic gut back to normal. One can even imagine an miRNA treatment plan designed to decrease the growth of pathogenic bacteria and boost the numbers of psychobiotics, thereby improving mood.

THE AMYLOID WARS

At this point in the treatment of Alzheimer's, it is generally understood that this form of debilitating progressive dementia is accompanied by abnormalities inside and outside the neurons in the brain. Proteins form these tau tangles and amyloid plaques. Similar molecules are made by all cells, including human, bacterial, protozoal, and archaeal cells, so they must be important to life itself.

For a long time, these cell abnormalities were considered the cause of Alzheimer's dementia. The 21st century has brought some major shifts in Alzheimer's research, though, and a new paradigm is emerging, one that sees the amyloid plaques and tau tangles not as causative, but merely as markers of something else entirely: a bacterial battle.

Much of this work has come from Rudolph Tanzi and Robert Moir at Harvard, who noticed similarities between amyloid proteins in the brain and antimicrobial peptides (AMPs) in the gut.[4] These gut peptides also link up to form sheets, ribbons, and threads, and can form a web around pathogens to immobilize them for later pickup by macrophages and the other roving beat cops of the immune system. Could amyloid be doing something similar?

Remarkably, when they tested this theory, amyloid did as well or better than AMPs at killing microbes. Further testing has buttressed this idea. Amyloid and tau, rather than causing dementia, may actually be saving the brain from a bacterial invasion.[5] The webs they erect are to trap and kill pathogens. They are, it seems, the firemen—not the arsonists.

> *Research by Tanzi and Moir shows that amyloid functions as an antimicrobial peptide via plaque formation, trapping invading microorganisms, including bacteria (such as* Salmonella enterica*), fungi (such as* Candida albicans*), viruses (such as herpes simplex virus), and protist parasites (such as* Toxoplasma gondii*). Amyloid plaque formation in response to infection could result in a neuro-inflammatory response and neurodegeneration due to collateral damage in plaque-surrounding tissue.*
>
> *We are studying how a healthy microbiota could contribute to preventing systemic infection by limiting pathogen growth, maintaining the BBB and training the host immune system, including microglia.*[6]

If this theory is true (and not everyone agrees), then trying to eliminate amyloid and tau is not only fruitless but also potentially dangerous—it may involve actually eliminating a powerful anti-microbial. Indeed, many drugs for treating Alzheimer's significantly increase the risk of infection. Still, in their zeal to trap bacteria, tau tangles in neurons can incapacitate and even kill the cell they are trying to protect. Perhaps we need to look at these proteins as more like cholesterol: A moderate amount is healthy and necessary, but too much can be deadly.

The final word has not been written on the function of amyloid and tau, but the evidence is starting to tilt toward an antimicrobial role for these molecules. If so, this is another piece of the puzzle in the remarkable new field of psychobiotics. Microbes in the brain, including protozoa, bacteria, and yeast, most commonly find their way there from a leaky gut. Perhaps we can harness beneficial microbes to address these leaks in both the gut and the brain. It's important to note that protein tangles are also features of other brain diseases, including Parkinson's, Lewy body dementia, and Huntington's disease. Unlocking the secrets of one could lead to cures or treatments for all of these intractable maladies.

GENETICALLY ENGINEERED BACTERIA

The new science of synthetic biology is a cross between biology and engineering. With powerful tools like CRISPR that can cut and paste genes, scientists are seeking ways to design and reassemble genetic components in a startling number of ways.

Several researchers are exploring possibilities in the gut microbiota, trying to design microbes that act like tiny doctors, testing the gut and then delivering medication whenever they detect something troubling. One of these engineered bacteria, created by Zhongyi Chen at Vanderbilt, produces a chemical called NAPE that the body uses to indicate satiety. Mice drinking water with these bacteria experienced a dramatic decrease in eating and body fat. Signs of diabetes and liver disease also decreased. Interestingly, the effects lasted for four weeks after they stopped spiking the water. That seems to imply that the bacteria managed to settle in, at least temporarily.[7]

Jeff Tabor at Rice University has reengineered commensal *E. coli* to detect dysbiosis and then produce metabolic molecules that can correct it, as if they are following a simple computer program that says, "If dysbiosis is detected, then secrete medicine." Tabor is also working to apply similar code to specifically target obesity and anxiety, two closely related conditions. One of the beauties of this approach is that all the action is local. The bacteria only sense what is in the immediate neighborhood, and their secretions stay local as well, which means side effects can be minimized or even eliminated. Tabor envisions a future in which manipulating gut microbes like this could treat or even cure diseases like autoimmune disorders, cancer, obesity—and depression and anxiety. He imagines that the delivery vehicle for these engineered bacteria could be as innocuous as a cup of specially programmed yogurt.[8]

John March at Cornell is also working on another commensal *E. coli* that produces a protein that causes stem cells, located deep in the crypts of the gut, to metamorphose into pancreas cells that can produce insulin. If he succeeds, he might be able to cure or treat type 1 diabetes—a disease strongly associated with depression.

The idea that genetic engineering could be on the cusp of curing major diseases, as well as depression and anxiety, is exciting. But because creating novel bacteria is involved, it may take some convincing before a public wary of both germs and GMOs accepts these treatments.

TREAT THE HOLOGENOME

In 1967, Lynn Margulis received the 15th rejection of her paper on the origin of mitochondria. That didn't stop her. Lynn was married to Carl Sagan at the time, and her paper "On the Origin of Mitosing

Cells" would at last be published later that year. It came out in the *Journal of Theoretical Biology* under the name Lynn Sagan.

The idea that mitochondria and chloroplasts—tiny **organelles** inside cells—were actually captured bacteria was brilliant and paradigm busting. It was also roundly attacked as absurd, the result of sloppy research. But 10 years later, experiments demonstrated the veracity of the theory, and by the 1980s, it was completely obvious to most biologists.

Margulis believed that wholesale gene transfer—even wholesale organism transfer—could make evolution dance to a faster beat. Although most biologists now accept that mitochondria—the energy machines of the cell—are captured bacteria, many of the ramifications of that concept are only now being fully realized.

Margulis introduced the idea of the hologenome, saying that you are far more than a human—you are an ecosystem composed of bacteria, viruses, protozoa, yeasts, and more—an idea you ought to be plenty familiar with by this point in this book. Each of your cells contains trapped bacteria, and the rest of your body is covered in microbes. When you are born, you inherit genes from all of these actors. Your human DNA comes from your father and mother, your mitochondrial DNA comes only from your mother, and your microbiota comes mostly from your mother.[9] "You" are really "y'all."

The more we know about the intimate relationship we have with our microbiota, the clearer the origins of disease become. A tendency toward Alzheimer's, for instance, may not be triggered until microbial dysbiosis allows bacteria to get into your brain. And that means something as simple as a good diet might outweigh your genetic inclination to many diseases. The future of genetics will likely include a readout of the entire set of genes that represent "you," and that won't be easy. Current computers are being pushed to the limit trying to deal with the comparatively small number of human genes; your hologenome—the sum total of your genes and those of your microbiota—contains one hundred times as many.

In light of the fact that "your genes" are 99 percent microbial, it behooves us to act appropriately and take care of that part of "you." Rethink using antibiotic soap, and realize it's akin to stripping off your skin. Taking oral antibiotics that wipe out your gut microbiota is tantamount to having an organ removed. It is probably time for all of us to be nicer to our little friends.

Today's personalized medicine is predicated on developing drugs specific to every individual patient. But basing these formulations on your human DNA may not be enough. Your health and your diseases, both physical and mental, intimately depend on your microbial DNA as well. To really make a difference, tomorrow's medicine will have to look at *all* your genes. Your hologenome is the key to the personalized medicine of the future.

THE PSYCHOBIOTIC REVOLUTION

As Yogi Berra said, it's hard to make predictions, especially about the future. Research in the field of psychobiotics is new, and dynamic, and happening right now. Where it ends up is anyone's guess, but many of the right questions are being asked—and the potential is enormous.

One of the first and most important revelations coming from the science of psychobiotics is the knowledge that depression and anxiety have a microbial component. This fact should reduce the stigma surrounding mental illness. Where is the moral failure in having gut dysbiosis? Mental issues will soon become understood as having an obvious biological origin, just like getting a cold or food poisoning. Mental illnesses such as depression and psychosis are increasingly viewed as disorders of the brain-gut axis. Psychoses are not "all in your head" after all.

Future doctors and psychiatrists will become more aware of and careful about the effect of antibiotics, not only on the digestive system but also on mood and mental state. When patients are admitted with mental distress of one kind or another, doctors will immediately test their guts, newly understanding that repairing an unhealthy gut may actually resolve some mental issues.

This progress will be difficult and controversial, to be sure. There are so many types of bacteria, both pathogens and commensals, so many psychobiotics, and so many ways they can be combined with each other—as well as with the microbes in the local environment— that the possible combinations grow exponentially. Everything is related to everything else. It's a giant problem, but one that new computer algorithms may soon be able to solve.

Meanwhile, now that you've learned about the wondrous partnership between you and your microbes, you can take better control. The power to improve your mood and your cognition is in your hands. It's up to you: The huge variation in flora from person to person means that there is no "one size fits all" solution. You need to experiment, and in this book we have given you tools to do so.

You can take charge of your gut to optimize your mind and your mood. If you want to be happier, get to it!

ACKNOWLEDGMENTS

The three of us can put our names on this book, but it took a small army of dedicated people to bring our book to life. Our agent, Victoria Pryor, has a keen eye. She saw the gem hiding in our rough proposal and helped to polish it up. Our editor, Susan Tyler Hitchcock, is a real trouper, overseeing every aspect of the book, from fact-checking to cover design. For putting up with a bunch of scientists, she deserves a medal. Other National Geographic troupers include assistant editor Michelle Cassidy, photography director Susan Blair, marketing vice president Heidi Vincent, publicity gurus Ann Day and Kathy Daneman, eagle-eyed production editor Mike O'Connor, and designer Katie Olsen. They worked under tight deadlines but made it all look easy.

Science is a team sport, and the work on which this book is based results from the research of dozens of amazing scientists who have come through our Cork-based labs. In particular, we would like to thank Ger Clarke, Siobhain O'Mahony, Harriet Schellekens, Niall Hyland, Gerry Moloney, Declan McKernan, Javier Bravo, Marcela Julio-Pieper, Olivia O'Leary, Romain Gosselin, Sinead Gibney, Sue Grenham, Joan O'Sullivan, Lieve Desbonnet, Dervla O'Malley, Peter Fitzgerald, Sinead O'Brien, Paul Scully, Una Dennison, Gabor Gazner, Paul Kennedy, Rachel Moloney, Pat Fitzgerald,

Andrew Allen, Kieran Rea, Anna Golubeva, Cristina Torres-Fuentes, Roman Stilling, Alan Hoban, Karen Scott, Karen-Anne McVey Neufeld, Monica Tramullas, Kieran Davey, Eileen Curran, Valeria Felice, Caroline Browne, Clion O'Mahony, Daniela Felice, Richard O'Connor, Eoin Sherwin, James Dollard, John Kelly, Sahar El Aidy, Elaine Patterson, Kevin Lomasney, Livia Morais, Veronica Peterson, Marcel van de Wouw, Sofia Cusotto, Matteo Pusceddo, Helene Savignac, Beate Finger, Angela Moya, Pauline Luczynski, Thorsten Becker, Gilliard Lach, Christine Fülling, Caitriona Long-Smith, Josh Lyte, Anand Gururajan, Barbara Chruscicka, Ana-Paula Ventura da Silva, Marcus Boehme, Emanuela Morelli, Valerie Ramirez, Kiran Sandhu, Clementine Druelle, Ana Paula Ramos Costa, Clara Seira Oriach, Pooja Jayaprakash, and Gonzalo Rabasa.

Moreover, we need to thank our many collaborators for making this psychobiotic journey so much fun, especially Eamonn Quigley, Catherine Stanton, Paul O'Toole, Colin Hill, Paul Ross, Paul Cotter, and Fergus Shanahan, all at the APC Microbiome Institute; John Bienenstock and Paul Forsythe at McMaster University; and our major funding sources, Science Foundation Ireland, the Health Research Board, Irish Research Council, and the Department of Agriculture, Food and the Marine.

APPENDIX

PROVEN PROBIOTIC
BACTERIA AND PRODUCTS

Table 1: Psychobiotics tested in controlled trials

This list of psychobiotic microbes includes references to peer-reviewed, controlled studies that have confirmed and detailed their effectiveness. Use this table to learn more about specific psychobiotic bacteria that may address your health needs or that you find listed in any product of interest. To see what conditions each psychobiotic has been tested for, look at the "Conditions reviewed in study" column. You can also compare the information in the "Standard dose CFUs/day" column to the amount listed on any given probiotic label.

Table 2: Tested products containing psychobiotics

This list of branded, compounded products that contain psychobiotics includes references to peer-reviewed, controlled studies that have confirmed and detailed their effectiveness. Look up the individual product to find out what it contains and the details of the research. You can learn more about the component bacteria and the conditions each has been tested for in Table 1.

Table I. Psychobiotics tested in controlled trials

Genus	Species	Strain	Location in body	This microbe produces
Bacteroides	*thetaiotaomicron*		distal ileum, cecum, colon	vitamin K2, acetate
Bifidobacterium	*animalis lactis*	BB-12	colon	GABA
Bifidobacterium	*animalis lactis*	W52	colon	GABA
Bifidobacterium	*bifidum*	MIMBb75	ileum, colon	GABA
Bifidobacterium	*bifidum*	W23	ileum, colon	GABA
Bifidobacterium	*breve*	4006	colon	GABA
Bifidobacterium	*infantis*	35624	colon	tryptophan, GABA
Bifidobacterium	*longum*	1714	colon	GABA
Bifidobacterium	*longum*	BB536-HGM	colon	GABA
Bifidobacterium	*longum*	R0175	colon	GABA
Clostridium	*butyricum*	588	cecum, colon	butyrate, bile-converting enzymes
Enterococcus	*durans*	LAB18s	colon ascending	serotonin
Escherichia	*coli*	Nissle 1917	ileum	GABA, vitamin K2, serotonin, norepinephrine
Faecalibacterium	*prausnitzii*	ATCC 27766, ATCC 27768	ileum, cecum, colon	butyrate
Lactobacillus	*acidophilus*	DDS-1	colon transverse	GABA, acetylcholine
Lactobacillus	*acidophilus*	W37	colon transverse	GABA, acetylcholine
Lactobacillus	*acidophilus*		colon transverse	GABA, acetylcholine
Lactobacillus	*brevis*	W63	colon transverse	tyramine, phenylethylamine, lactic acid, ethanol, GABA
Lactobacillus	*casei*	DN-114001	colon transverse	GABA, acetylcholine
Lactobacillus	*casei*	LBC80R	colon transverse	GABA, acetylcholine
Lactobacillus	*casei*	W56	colon transverse	GABA, acetylcholine
Lactobacillus	*casei*		colon transverse	GABA, acetylcholine
Lactobacillus	*delbrueckii bulgaricus*		colon transverse	tryptomine
Lactobacillus	*farciminis*		colon transverse	NO
Lactobacillus	*gasseri*		colon transverse	GABA, acetylcholine
Lactobacillus	*helveticus*	NS8	colon transverse	GABA, acetylcholine
Lactobacillus	*helveticus*	R0052	colon transverse	GABA, acetylcholine
Lactobacillus	*plantarum*	299v	colon transverse	GABA, acetylcholine
Lactobacillus	*reuteri*	DSM 17938, ATCC 55730, ATCC 6475	colon transverse	GABA, acetylcholine, serotonin
Lactobacillus	*rhamnosus*	GG (ATCC 53103)	colon transverse	GABA
Lactobacillus	*rhamnosus*	HN001	colon transverse	histamine, acetylcholine
Lactobacillus	*salivarius*	W24	colon transverse	GABA, acetylcholine
Lactococcus	*lactis*	W19, W58	duodenum, ileum, cecum, colon	lactic acid, GABA
Saccharomyces	*boulardii*		ileum, colon	Protease
Streptococcus	*thermophilus*		stomach	folic acid, formic acid, serotonin

Appendix

References	Conditions reviewed in study	Standard dose (CFUs/day)
Wrzosek et al. (2013)	malnutrition, leaky gut, anxiety	10B
Merenstein et al. (2015), Jungersen et al. (2014), Mohammadi et al. (2016), Pitkala et al. (2007)	pathogen inhibition, gut integrity, immune modulator, antibiotic diarrhea, depression, IBS, constipation	10M–1B
Steenbergen et al. (2015)	pathogen inhibition, gut integrity, immune modulator, antibiotic diarrhea, depression, IBS	2B
Guglielmetti et al. (2011), Saavedra et al. (1994), Akkasheh et al. (2016)	IBS, diarrhea, major depression	6B
Steenbergen et al. (2015)	IBS, diarrhea, depression	2B
Shimakawa et al. (2003), Tanaka et al. (1983), Kondo et al. (2010), Mohammadi et al. (2016)	pathogen inhibition, adiposity, inflammation reduction, depression	10B
Konieczna et al. (2013), Whorwell et al. (2006)	IBS, diarrhea, depression	100M
Savignac et al. (2015), Allen et al. (2016)	cognition, anxiety, depression	1B
Lee et al. (2015), Sugahara et al. (2015)	pathogen inhibition, diarrhea, allergy, depression	1B
Messaoudi et al. (2011), Mohammadi et al. (2016)	anxiety, depression	3B
Yang et al. (2016)	depression	5B
Pieniz et al. (2014)	pathogen inhibition, selenium accumulation	1B
Kruis et al. (2004), Wehkamp et al. (2004), Kleta et al. (2014)	UC, IBD, constipation, Crohn's, IBS	100M
Hold et al. (2003), Flint et al. (2012), Sokol et al. (2008)	IBD, UC, inflammation	5B
Sinn et al. (2008)	depression	30B
Steenbergen et al. (2015)	depression	2B
Sinn et al. (2008), Kailasapathy et al. (2000), Akkasheh et al. (2016)	major depression, pathogen inhibition	6B
Steenbergen et al. (2015)	depression	2B
Pawłowska et al. (2007)	post-liver transplant, anxiety	30M–6B
Gao et al. (2010)	antibiotic diarrhea, anxiety	30M–6B
Steenbergen et al. (2015)	depression, anxiety	3B
Akkasheh et al. (2016)	major depression, pathogen inhibition, anxiety	2B
Mohammadi et al. (2016)	depression	30B
Ait-Belgnaoui et al. (2012)	inflammation, anxiety	1B
Nishihira et al. (2010)	anxiety	1B
Liang et al. (2015)	anxiety, depression	1B
Messaoudi et al. (2011)	anxiety, depression	3B
Niedzielin et al. (2001)	IBS, C. diff	1B
Shornikova et al. (1997)	inflammation, anxiety	1B–100B
Basu et al. (2009)	diarrhea, antibiotic diarrhea	30B
Basu et al. (2009), Mohammadi et al. (2016)	depression, antibiotic diarrhea, anxiety, excema	10B
Steenbergen et al. (2015)	depression	3B
Steenbergen et al. (2015)	depression	3B
Kelesidis et al. (2012), McFarland and Bernasconi (1993)	diarrhea, IBS, anxiety	5B
Saavedra et al. (1994), Mohammadi et al. (2016)	diarrhea, depression	30B

Table 2. Tested products containing psychobiotics

Product name (company)	Bacterial strains used in product	References * = Study conducted or funded partially or wholly by manufacturer	Conditions reviewed in study	Standard dose (CFUs/day)
Activia (Dannon, White Plains, NY)	*S. thermophilus, L. bulgaricus, B. lactis* DN 173-010	Tillisch et al. (2013)*, De Paula et al. (2008)	Mood improvement, constipation	5–10B
Align (Proctor & Gamble, Cincinnati, OH)	*Bifidobacterium infantis* 35624	Whorwell et al. (2006)*, O'Mahony et al. (2005)	IBS, depression	1B
BioGaia (Everidis Health Sciences, St. Louis, MO)	*L. reuteri protectis* SD2112 (ATCC 55730 or DSM 17938)	Valeur et al. (2004)*	Infectious diarrhea treatment	100M
Bio-K+ (Bio-K plus International Inc., Laval, QC, Canada)	*L. acidophilus* CL1285 and *L. casei* LBC80R	Mubasher et al. (2009)*	Antibiotic diarrhea prevention, *C. diff* prevention	100B
Culturelle (Valio, Helsinki, Finland)	*L. rhamnosus* GG (LGG)	Pedersen et al. (2014), Feleszko et al. (2007)	Antibiotic and infectious diarrhea prevention, *C. diff* prevention, IBS	10B
DanActive (Dannon, White Plains, NY)	*Lactobacillus casei* DN-114-001	Merenstein et al. (2010)*	Antibiotic and infectious diarrhea prevention, *C. diff* prevention	10B
Florastor (Biocodex, Inc., Creswell, OR)	*Saccharomyces boulardii*	McFarland et al. (2010)	Antibiotic and infectious diarrhea prevention, *C. diff* prevention	5B
Mutaflor (Ardeypharm, Herdecke, Germany)	*E. coli* Nissle 1917 (ECN)	Boudeau et al. (2003), McCann et al. (1994)	UC induction and maintenance, anxiety	10B
Probio'Stick (Lallemand, Montreal, Canada) and ProbioMood (Pure Encapsulations, Inc., Sudbury, MA)	*L. acidophilus* R-52 and *B. longum* R-175	Messaoudi et al. (2011)*, Diop et al. (2008)*	Stress, anxiety, abdominal pain	3B
VSL*3 (Sigma-Tau Pharmaceuticals, Inc., Towson, MD)	*Streptococcus thermophilus, B. breve, B. longum, B infantis, L. acidophilus, L. plantarum, L. paracasei, L. helveticus*	Kim et al. (2003), Sood et al. (2009)	UC induction and maintenance, pouchitis, IBS	125–900B
Yakult (Yakult Honsha Co., Ltd., Tokyo, Japan)	*L. casei* Shirota	Kato-Kataoka et al. (2016)*, Rao et al. (2009)*	Constipation, gut maintenance, mood, cognition	24B

TABLE REFERENCES

Ait-Belgnaoui, Afifa, Henri Durand, Christel Cartier, Gilles Chaumaz, Hélène Eutamene, Laurent Ferrier, Eric Houdeau, Jean Fioramonti, Lionel Bueno, and Vassilia Theodorou. "Prevention of Gut Leakiness by a Probiotic Treatment Leads to Attenuated HPA Response to an Acute Psychological Stress in Rats." *Psychoneuroendocrinology* 37, no. 11 (November 2012): 1885–95. doi:10.1016/j.psyneuen.2012.03.024.

Akkasheh, G., Z. Kashani-Poor, M. Tajadadi-Ebrahimi, P. Jafari, H. Akbari, M. Taghizadeh, et al. "Clinical and Metabolic Response to Probiotic Administration in Patients With Major Depressive Disorder: A Randomized, Double-Blind, Placebo Controlled Trial." *Nutrition* 32 (2016): 315–20.

Allen, A. P., W. Hutch, Y. E. Borre, P. J. Kennedy, A. Temko, G. Boylan, E. Murphy, J. F. Cryan, T. G. Dinan, and G. Clarke. "*Bifidobacterium longum* 1714 as a Translational Psychobiotic: Modulation of Stress, Electrophysiology and Neurocognition in Healthy Volunteers." *Translational Psychiatry* 6, no. 11 (November 1, 2016): e939. doi:10.1038/tp.2016.191.

Basu, S., D. K. Paul, S. Ganguly, M. Chatterjee, and P. K. Chandra. "Efficacy of High-dose *Lactobacillus rhamnosus* GG in Controlling Acute Watery Diarrhea in Indian Children: A Randomized Controlled Trial." *Journal of Clinical Gastroenterology* 43, no. 3 (March 2009): 208–13. doi:10.1097/MCG.0b013e31815a5780.

Boudeau, J., A. L. Glasser, S. Julien, J. F. Colombel, and A. Darfeuille-Michaud. "Inhibitory Effect of Probiotic *Escherichia coli* Strain Nissle 1917 on Adhesion to and Invasion of Intestinal Epithelial Cells by Adherent-Invasive *E. Coli* Strains Isolated From Patients With Crohn's Disease." *Alimentary Pharmacology & Therapeutics* 18, no. 1 (July 1, 2003): 45–56.

De Paula, J. A., E. Carmuega, and R. Weill. "Effect of the Ingestion of a Symbiotic Yogurt on the Bowel Habits of Women With Functional Constipation." *Acta Gastroenterologica Latinoamericana* 38, no. 1 (March 2008): 16–25.

Diop, Laurent, Sonia Guillou, and Henri Durand. "Probiotic Food Supplement Reduces Stress-Induced Gastrointestinal Symptoms in Volunteers: A Double-Blind, Placebo-Controlled, Randomized Trial." *Nutrition Research* 28, no. 1 (January 2008): 1–5. doi:10.1016/j.nutres.2007.10.001.

Feleszko, W., J. Jaworska, R. D. Rha, S. Steinhausen, A. Avagyan, A. Jaudszus, B. Ahrens, D. A. Groneberg, U. Wahn, and E. Hamelmann. "Probiotic-Induced Suppression of Allergic Sensitization and Airway Inflammation Is Associated With an Increase of T Regulatory-Dependent Mechanisms in a Murine Model of Asthma." *Clinical & Experimental Allergy* 37, no. 4 (April 1, 2007): 498–505. doi:10.1111/j.1365-2222.2006.02629.x.

Flint, H. J., K. P. Scott, S. H. Duncan, P. Louis, E. Forano. "Microbial Degradation of Complex Carbohydrates in the Gut." *Gut Microbes* 3, no. 4: 289–306. doi: 10.4161/gmic.19897.

Gao, X. W., M. Mubasher, C. Y. Fang, C. Reifer, L. E. Miller. "Dose-Response Efficacy of a Proprietary Probiotic Formula of *Lactobacillus acidophilus* CL1285 and *Lactobacillus casei* LBC80R for Antibiotic-Associated Diarrhea and *Clostridium difficile*–Associated Diarrhea Prophylaxis in Adult Patients." *American Journal of Gastroenterology* 105 (2009): 1636–41. doi: 10.1038/ajg.2010.11.

Guglielmetti, S., D. Mora, M. Gschwender, and K. Popp. "Randomised Clinical Trial: *Bifidobacterium bifidum* MIMBb75 Significantly Alleviates Irritable Bowel Syndrome and Improves Quality of Life—A Double-Blind, Placebo-Controlled Study." *Alimentary Pharmacology & Therapeutics* 33, no. 10 (May 1, 2011): 1123–32.

Hold, G. L., A. Schwiertz, R. I. Aminov, M. Blaut, and H. J. Flint. "Oligonucleotide Probes That Detect Quantitatively Significant Groups of Butyrate-Producing Bacteria in Human Feces." *Applied and Environmental Microbiology* 69, no. 7 (2009): 4320–24. doi: 10.1128/AEM.69.7.4320-4324.2003.

Jungersen, Mikkel, Anette Wind, Eric Johansen, Jeffrey E. Christensen, Birgitte Stuer-Lauridsen, and Dorte Eskesen. "The Science Behind the Probiotic Strain *Bifidobacterium animalis* subsp. *lactis* BB-12®." *Microorganisms* 2, no. 2 (March 28, 2014): 92–110. doi:10.3390/microorganisms2020092.

Kailasapathy, Kaila, and James Chin. "Survival and Therapeutic Potential of Probiotic Organisms With Reference to *Lactobacillus acidophilus* and *Bifidobacterium* spp." *Immunology and Cell Biology* 78, no. 1 (February 2000): 80–88. doi:10.1046/j.1440-1711.2000.00886.x.

Kato-Kataoka, A., K. Nishida, M. Takada, K. Suda, M. Kawai, K. Shimizu, A. Kushiro, et al. "Fermented Milk Containing *Lactobacillus casei* Strain Shirota Prevents the Onset of Physical Symptoms in Medical Students Under Academic Examination Stress." *Beneficial Microbes* 7, no. 2 (2016): 153–56. doi:10.3920/BM2015.0100.

Kelesidis, Theodoros, and Charalabos Pothoulakis. "Efficacy and Safety of the Probiotic *Saccharomyces boulardii* for the Prevention and Therapy of Gastrointestinal Disorders." *Therapeutic Advances in Gastroenterology* 5, no. 2 (March 2012): 111–25. doi:10.1177/1756283X11428502.

Kim, H. J., M. Camilleri, S. Mckinzie, M. B. Lempke, D. D. Burton, G. M. Thomforde, and A. R. Zinsmeister. "A Randomized Controlled Trial of a Probiotic, VSL#3, on Gut Transit and Symptoms in Diarrhoea-Predominant Irritable Bowel Syndrome." *Alimentary Pharmacology & Therapeutics* 17, no. 7 (April 1, 2003): 895–904. doi:10.1046/j.1365-2036.2003.01543.x.

Kleta, Sylvia, Marcel Nordhoff, Karsten Tedin, Lothar H. Wieler, Rafal Kolenda, Sibylle Oswald, Tobias A. Oelschlaeger, Wilfried Bleiss, and Peter Schierack. "Role of F1C Fimbriae, Flagella, and Secreted Bacterial Components in the Inhibitory Effect of Probiotic *Escherichia coli* Nissle 1917 on Atypical Entero-pathogenic *E. Coli* Infection." *Infection and Immunity* 82, no. 5 (May 1, 2014): 1801–12. doi:10.1128/IAI.01431-13.

Kondo, Shizuki, Jin-zhong Xiao, Takumi Satoh, Toshitaka Odamaki, Sachiko Takahashi, Hirosuke Sugahara, Tomoko Yaeshima, Keiji Iwatsuki, Asuka Kamei, and Keiko Abe. "Antiobesity Effects of *Bifidobacterium breve* Strain B-3 Supplementation in a Mouse Model With High-Fat Diet-Induced Obesity." *Bioscience, Biotechnology, and Biochemistry* 74, no. 8 (2010): 1656–61. doi:10.1271/bbb.100267.

Konieczna, P., R. Ferstl, M. Ziegler, R. Frei, D. Nehrbass, R. P. Lauener, et al. "Immunomodulation by *Bifidobacterium infantis* 35624 in the Murine Lamina Propria Requires Retinoic Acid–Dependent and Independent Mechanisms." *PLoS ONE* 8, no. 5 (May 21, 2013): e62617. doi: 10.1371/journal.pone.0062617.

Kruis, W., P. Frič, J. Pokrotnieks, M. Lukáš, B. Fixa, M. Kaščák, M. A. Kamm, et al. "Maintaining Remission of Ulcerative Colitis with the Probiotic *Escherichia coli* Nissle 1917 Is as Effective as With Standard Mesalazine." *Gut* 53, no. 11 (November 1, 2004): 1617–23. doi:10.1136/gut.2003.037747.

Lee, D. K., J. E. Park, M. J. Kim, J. G. Seo, J. H. Lee, and N. J. Ha. Probiotic Bacteria, *B. longum* and *L. acidophilus* Inhibit Infection by Rotavirus in Vitro and Decrease the Duration of Diarrhea in Pediatric Patients. *Clinics and Research in Hepatology Gastroenterology* 39, no. 2 (April 2015): 237–44. doi: 10.1016/j.clinre.2014.09.006.

Liang, S., T. Wang, X. Hu, J. Luo, W. Li, X. Wu, Y. Duan, and F. Jin. "Administration of *Lactobacillus helveticus* NS8 Improves Behavioral, Cognitive, and Biochemical Aberrations Caused by Chronic Restraint Stress." *Neuroscience* 310 (December 3, 2015): 561–77. doi:10.1016/j.neuroscience.2015.09.033.

McCann, M. L., R. S. Abrams, and R. P. Nelson. "Recolonization Therapy With Nonadhesive *Escherichia coli* for Treatment of Inflammatory Bowel Disease." *Annals of the New York Academy of Sciences* 730 (August 15, 1994): 243–45.

McFarland, L. V., and P. Bernasconi. "*Saccharomyces boulardii.*' A Review of an Innovative Biotherapeutic Agent." *Microbial Ecology in Health and Disease* 6, no. 4 (January 1, 1993): 157–71. doi:10.3109/08910609309141323.

McFarland, Lynne V. "Systematic Review and Meta-Analysis of *Saccharomyces boulardii* in Adult Patients." *World Journal of Gastroenterology* 16, no. 18 (2010): 2202–22.

Merenstein, D., M. Murphy, A. Fokar, R. K. Hernandez, H. Park, H. Nsouli, M. E. Sanders, et al. "Use of a Fermented Dairy Probiotic Drink Containing

Lactobacillus casei (DN-114 001) to Decrease the Rate of Illness in Kids: The DRINK Study. A Patient-Oriented, Double-Blind, Cluster-Randomized, Placebo-Controlled, Clinical Trial." *European Journal of Clinical Nutrition* 64, no. 7 (July 2010): 669–77. doi:10.1038/ejcn.2010.65.

Merenstein, Daniel J., Tina P. Tan, Aleksey Molokin, Keisha Herbin Smith, Robert F. Roberts, Nawar M. Shara, Mihriye Mete, Mary Ellen Sanders, and Gloria Solano-Aguilar. "Safety of *Bifidobacterium animalis* subsp. *lactis (B. lactis)* Strain BB-12-Supplemented Yogurt in Healthy Adults on Antibiotics: A Phase I Safety Study." *Gut Microbes* 6, no. 1 (2015): 66–77. doi:10.1080/19490976.20 15.1005484.

Messaoudi, M., R. Lalonde, N. Violle, H. Javelot, D. Desor, A. Nejdi, et al. "Assessment of Psychotropic-Like Properties of a Probiotic Formulation (*Lactobacillus helveticus* R0052 and *Bifidobacterium longum* R0175) in Rats and Human Subjects." *British Journal of Nutrition* 105 (2011): 755–64.

Mohammadi, Ali Akbar, Shima Jazayeri, Kianoush Khosravi-Darani, Zahra Solati, Nakisa Mohammadpour, Zatollah Asemi, Zohre Adab, et al. "The Effects of Probiotics on Mental Health and Hypothalamic-Pituitary-Adrenal Axis: A Randomized, Double-Blind, Placebo-Controlled Trial in Petrochemical Workers." *Nutritional Neuroscience* 19, no. 9 (November 2016): 387–95. doi:10.1179 /1476830515Y.0000000023.

Mubasher, Mohamed. "Dose Response Effects of BIO-K+CL-1285° on Antibiotic-Associated Diarrhea (AAD) and Incidence of *Clostridium difficile (C. diff.)*." ISDA, 2009. https://idsa.confex.com/idsa/2009/webprogram/Paper29620.html.

Niedzielin, K., H. Kordecki, and B. Birkenfeld. "A Controlled, Double-Blind, Randomized Study on the Efficacy of *Lactobacillus plantarum* 299V in Patients With Irritable Bowel Syndrome." *European Journal of Gastroenterology & Hepatology* 13, no. 10 (October 2001): 1143–47.

Nishihira, J., H. Kagami-Katsuyama, A. Tanaka, M. Nishimura, T. Kobayashi, and Y. Kawasaki. "Elevation of Natural Killer Cell Activity and Alleviation of Mental Stress by the Consumption of Yogurt Containing *Lactobacillus gasseri* SBT2055 and *Bifidobacterium longum* SBT2928 in a Double-Blind, Placebo-Controlled Clinical Trial." *Journal of Functional Foods* 11 (2014): 261–68.

O'Mahony, Liam, Jane McCarthy, Peter Kelly, George Hurley, Fangyi Luo, Kersang Chen, Gerald C. O'Sullivan, et al. "*Lactobacillus* and *Bifidobacterium* in Irritable Bowel Syndrome: Symptom Responses and Relationship to Cytokine Profiles." *Gastroenterology* 128, no. 3 (March 2005): 541–51.

Pawłowska, J., E. Klewicka, P. Czubkowski, I. Motyl, I. Jankowska, Z. Libudzisz, M. Teisseyre, D. Gliwicz, and B. Cukrowska. "Effect of *Lactobacillus casei* DN-114001 Application on the Activity of Fecal Enzymes in Children After

Liver Transplantation." *Transplantation Proceedings* 39, no. 10 (December 2007): 3219–21. doi:10.1016/j.transproceed.2007.03.101.

Pedersen, Natalia, Nynne Nyboe Andersen, Zsuzsanna Végh, Lisbeth Jensen, Dorit Vedel Ankersen, Maria Felding, Mette Hestetun Simonsen, Johan Burisch, and Pia Munkholm. "Ehealth: Low FODMAP Diet vs *Lactobacillus rhamnosus* GG in Irritable Bowel Syndrome." *World Journal of Gastroenterology* 20, no. 43 (November 21, 2014): 16215. doi:10.3748/wjg.v20.i43.16215.

Pieniz, S., R. Andreazza, T. Anghinoni, F. Camargo, A. Brandelli. "Probiotic Potential, Antimicrobial and Antioxidant Activities of *Enterococcus durans* Strain LAB18s." *Food Control* 37, no 1 (March 2014): 251–56. doi: 10.1016/j.foodcont .2013.09.055.

Pitkala K. H., Strandberg T. E., Finne Soveri U. H., Ouwehand A. C., Poussa T., Salminen "S. Fermented Cereal With Specific Bifidobacteria Normalizes Bowel Movements in Elderly Nursing Home Residents: A Randomized Controlled Trial." *J. Nutr. Health Agents* 11 (2007): 305–11.

Rao, A. Venket, Alison C. Bested, Tracey M. Beaulne, Martin A. Katzman, Christina Iorio, John M. Berardi, and Alan C. Logan. "A Randomized, Double-Blind, Placebo-Controlled Pilot Study of a Probiotic in Emotional Symptoms of Chronic Fatigue Syndrome." *Gut Pathogens* 1 (2009): 1–6. doi:10.1186/1757-4749-1-6.

Saavedra, J. M, N. A. Bauman, J. A. Perman, R. H. Yolken, and I. Oung. "Feeding of *Bifidobacterium bifidum* and *Streptococcus thermophilus* to Infants in Hospital for Prevention of Diarrhoea and Shedding of Rotavirus." *Lancet* 344, no. 8929 (October 15, 1994): 1046–49. doi:10.1016/S0140-6736(94)91708-6.

Savignac, H. M., M. Tramullas, B. Kiely, T. G. Dinan, and J. F. Cryan. "*Bifidobacteria* Modulate Cognitive Processes in an Anxious Mouse Strain." *Behavioural Brain Research* 287 (2015): 59–72. doi:10.1016/j.bbr.2015.02.044.

Shimakawa Y., S. Matsubara, N. Yuki, M. Ikeda, and F. Ishikawa. "Evaluation of *Bifidobacterium breve* Yakult-Fermented Soymilk as a Probiotic Food." *International Journal of Food Microbiology* 81, no 2 (April 2003) 131–36. doi: 10.1016/S0168-1605(02)00224-6.

Shornikova, A. V., I. A. Casas, E. Isolauri, H. Mykkänen, and T. Vesikari. "*Lactobacillus reuteri* as a Therapeutic Agent in Acute Diarrhea in Young Children." *Journal of Pedriatiric Gastroenterology and Nutrition* 24, no. 4 (May 1997) 399–404. doi: 10.1097/00005176-199704000-00008.

Sinn, D. H., J. H. Song, H. J. Kim, J. H. Lee, H. J. Son, D. K. Chang, et al. "Therapeutic Effect of *Lactobacillus acidophilus*-SDC 2012, 2013 in Patients With Irritable Bowel Syndrome." *Digestive Diseases and Sciences* 53, no 10 (October 2008): 2714–18. doi: 10.1007/s10620-007-0196-4.

Sokol, Harry, Bénédicte Pigneur, Laurie Watterlot, Omar Lakhdari, Luis G. Bermúdez-Humarán, Jean-Jacques Gratadoux, Sébastien Blugeon, et al. "*Faecalibacterium prausnitzii* Is an Anti-Inflammatory Commensal Bacterium Identified by Gut Microbiota Analysis of Crohn Disease Patients." *Proceedings of the National Academy of Sciences* 105, no. 43 (October 28, 2008): 16731–36. doi:10.1073/pnas.0804812105.

Sood, Ajit, Vandana Midha, Govind K. Makharia, Vineet Ahuja, Dinesh Singal, Pooja Goswami, and Rakesh K. Tandon. "The Probiotic Preparation, VSL#3 Induces Remission in Patients With Mild-to-Moderately Active Ulcerative Colitis." *Clinical Gastroenterology and Hepatology* 7, no. 11 (November 2009): 1202–09.e1. doi:10.1016/j.cgh.2009.07.016.

Steenbergen, L., R. Sellaro, S. van Hemert, J. A. Bosch, and L. S. Colzato. "A Randomized Controlled Trial to Test the Effect of Multispecies Probiotics on Cognitive Reactivity to Sad Mood." *Brain, Behavior, and Immunity* 48 (2015): 258–64.

Sugahara, Hirosuke, Toshitaka Odamaki, Shinji Fukuda, Tamotsu Kato, Jin-zhong Xiao, Fumiaki Abe, Jun Kikuchi, and Hiroshi Ohno. "Probiotic *Bifidobacterium longum* Alters Gut Luminal Metabolism Through Modification of the Gut Microbial Community." *Scientific Reports* 5 (August 28, 2015): 13548. doi:10.1038/srep13548.

Tanaka, Ryuichiro, Hiroo Takayama, Masami Morotomi, Toshikata Kuroshima, Sadao Ueyama, Keisuke Matsumoto, Akio Kuroda, and Masahiko Mutai. "Effects of Administration of TOS and *Bifidobacterium breve* 4006 on the Human Fecal Flora." *Bifidobacteria and Microflora* 2, no. 1 (1983): 17–24. doi:10.12938/bifidus1982.2.1_17.

Tillisch, Kirsten, Jennifer Labus, Lisa Kilpatrick, Zhiguo Jiang, Jean Stains, Bahar Ebrat, Denis Guyonnet, et al. "Consumption of Fermented Milk Product With Probiotic Modulates Brain Activity." *Gastroenterology* 144, no. 7 (June 2013): 1394–1401, 1401–04. doi:10.1053/j.gastro.2013.02.043.

Valeur, Nana, Peter Engel, Noris Carbajal, Eamonn Connolly, and Karin Ladefoged. "Colonization and Immunomodulation by *Lactobacillus reuteri* ATCC 55730 in the Human Gastrointestinal Tract." *Applied and Environmental Microbiology* 70, no. 2 (February 1, 2004): 1176–81. doi:10.1128/AEM.70.2.1176-1181.2004.

Wehkamp, Jan, Jürgen Harder, Kai Wehkamp, Birte Wehkamp von Meissner, Miriam Schlee, Corinne Enders, Ulrich Sonnenborn, et al. "NF-κB- and AP-1-Mediated Induction of Human Beta Defensin-2 in Intestinal Epithelial Cells by *Escherichia coli* Nissle 1917: A Novel Effect of a Probiotic Bacterium." *Infection and Immunity* 72, no. 10 (October 1, 2004): 5750–58. doi:10.1128/IAI.72.10.5750-5758.2004.

Whorwell, Peter J., Linda Altringer, Jorge Morel, Yvonne Bond, Duane Charbonneau, Liam O'Mahony, Barry Kiely, Fergus Shanahan, and Eamonn M. M. Quigley. "Efficacy of an Encapsulated Probiotic *Bifidobacterium infantis* 35624 in Women With Irritable Bowel Syndrome." *American Journal of Gastroenterology* 101, no. 7 (July 2006): 1581–90. doi:10.1111/j.1572-0241.2006.00734.x.

Wrzosek, Laura, Sylvie Miquel, Marie-Louise Noordine, Stephan Bouet, Marie Joncquel Chevalier-Curt, Véronique Robert, Catherine Philippe, et al. "*Bacteroides thetaiotaomicron* and *Faecalibacterium prausnitzii* Influence the Production of Mucus Glycans and the Development of Goblet Cells in the Colonic Epithelium of a Gnotobiotic Model Rodent." *BMC Biology* 11 (2013): 61. doi:10.1186/1741-7007-11-61.

Yang, Hui, Xiaoyun Zhao, Shan Tang, Hua Huang, Xiulan Zhao, Zhuohui Ning, Xiurong Fu, and Caihong Zhang. "Probiotics Reduce Psychological Stress in Patients Before Laryngeal Cancer Surgery." *Asia-Pacific Journal of Clinical Oncology* 12, no. 1 (March 2016): e92–96. doi:10.1111/ajco.12120.

GLOSSARY

amygdala: A pair of almond-shaped structures in the brain involved with processing emotions and forming memories.

antibiotics: These are broad-spectrum, lifesaving chemicals that kill bacteria, typically produced by bacteria and yeasts. They can be abused, however, leading to dysbiosis and mood disruption.

antibiotic resistance: This is a phenomenon in which bacteria become resistant to antibiotics, typically by overuse.

antibody: This is a molecule created by your adaptive immune system that latches on to antigens. The immune system creates millions of antibodies that are then filtered to eliminate those that react to your own tissue. Foreign antigens tagged by antibodies can then be removed by the white cells of your immune system.

antigen: An antigen is a substance that generates antibodies. Most pathogens have cell walls that are antigenic. When they die, pieces of the cell walls can generate a strong immune reaction to these antigens. If your body decides that your own cells are antigens, it will trigger an autoimmune reaction.

antimicrobial peptides (AMPs): These are chemicals excreted by the cells lining your gut to kill pathogens. They are like homegrown antibiotics.

anxiety: This is a normal emotion that is your body's way of drawing your attention to something problematic. The nerves you feel before taking a test or making a speech are examples of anxiety. However, if anxiety is persistent, it can become a disabling disorder. Anxiety is highly correlated with gut dysbiosis, and often healing the gut can rid you of anxiety behaviors.

B cell: A cell of the adaptive immune system that develops in the bone marrow. It secretes antibodies and cytokines that can lead an attack on pathogens.

bacteria: One-celled animals that rule the planet. The word is, confusingly, plural. If you just have one, it's a bacterium.

bacterial strains: Most bacteria are defined by their genus and species, but within a species there can be many subtle varieties, called strains.

bacteriocin: A toxin secreted by one bacterial species to kill or inhibit a closely related species. For instance, *E. coli* produces a bacteriocin called colicin that kills related *E. coli*. Bacteriocins may represent a new way to carefully target specific pathogens, rather than broad-spectrum antibiotics that kill the good with the bad.

bacteriophage: This is a virus that preys on bacteria. It invades a bacterium and commandeers its protein machinery to replicate in such numbers that the bacterium explodes, spewing more bacteriophages into the environment. Also called simply phage.

Bacteroidetes: A phylum of bacteria, these represent one of the major groups of bacteria in the gut, along with Firmicutes.

Bifidobacteria (Bifido): A genus of bacteria that is found in humans from the time they are breast-fed to the day they die. *Bifidobacteria* are also the bacterial species that turn milk into yogurt. Many species of *Bifidobacteria* are considered to be psychobiotics. They eat fiber in your diet and produce butyric acid, a beneficial gut and brain chemical.

biofilm: This refers to a community of microbes that gather together and produce a tenacious goo to bind them all into a film. Thus ensconced, they can work together very much like a multicelled creature to process food, pump nutrients around, and communicate with each other. Biofilms cover a large percentage of your intestines, and a good biofilm protects against pathogens.

blood-brain barrier (BBB): This is a protective barrier made of cell appendages that surrounds every single blood vessel and capillary in your brain. The barrier is designed to keep pathogens out while simultaneously letting in nutrients.

brain-gut axis: This refers to the set of communication channels that convey information between the gut and the brain. When the gut is dysbiotic, the brain may respond with feelings of anxiety or depression. Because microbes in the gut are involved, this is also referred to as the gut-brain-microbiota axis.

butyric acid or butyrate: This is a short-chain fatty acid (SCFA) that can be produced by many commensal bacteria. It can pass through the cells lining your gut and the blood-brain barrier (BBB) and can improve your mood.

Clostridia: This is a class of Firmicutes bacteria that enjoy the warm oxygen-free environment in your colon. They are normal citizens of your gut, as long as their numbers are small. They can be deadly when they get out of control. Because they can create spores, they are highly resistant to most broad-spectrum antibiotics. That means they can survive treatment to be the last microbe standing. That's how *Clostridium difficile (C. diff)* causes problems. You can also thank *Clostridia* for gangrene, tetanus, and botulism.

commensals: Latin for "sharing a table," these are the "good" bacteria that behave themselves in your gut, and are considered to be symbiotic. Take care of your commensals, and they will take care of you.

cytokine: This is a class of chemicals used by immune cells for communication. There are hundreds of different cytokines, including many variations of interleukin and interferon. They spread out through tissues, calling on other immune cells for help.

dendritic cell: This is an amoeboid cell of the immune system that cruises through the tissues of your gut, sampling the environment and capturing bacteria.

depression: This is a state of mind associated with bereavement, sickness behavior, and low mood. When you are sick, you want to curl up in bed and be left alone. That is a form of depression, but when it persists, it can become major depressive disorder. Often there is an obvious reason for depression, but it is also associated with gut dysbiosis. Once the dysbiosis is cured, the depression often lifts.

dopamine: This is a neurotransmitter that is used in your brain and your gut. In your brain it contributes to the reward system, which can make you feel good, and underlies addiction. In the gut, it reduces peristaltic action, and thus opposes serotonin.

dysbiosis: When your gut is behaving well, it can be said to be in balance; no single species is dominant, and there is a lot of diversity. When the balance is disturbed, say by infection or dominating pathogens, it is said to be dysbiotic. Dysbiosis can be caused by antibiotics, infections, or just aging. It contributes to IBS, allergies, obesity, depression, and anxiety.

enteric nervous system: This is your "second brain" in your guts. Your intestines are completely wrapped in a fine network of nerves that can pump your food autonomously, without interference from your "first brain." It responds to signals from sensory cells along the intestines to do things like vomit or instantly evacuate.

enterochromaffin cells (ECs): These are cells located throughout your gut that are designed to sense certain chemicals and then respond with the secretion of serotonin to increase peristalsis.

enterocytes: These are cells lining your gut that absorb nutrients from your food. This is where the digested meets the digester. These cells line your intestines, soaking up every available nutrient they can get. As with all the cells lining the gut, they suffer great abuse. Replacements arrive continually, derived from stem cells in deeper tissues. They have a favorite fuel: butyrate.

epigenetic: You are born with a complete set of genes, but their conversion into proteins—their expression—can be turned on and off. To make a liver cell, you need to turn off all the genes that aren't required to make a liver cell. These changes to the expression of genes are called epigenetic. Different chemicals in the body, including stress chemicals, can affect gene expression throughout the body, including the brain.

enzymes: These are proteins that can encourage and speed up chemical reactions in living creatures. Without enzymes, organic reactions would be too slow to be effective.

fecal transplant: This is a procedure that transfers a complete microbiota from one person to another. It has shown great success in repopulating the gut of people with *C. diff* infections.

fermentation: This is the process that bacteria and yeast use to convert sugars to gas, alcohol, and fatty acids. This is how wine and bread are made, and it underlies the action of psychobiotics in your gut.

fiber: This is not tree bark, but rather complex sugars that your intestines cannot break down. That means they make it all the way to the colon, where the fiber-eating microbes live. They eat the fiber and produce fatty acids like butyrate, acetate, and propionate.

Firmicutes: A phylum of bacteria, these are one of the major groups of bacteria in the gut, along with Bacteroidetes. This phylum contains *Lactobacilli* and *Clostridia.*

fungi or fungus: These tiny creatures include molds and yeasts, and they are very important to the food industry. They are used to make wine, bread, and cheese, arguably the perfect picnic layout. Some fungi, like *Saccharomyces boulardii,* are beneficial. Others, like *Candida albicans,* can be pathogenic.

GABA: An acronym for gamma-aminobutyric acid, this is the main inhibitory neurotransmitter in the brain, and as such it reduces excitability in the brain.

gnotobiotic: Latin for "known life," this term refers to animals that have a known and well-described microbiota.

gut-brain axis: Same as the brain-gut axis, but from a gastroenterologist's point of view.

hippocampus: This is a seahorse-shaped part of the brain that is involved with both memory and emotion. It needs a well-balanced microbiota to develop correctly. The hippocampus shrinks in people with depression.

homeostasis: This is the amazing ability of living systems to maintain equilibrium in the face of a changing environment. A typical example is thermoregulation that causes you to sweat when you're hot and shiver when you're cold as a way to keep your temperature stable. Your microbiota also tries to maintain a homeostatic environment and will push back if you try to change it.

HPA axis: The hypothalamus-pituitary-adrenal axis is a homeostatic controller of the flight-or-fight system. It responds to stressful situations like an attacking lion, filling your muscles with fuel and allowing you to run or fight. The HPA axis is affected by your gut bacteria, and if stimulation persists, it can result in depression or anxiety.

hypothalamus: This is part of your limbic system. It is central to your mood, motivation, hunger, and sleep.

IBD: Inflammatory bowel disease. This is a group of GI diseases that includes Crohn's disease and ulcerative colitis. It seems to be an autoimmune disease and also has a high correlation to depression and anxiety.

IBS: Irritable bowel syndrome. This is a disease without a well-known cause or cure. It also has a high correlation to depression and anxiety.

Lactobacillus (Lacto): A genus of bacteria that is found in humans from the time they are born to the time they die. *Lactobacillus* is also one of the bacterial species that turn milk into yogurt and cabbage into sauerkraut. Many species of *Lactobacillus* are considered to be psychobiotics.

macrophage: Meaning "big eater," this is an immune cell that can surround and dissolve toxins and bacteria.

metabolites: These are the products of metabolism, the basic activity of living. They are, basically, excretions. In bacteria, these metabolites are often short-chain fatty acids (SCFAs), like butyrate, that are excreted when the microbes eat oligosaccharides.

microbe: A great inclusive word for all the little critters of the world. It includes viruses, bacteria, archaea, fungus, protists, and other single-celled life-forms.

microbiome: This is the collection of genes that belong to all the microbes that coat your body and live in major population centers in your colon. You have some 100 times as many microbe genes as human genes. They provide you with a huge, flexible set of proteins that can nourish you and fight off pathogens. The word is often used interchangeably with microbiota.

microbiota: This refers to the collection of microbes that thrive on your skin and throughout your intestines. It is often used interchangeably with microbiome.

microglia: These are the immune cells of the brain. Normally, they are at rest in the brain, but when stimulated by pathogens, they become activated and are able to move like an amoeba throughout the brain, destroying the invaders.

microvilli: These are hairlike protrusions from the cells lining your gut, vastly increasing the surface area for absorption of nutrients from your food.

mucus: This is snot, and it coats your gut from your mouth to your anus. It is the first layer of defense against microbes. There are multiple layers of mucus lining your gut, and the outermost layer occasionally sloughs off, with millions of bacteria in tow.

natural killer (NK) cells: These are cells of the innate immune system that target known classes of bacteria and then kill them.

neurons: These are the basic cells of your brain that are in charge of computing, memory, and messaging. They have dendrites like tree branches coming off of their cell body, and typically have a long axon that communicates a nerve impulse over distances.

neurotransmitters: These are the chemicals that your brain uses to communicate. Neurons don't actually touch each other. There is a gap between them called a synapse, and neurotransmitters are tiny chemical packets that bridge that gap. Because of their centrality to proper brain function, they are a frequent target of antidepressants and antianxiety medications.

oligosaccharides: These are chains of three to ten sugars linked together into a molecule that the human gut cannot digest. They can, however, be consumed by bacteria, which produce short-chain fatty acids (SCFAs) as a result.

organelles: Like the organs in your body, these are tiny organs within your cells. Organelles include nuclei, mitochondria, and vacuoles. Some of them, like mitochondria, are bacteria that were captured by the cell billions of years ago. Bacteria themselves lack these kinds of internal structures.

pathogens: These are the "bad" bacteria that plague you and cause disease. This is often situational, as so-called pathogens can live in harmony in your gut—at least until the balance gets upset and they try to take over.

peristalsis: This is the pumping action that moves food through your digestive tract. When you get food poisoning, it will go into overdrive and you would be wise to find a bathroom, ASAP.

phage: See bacteriophage.

phagocyte: Meaning "eating cell," this is an amoeboid cell of your immune system that cruises through your lymphatic system and other tissues, looking for pathogens that it then consumes.

polyphenols: These are chemicals found in plants that act as antioxidants, protecting you against pathogens.

prebiotics: These are food for probiotics. Prebiotics are complex sugars, called fiber, that make it through the guts to the colon, where bacteria eat them. A common prebiotic is a chain of fructose sugars called fructo-oligosaccharide, or FOS. Chains of galactose are called GOS, and chains of mannan are called MOS. They are commonly found in good old-fashioned vegetables, but especially in chicory, artichokes, leeks, and garlic.

probiotics: These are microbes that, in sufficient quantities, can improve your health, especially your gut and immune system. They are typically bacteria like *Lactobacillus* or *Bifidobacteria,* but they can include fungi like *Saccharomyces boulardii.*

psychobiotics: These are microbes that, taken in sufficient quantity, yield positive psychiatric effects and can improve mental health, including depression and anxiety.

SCFAs: Short-chain fatty acids, the excretions of oligosaccharide-munching bacteria, can pass through the BBB and directly enter the brain. The main SCFAs are acetate, propionate, and butyrate.

serotonin: This is a neurotransmitter that is used in your brain and your gut. In your brain it contributes to feelings of well-being and happiness. In your gut, it contributes to peristalsis, the pumping action that moves food through your digestive system.

stress: This refers to external events that can threaten your health or mood. Some amount of stress is good. Like exercise, stress can make you stronger. But unrelieved stress can cause your HPA axis to overreact, potentially resulting in anxiety or depression.

synapses: These are the gaps between neurons that are bridged by chemicals called neurotransmitters.

T cells: These are cells of the adaptive immune system that are targeted to specific pathogens by passage through the thymus gland.

T-regs: These are important cells of the immune system. They are specialized T-cells that can regulate an inflammation, typically to dampen it.

vacuoles: These are tiny intracellular balloons, filled with liquid. They can hold items, like bacteria, in jail—or they can hit them with chemicals and dissolve them. These are multipurpose organelles.

vagus nerve: This is a nerve that wanders from the brain through your torso, sending projections to all your organs. It is an important component of the gut-brain axis, connecting your intestines to your brain.

villi: These are fingerlike protrusions that carpet the small intestine like a shag rug. They increase the surface area for absorbing nutrients from your food.

virus: Even tinier than bacteria, viruses are barely considered to be alive. If all living things died, viruses would be doomed, because they depend on a living host to reproduce. They cannot do it on their own, due to their comparatively puny DNA (or RNA). Some kinds of viruses called phages infect bacteria, reproducing to the extent that they cause the bacteria to explode, spreading around more viruses.

NOTES

CHAPTER 1

1. Timothy G. Dinan, Catherine Stanton, and John F. Cryan, "Psychobiotics: A Novel Class of Psychotropic," *Biological Psychiatry* 74, no. 10 (November 15, 2013): 720–26, doi:10.1016/j.biopsych.2013.05.001.

2. Amar Sarkar, Soili M. Lehto, Siobhán Harty, Timothy G. Dinan, John F. Cryan, and Philip W. J. Burnet, "Psychobiotics and the Manipulation of Bacteria–Gut–Brain Signals," *Trends in Neurosciences* 39, no. 11 (November 1, 2016): 763–81, doi:10.1016/j.tins.2016.09.002.

3. John R. Kelly, Yuliya Borre, Ciaran O'Brien, Elaine Patterson, Sahar El Aidy, Jennifer Deane, Paul J. Kennedy, et al., "Transferring the Blues: Depression-Associated Gut Microbiota Induces Neurobehavioural Changes in the Rat," *Journal of Psychiatric Research* 82 (November 2016): 109–18, doi:10.1016/j.jpsychires.2016.07.019.

CHAPTER 2

1. Byron Robinson, *The Abdominal Brain and Automatic Visceral Ganglia* (Chicago: Clinic Publishing Company, 1899).

2. Michael Gershon, *The Second Brain: The Scientific Basis of Gut Instinct and a Groundbreaking New Understanding of Nervous Disorders of the Stomach and Intestines* (New York: Harper, 1998).

3. "Special Correspondence," *British Medical Journal* 1, no. 2359 (March 17, 1906): 647, doi:10.1136/bmj.1.2359.647-a.

4. Russell W. Schaedler, René Dubos, and Richard Costello, "The Development of the Bacterial Flora in the Gastrointestinal Tract of Mice," *Journal of Experimental Medicine* 122, no. 1 (July 1, 1965): 59–66.

5. Nobuyuki Sudo et al., "Postnatal Microbial Colonization Programs the Hypothalamic-Pituitary-Adrenal System for Stress Response in Mice,"

Journal of Physiology 558, pt. 1 (July 1, 2004): 263–75, doi:10.1113/
jphysiol.2004.063388.

6. Gerard Clarke et al., "The Microbiome-Gut-Brain Axis During Early Life Regulates the Hippocampal Serotonergic System in a Sex-Dependent Manner," *Molecular Psychiatry* 18, no. 6 (June 2013): 666–73, doi:10.1038/mp.2012.77.

7. John K. Marshall et al., "Eight Year Prognosis of Postinfectious Irritable Bowel Syndrome Following Waterborne Bacterial Dysentery," *Gut* 59, no. 5 (May 1, 2010): 605–11, doi:10.1136/gut.2009.202234.

8. Stephanie K. Lathrop et al., "Peripheral Education of the Immune System by Colonic Commensal Microbiota," *Nature* 478, no. 7368 (October 13, 2011): 250–54, doi:10.1038/nature10434.

9. Hachung Chung et al., "Gut Immune Maturation Depends on Colonization With a Host-Specific Microbiota," *Cell* 149, no. 7 (June 22, 2012): 1578–93, doi:10.1016/j.cell.2012.04.037.

10. Merete Ellekilde et al., "Transfer of Gut Microbiota From Lean and Obese Mice to Antibiotic-Treated Mice," *Scientific Reports* 4 (August 1, 2014), doi:10.1038/srep05922.

11. John R. Kelly, Yuliya Borre, Ciaran O'Brien, Elaine Patterson, Sahar El Aidy, Jennifer Deane, Paul J. Kennedy, et al., "Transferring the Blues: Depression-Associated Gut Microbiota Induces Neurobehavioural Changes in the Rat," *Journal of Psychiatric Research* 82 (November 2016): 109–18, doi:10.1016/j.jpsychires.2016.07.019.

12. Guillaume Sarrabayrouse, Joudy Alameddine, Frédéric Altare, and Francine Jotereau, "Microbiota-Specific CD4CD8αα Tregs: Role in Intestinal Immune Homeostasis and Implications for IBD," *Frontiers in Immunology* 6 (October 8, 2015), doi:10.3389/fimmu.2015.00522.

13. A. Houlden et al., "Brain Injury Induces Specific Changes in the Caecal Microbiota of Mice via Altered Autonomic Activity and Mucoprotein Production," *Brain, Behavior, and Immunity* (April 6, 2016), doi:10.1016/j.bbi.2016.04.003.

14. Jari Huuskonen, Tiina Suuronen, Tapio Nuutinen, Sergiy Kyrylenko, and Antero Salminen, "Regulation of Microglial Inflammatory Response by Sodium Butyrate and Short-Chain Fatty Acids," *British Journal of Pharmacology* 141, no. 5 (March 2004): 874–80, doi:10.1038/sj.bjp.0705682.

15. Frederick A. Schroeder, Cong Lily Lin, Wim E. Crusio, and Schahram Akbarian, "Antidepressant-Like Effects of the Histone Deacetylase Inhibitor, Sodium Butyrate, in the Mouse," *Biological Psychiatry* 62, no. 1 (July 1, 2007): 55–64, doi:10.1016/j.biopsych.2006.06.036.

16. Christel Rousseaux, Xavier Thuru, Agathe Gelot, Nicolas Barnich, Christel Neut, Laurent Dubuquoy, and Caroline Dubuquoy, "*Lactobacillus*

Acidophilus Modulates Intestinal Pain and Induces Opioid and Cannabinoid Receptors," *Nature Medicine* 13, no. 1 (January 2007): 35–37, doi:10.1038/nm1521.

17. T. D. Swartz, F. A. Duca, T. de Wouters, Y. Sakar, and M. Covasa, "Up-Regulation of Intestinal Type 1 Taste Receptor 3 and Sodium Glucose Luminal Transporter-1 Expression and Increased Sucrose Intake in Mice Lacking Gut Microbiota," *British Journal of Nutrition* 107, no. 5 (March 2012): 621–30, doi:10.1017/S0007114511003412.

18. G. Oliver, J. Wardle, and E. L. Gibson, "Stress and Food Choice: A Laboratory Study," *Psychosomatic Medicine* 62, no. 6 (December 2000): 853–65.

19. Alexander D. Miras and Carel W. le Roux. "Mechanisms Underlying Weight Loss After Bariatric Surgery," *Nature Reviews Gastroenterology and Hepatology* 10, no. 10 (October 2013): 575–84, doi:10.1038/nrgastro.2013.119.

20. Jacqueline W. Njoroge, Y. Nguyen, Meredith M. Curtis, Cristiano G. Moreira, and Vanessa Sperandio, "Virulence Meets Metabolism: Cra and KdpE Gene Regulation in Enterohemorrhagic *Escherichia coli*," *mBio* 3, no. 5 (2012): e00280-212, doi:10.1128/mBio.00280-12.

21. Aja L. Gore and Shelley M. Payne, "CsrA and Cra Influence *Shigella flexneri* Pathogenesis," *Infection and Immunity* 78, no. 11 (November 2010): 4674–82, doi:10.1128/IAI.00589-10.

22. Mehrdad Yazdani, Bryn C. Taylor, Justine W. Debelius, Weizhong Li, Rob Knight, and Larry Smarr, "Using Machine Learning to Identify Major Shifts in Human Gut Microbiome Protein Family Abundance in Disease," in *2016 IEEE International Conference on Big Data (Big Data)* (2016): 1272–80, doi:10.1109/BigData.2016.7840731.

CHAPTER 3

1. Kjersti Aagaard, Jun Ma, Kathleen M. Antony, Radhika Ganu, Joseph Petrosino, and James Versalovic, "The Placenta Harbors a Unique Microbiome," *Science Translational Medicine* 6, no. 237 (May 21, 2014): 237ra65, doi:10.1126/scitranslmed.3008599.

2. Angela B. Javurek, William G. Spollen, Amber M. Mann Ali, Sarah A. Johnson, Dennis B. Lubahn, Nathan J. Bivens, Karen H. Bromert, Mark R. Ellersieck, Scott A. Givan, and Cheryl S. Rosenfeld, "Discovery of a Novel Seminal Fluid Microbiome and Influence of Estrogen Receptor Alpha Genetic Status," *Scientific Reports* 6 (March 14, 2016): 23027, doi:10.1038/srep23027.

3. Diane M. B. Dodd, "Reproductive Isolation as a Consequence of Adaptive Divergence in *Drosophila pseudoobscura*," *Evolution* 43, no. 6 (1989): 1308–11, doi:10.2307/2409365.

4. Gil Sharon, Daniel Segal, John M. Ringo, Abraham Hefetz, Ilana Zilber-Rosenberg, and Eugene Rosenberg, "Commensal Bacteria Play a Role in Mating Preference of *Drosophila melanogaster*," *Proceedings of the National Academy of Sciences* 107, no. 46 (November 16, 2010): 20051–56, doi:10.1073/pnas.1009906107.

5. Natsumi Fujiwara, Keiko Tsuruda, Yuko Iwamoto, Fuminori Kato, Teruko Odaki, Nobuko Yamane, Yuriko Hori, et al., "Significant Increase of Oral Bacteria in the Early Pregnancy Period in Japanese Women," *Journal of Investigative and Clinical Dentistry* (September 1, 2015), doi:10.1111/jicd.12189.

6. Michelle L. Holland, Robert Lowe, Paul W. Caton, Carolina Gemma, Guillermo Carbajosa, Amy F. Danson, Asha A. M. Carpenter, Elena Loche, Susan E. Ozanne, and Vardhman K. Rakyan, "Early-Life Nutrition Modulates the Epigenetic State of Specific rDNA Genetic Variants in Mice," *Science* (July 7, 2016): aaf7040, doi:10.1126/science.aaf7040.

7. Daniel B. DiGiulio, Benjamin J. Callahan, Paul J. McMurdie, Elizabeth K. Costello, Deirdre J. Lyell, Anna Robaczewska, Christine L. Sun, et al., "Temporal and Spatial Variation of the Human Microbiota During Pregnancy," *Proceedings of the National Academy of Sciences* 112, no. 35 (September 1, 2015): 11060–65, doi:10.1073/pnas.1502875112.

8. Jill Astbury, "Gender Disparities in Mental Health" (Geneva, Switzerland: World Health Organization, 2001), http://www.who.int/mental_health/media/en/242.pdf.

9. Omry Koren, Julia K. Goodrich, Tyler C. Cullender, Aymé Spor, Kirsi Laitinen, Helene Kling Bäckhed, Antonio Gonzalez, et al., "Host Remodeling of the Gut Microbiome and Metabolic Changes During Pregnancy." *Cell* 150, no. 3 (August 3, 2012): 470–80, doi:10.1016/j.cell.2012.07.008.

10. Esther Jiménez, Leonides Fernández, María L. Marín, Rocío Martín, Juan M. Odriozola, et al., "Isolation of Commensal Bacteria From Umbilical Cord Blood of Healthy Neonates Born by Cesarean Section," *Current Microbiology* 51 (2005): 270–74, doi:10.1007/s00284-005-0020-3.

11. Caroline Bearfield, Elizabeth S. Davenport, Vythil Sivapathasundaram, and Robert P. Allaker, "Possible Association Between Amniotic Fluid Micro-Organism Infection and Microflora in the Mouth," *BJOG* 109 (2002): 527–33, doi:10.1111/j.1471-0528.2002.01349.x.

12. Samuli Rautava, Maria Carmen Collado, Seppo Salminen, and Erika Isolauri, "Probiotics Modulate Host-Microbe Interaction in the Placenta and Fetal Gut: A Randomized, Double-Blind, Placebo-Controlled Trial," *Neonatology* 102 (2012): 178–84, doi:10.1159/000339182.

13. E. Jiménez, M. L. Marín, R. Martín, J. M. Odriozola, M. Olivares, et al., "Is Meconium From Healthy Newborns Actually Sterile?" *Research in Microbiology* 159 (2008): 187–93, doi:10.1016/j.resmic.2007.12.007.

14. Josef Neu and Jona Rushing, "Cesarean Versus Vaginal Delivery: Long-Term Infant Outcomes and the Hygiene Hypothesis," *Clinics in Perinatology* 38, no. 2 (June 2011): 321–31, doi:10.1016/j.clp.2011.03.008.

15. Derrick M. Chu, Jun Ma, Amanda L. Prince, Kathleen M. Antony, Maxim D. Seferovic, and Kjersti M. Aagaard, "Maturation of the Infant Microbiome Community Structure and Function Across Multiple Body Sites and in Relation to Mode of Delivery," *Nature Medicine,* advance online publication (January 23, 2017), doi:10.1038/nm.4272.

16. Daniel B. DiGiulio, Benjamin J. Callahan, Paul J. McMurdie, Elizabeth K. Costello, Deirdre J. Lyell, Anna Robaczewska, Christine L. Sun, et al., "Temporal and Spatial Variation of the Human Microbiota During Pregnancy," *Proceedings of the National Academy of Sciences* 112, no. 35 (September 1, 2015): 11060–65, doi:10.1073/pnas.1502875112.

17. Roman M. Stilling, Feargal J. Ryan, Alan E. Hoban, Fergus Shanahan, Gerard Clarke, Marcus J. Claesson, Timothy G. Dinan, and John F. Cryan, "Microbes & Neurodevelopment—Absence of Microbiota During Early Life Increases Activity Related Transcriptional Pathways in the Amygdala," *Brain, Behavior, and Immunity* 50 (November 2015): 209–20, doi:10.1016/j.bbi.2015.07.009.

18. Ebere S. Ogbonnaya, Gerard Clarke, Fergus Shanahan, Timothy G. Dinan, John F. Cryan, and Olivia F. O'Leary. "Adult Hippocampal Neurogenesis Is Regulated by the Microbiome," *Biological Psychiatry* 78, no. 4 (August 15, 2015): e7–9, doi:10.1016/j.biopsych.2014.12.023.

19. A. E. Hoban, R. M. Stilling, F. J. Ryan, F. Shanahan, T. G. Dinan, M. J. Claesson, G. Clarke, and J. F. Cryan. "Regulation of Prefrontal Cortex Myelination by the Microbiota," *Translational Psychiatry* 6, no. 4 (April 5, 2016): e774, doi:10.1038/tp.2016.42.

20. Lisa J. Funkhouser and Seth R. Bordenstein, "Mom Knows Best: The Universality of Maternal Microbial Transmission," *PLOS Biology* 11, no. 8 (August 20, 2013): e1001631, doi:10.1371/journal.pbio.1001631.

21. Ibid.

22. Karen-Anne McVey Neufeld, Pauline Luczynski, Clara Seira Oriach, Timothy G. Dinan, and John F. Cryan, "What's Bugging Your Teen?—The Microbiota and Adolescent Mental Health," *Neuroscience and Biobehavioral Reviews* 70 (November 2016): 300–312, doi:10.1016/j.neubiorev.2016.06.005.

23. Elena Biagi, Marco Candela, Claudio Franceschi, and Patrizia Brigidi, "The Aging Gut Microbiota: New Perspectives," *Ageing Research Reviews* 10, no. 4 (September 2011): 428–29, doi:10.1016/j.arr.2011.03.004.

24. Stephan C. Bischoff, "Microbiota and Aging," *Current Opinion in Clinical Nutrition and Metabolic Care* 19, no. 1 (January 2016): 26–30, doi:10.1097/MCO.0000000000000242.

25. Paul W. O'Toole and Ian B. Jeffery, "Gut Microbiota and Aging," *Science* 350, no. 6265 (December 4, 2015): 1214–15, doi:10.1126/science.aac8469.

26. Sitaraman Saraswati and Ramakrishnan Sitaraman, "Aging and the Human Gut Microbiota—From Correlation to Causality," *Frontiers in Microbiology* 5 (January 12, 2015), doi:10.3389/fmicb.2014.00764.

27. Alexander E. Pozhitkov, Rafik Neme, Tomislav Domazet-Loso, Brian Leroux, Shivani Soni, Diethard Tautz, and Peter Anthony Noble, "Thanatotranscriptome: Genes Actively Expressed After Organismal Death," *bioRxiv* (June 11, 2016): 58305, doi:10.1101/058305.

CHAPTER 4

1. James J. Galligan, "Pharmacology of Synaptic Transmission in the Enteric Nervous System," *Current Opinion in Pharmacology,* 2, no. 6 (December 1, 2002): 623–29. doi:10.1016/S1471-4892(02)00212-6.

2. P. Bercik, A. J. Park, D. Sinclair, A. Khoshdel, J. Lu, X. Huang, Y. Deng, et al., "The Anxiolytic Effect of *Bifidobacterium longum* NCC3001 Involves Vagal Pathways for Gut-Brain Communication," *Neurogastroenterology and Motility: The Official Journal of the European Gastrointestinal Motility Society* 23, no. 12 (December 2011): 1132–39, doi:10.1111/j.1365-2982.2011.01796.x.

3. A. Chua, J. Keating, D. Hamilton, P. W. Keeling, and T. G. Dinan, "Central Serotonin Receptors and Delayed Gastric Emptying in Non-Ulcer Dyspepsia," *BMJ* 305, no. 6848 (1992): 280–282; J. Tack, D. Broekaert, B. Fischler, L. Van Oudenhove, A. M. Gevers, and J. Janssens, "A Controlled Crossover Study of the Selective Serotonin Reuptake Inhibitor Citalopram in Irritable Bowel Syndrome," *Gut 55*, no. 8 (August 1, 2006): 1095–1103. doi:10.1136/gut .2005.077503.

CHAPTER 5

1. John F. Cryan and Timothy G. Dinan, "Mind-Altering Microorganisms: The Impact of the Gut Microbiota on Brain and Behaviour," *Nature Reviews Neuroscience* 13, no. 10 (October 2012): 701–12, doi:10.1038/nrn3346.

2. Kevin J. Tracey, "The Inflammatory Reflex," *Nature* 420, no. 6917 (2002): 853–59.

3.   Marc Udina et al., "Cytokine-Induced Depression: Current Status and Novel Targets for Depression Therapy," *CNS & Neurological Disorders—Drug Targets* 13, no. 6 (June 12, 2014): 1066–74, doi:10.2174/1871527313666140612121921.

4.   Rafael Campos-Rodríguez et al., "Stress Modulates Intestinal Secretory Immunoglobulin A," *Frontiers in Integrative Neuroscience* 7 (2013): 86, doi:10.3389/fnint.2013.00086.

5.   Li Wei, Lasantha Ratnayake, Gabby Phillips, Chris C. McGuigan, Steve V. Morant, Robert W. Flynn, Isla S. Mackenzie, and Thomas M. MacDonald, "Acid Suppression Medications and Bacterial Gastroenteritis: A Population-Based Cohort Study," *British Journal of Clinical Pharmacology* (January 1, 2016), doi:10.1111/bcp.13205.

6.   S. F. Altekruse, N. J. Stern, P. I. Fields, and D. L. Swerdlow, "*Campylobacter jejuni*—An Emerging Foodborne Pathogen," *Emerging Infectious Diseases* 5, no. 1 (1999): 28–35, doi 10.3201/eid0501.990104.

7.   Raffaella Campana, Sara Federici, Eleonora Ciandrini, and Wally Baffone, "Antagonistic Activity of *Lactobacillus acidophilus* ATCC 4356 on the Growth and Adhesion/Invasion Characteristics of Human *Campylobacter jejuni,*" *Current Microbiology* 64, no. 4 (April 2012): 371–78, doi:10.1007/s00284 -012-0080-0.

8.   A. Munck, P. M. Guyre, and N. J. Holbrook, "Physiological Functions of Glucocorticoids in Stress and Their Relation to Pharmacological Actions," *Endocrine Reviews* 5, no. 1 (1984): 25–44, doi:10.1210/edrv-5-1-25.

9.   Hans Linde Nielsen, Jørgen Engberg, Tove Ejlertsen, and Henrik Nielsen, "Psychometric Scores and Persistence of Irritable Bowel After *Campylobacter concisus* Infection," *Scandinavian Journal of Gastroenterology* 49, no. 5 (May 2014): 545–51, doi:10.3109/00365521.2014.886718.

10. Lukas Van Oudenhove et al., "Fatty Acid–Induced Gut-Brain Signaling Attenuates Neural and Behavioral Effects of Sad Emotion in Humans," *Journal of Clinical Investigation* 121, no. 8 (August 1, 2011): 3094–99, doi:10.1172/ JCI46380.

11. Sandy R. Shultz et al., "Intracerebroventricular Injections of the Enteric Bacterial Metabolic Product Propionic Acid Impair Cognition and Sensorimotor Ability in the Long–Evans Rat: Further Development of a Rodent Model of Autism," *Behavioural Brain Research* 200, no. 1 (June 8, 2009): 33–41, doi:10.1016/j.bbr.2008.12.023.

12. C. Tana et al., "Altered Profiles of Intestinal Microbiota and Organic Acids May Be the Origin of Symptoms in Irritable Bowel Syndrome," *Neurogastroenterology and Motility: The Official Journal of the European Gastrointestinal Motility Society* 22, no. 5 (May 2010): 512–19, e114–15, doi:10.1111/j.1365-2982.2009.01427.x.

13. Roman M. Stilling, Marcel van de Wouw, Gerard Clarke, Catherine Stanton, Timothy G. Dinan, and John F. Cryan, "The Neuropharmacology of Butyrate: The Bread and Butter of the Microbiota-Gut-Brain Axis?" *Neurochemistry International* 99 (October 2016): 110–32, doi:10.1016/j.neuint.2016.06.011.

14. Sahar El Aidy, Timothy G. Dinan, and John F. Cryan, "Gut Microbiota: The Conductor in the Orchestra of Immune-Neuroendocrine Communication," *Clinical Therapeutics* 37, no. 5 (May 1, 2015): 954–67, doi:10.1016/j.clinthera.2015.03.002.

15. M. Lyte and S. Ernst, "Catecholamine Induced Growth of Gram Negative Bacteria," *Life Sciences* 50, no. 3 (1992): 203–12.

16. Phyllis M. O'Donnell et al., "Enhancement of In Vitro Growth of Pathogenic Bacteria by Norepinephrine: Importance of Inoculum Density and Role of Transferrin," *Applied and Environmental Microbiology* 72, no. 7 (July 1, 2006): 5097–99, doi:10.1128/AEM.00075-06.

17. Simon R. Knowles, Elizabeth A. Nelson, and Enzo A. Palombo, "Investigating the Role of Perceived Stress on Bacterial Flora Activity and Salivary Cortisol Secretion: A Possible Mechanism Underlying Susceptibility to Illness," *Biological Psychology* 77, no. 2 (February 2008): 132–37, doi:10.1016/j.biopsycho.2007.09.010.

CHAPTER 6

1. Jean M. Twenge, "Time Period and Birth Cohort Differences in Depressive Symptoms in the U.S., 1982–2013," *Social Indicators Research* 121, no. 2 (June 5, 2014): 437–54, doi:10.1007/s11205-014-0647-1.

2. Ronald Ross Watson, George Grimble, Victor R. Preedy, and Sherma Zibadi, eds., *Nutrition in Infancy* (New York: Humana, 2013).

3. J. George Porter Phillips, "The Treatment of Melancholia by the Lactic Acid Bacillus," *British Journal of Nursing* (May 29, 1909): 426.

4. C. J. Tsay, "Julius Wagner-Jauregg and the Legacy of Malarial Therapy for the Treatment of General Paresis of the Insane," *Yale Journal of Biology and Medicine* 86 (2013): 245–54.

5. F. R. Frankenburg and R. J. Baldessarini, "Neurosyphilis, Malaria, and the Discovery of Antipsychotic Agents," *Harvard Review of Psychiatry* 16 (2008): 299–307.

6. P. V. Luisada, "The Phencyclidine Psychosis: Phenomenology and Treatment," in *Phencyclidine (PCP) Abuse: An Appraisal,* ed. R. C. Petersen and R. C. Stillman (Rockville, Maryland: National Institute on Drug Abuse, 1978).

7. Rama Saad, Mariam R. Rizkallah, and Ramy K. Aziz, "Gut Pharmacomicrobiomics: The Tip of an Iceberg of Complex Interactions Between Drugs and

Gut-Associated Microbes," *Gut Pathogens* 4 (November 30, 2012): 16, doi:10.1186/1757-4749-4-16.

CHAPTER 7

1. María X. Maldonado-Gómez, Inés Martínez, Francesca Bottacini, Amy O'Callaghan, Marco Ventura, Douwe van Sinderen, Benjamin Hillmann, et al., "Stable Engraftment of *Bifidobacterium longum* AH1206 in the Human Gut Depends on Individualized Features of the Resident Microbiome," *Cell Host & Microbe,* accessed October 6, 2016, doi:10.1016/j. chom.2016.09.001.

2. Marina Elli, Maria Luisa Callegari, Susanna Ferrari, Elena Bessi, Daniela Cattivelli, Sara Soldi, Lorenzo Morelli, Nathalie Goupil Feuillerat, and Jean-Michel Antoine, "Survival of Yogurt Bacteria in the Human Gut," *Applied and Environmental Microbiology* 72, no. 7 (July 2006): 5113–17, doi:10.1128/ AEM.02950-05.

3. Premysl Bercik, Elena F. Verdu, Jane A. Foster, Joseph Macri, Murray Potter, Xiaxing Huang, Paul Malinowski, et al., "Chronic Gastrointestinal Inflammation Induces Anxiety-Like Behavior and Alters Central Nervous System Biochemistry in Mice," *Gastroenterology* 139, no. 6 (December 2010): 2102– 12.e1, doi:10.1053/j.gastro.2010.06.063.

4. H. M. Savignac, M. Tramullas, B. Kiely, T. G. Dinan, and J. F. Cryan., "*Bifidobacteria* Modulate Cognitive Processes in an Anxious Mouse Strain," *Behavioural Brain Research* 287 (2015): 59–72, doi:10.1016/j.bbr.2015.02.044.

5. Michaël Messaoudi, Robert Lalonde, Nicolas Violle, Hervé Javelot, Didier Desor, Amine Nejdi, Jean-François Bisson, et al., "Assessment of Psychotropic-Like Properties of a Probiotic Formulation (*Lactobacillus helveticus* R0052 and *Bifidobacterium longum* R0175) in Rats and Human Subjects," *British Journal of Nutrition* 105, no. 5 (March 2011): 755–64, doi:10.1017/ S0007114510004319.

6. A. P. Allen, W. Hutch, Y. E. Borre, P. J. Kennedy, A. Temko, G. Boylan, E. Murphy, J. F. Cryan, T. G. Dinan, and G. Clarke. "*Bifidobacterium longum* 1714 as a Translational Psychobiotic: Modulation of Stress, Electrophysiology and Neurocognition in Healthy Volunteers," *Translational Psychiatry* 6, no. 11 (November 1, 2016): e939, doi:10.1038/tp.2016.191.

7. Friedrich Altmann, Paul Kosma, Amy O'Callaghan, Sinead Leahy, Francesca Bottacini, Evelyn Molloy, Stephan Plattner, et al., "Genome Analysis and Characterisation of the Exopolysaccharide Produced by *Bifidobacterium longum* Subsp. *longum* 35624™," *PLOS ONE* 11, no. 9 (September 22, 2016): e0162983, doi:10.1371/journal.pone.0162983.

8. H. M. Savignac, B. Kiely, T. G. Dinan, and J. F. Cryan, "*Bifidobacteria* Exert Strain-Specific Effects on Stress-Related Behavior and Physiology in BALB/c Mice," *Neurogastroenterology and Motility: The Official Journal of the European Gastrointestinal Motility Society* 26, no. 11 (November 2014): 1615–27, doi:10.1111/nmo.12427.

9. Yudong Li, Toshiaki Shimizu, Atsuto Hosaka, Noritsugu Kaneko, Yoshikazu Ohtsuka, and Yuichiro Yamashiro, "Effects of *Bifidobacterium breve* Supplementation on Intestinal Flora of Low Birth Weight Infants," *Pediatrics International: Official Journal of the Japan Pediatric Society* 46, no. 5 (October 2004): 509–15, doi:10.1111/j.1442-200x.2004.01953.x.

10. Jian-jun Ren, Zhao Yu, Feng-Ling Yang, Dan Lv, Shi Hung, Jie Zhang, Ping Lin, Shi-Xi Liu, Nan Zhang, and Claus Bachert, "Effects of *Bifidobacterium breve* Feeding Strategy and Delivery Modes on Experimental Allergic Rhinitis Mice," *PloS One* 10, no. 10 (2015): e0140018, doi:10.1371/journal.pone.0140018.

11. R. Fuller, "Probiotics in Human Medicine," *Gut* 32, no. 4 (April 1991): 439–42.

12. H. M. Savignac, B. Kiely, T. G. Dinan, and J. F. Cryan, "*Bifidobacteria* Exert Strain-Specific Effects on Stress-Related Behavior and Physiology in BALB/c Mice," *Neurogastroenterology and Motility: The Official Journal of the European Gastrointestinal Motility Society* 26, no. 11 (November 2014): 1615–27, doi:10.1111/nmo.12427.

13. Yezaz A. Ghouri, David M Richards, Erik F Rahimi, Joseph T Krill, Katherine A Jelinek, and Andrew W DuPont, "Systematic Review of Randomized Controlled Trials of Probiotics, Prebiotics, and Synbiotics in Inflammatory Bowel Disease," *Clinical and Experimental Gastroenterology* 7 (December 9, 2014): 473–87, doi:10.2147/CEG.S27530.

14. D. Guyonnet, O. Chassany, P. Ducrotte, C. Picard, M. Mouret, C. H. Mercier, and C. Matuchansky, "Effect of a Fermented Milk Containing *Bifidobacterium animalis* DN-173 010 on the Health-Related Quality of Life and Symptoms in Irritable Bowel Syndrome in Adults in Primary Care: A Multicentre, Randomized, Double-Blind, Controlled Trial," *Alimentary Pharmacology & Therapeutics* 26, no. 3 (August 1, 2007): 475–86, doi:10.1111/j.1365-2036.2007.03362.x.

15. M. Ahmed, J. Prasad, H. Gill, L. Stevenson, and P. Gopal, "Impact of Consumption of Different Levels of *Bifidobacterium lactis* HN019 on the Intestinal Microflora of Elderly Human Subjects," *Journal of Nutrition, Health & Aging* 11, no. 1 (February 2007): 26–31.

16. Ryan Rieder, Paul J. Wisniewski, Brandon L. Alderman, and Sara C. Campbell, "Microbes and Mental Health: A Review," *Brain, Behavior, and Immunity* (January 25, 2017), doi:10.1016/j.bbi.2017.01.016.

17. Ghodarz Akkasheh, Zahra Kashani-Poor, Maryam Tajabadi-Ebrahimi, Parvaneh Jafari, Hossein Akbari, Mohsen Taghizadeh, Mohammad Reza Memarzadeh, Zatollah Asemi, and Ahmad Esmaillzadeh, "Clinical and Metabolic Response to Probiotic Administration in Patients with Major Depressive Disorder: A Randomized, Double-Blind, Placebo-Controlled Trial," *Nutrition* 32, no. 3 (March 2016): 315–20, doi:10.1016/j.nut.2015.09.003.

18. Christel Rousseaux, Xavier Thuru, Agathe Gelot, Nicolas Barnich, Christel Neut, Laurent Dubuquoy, Caroline Dubuquoy, et al., "*Lactobacillus acidophilus* Modulates Intestinal Pain and Induces Opioid and Cannabinoid Receptors," *Nature Medicine* 13, no. 1 (January 2007): 35–37, doi:10.1038/nm1521.

19. Raffaella Campana, Sara Federici, Eleonora Ciandrini, and Wally Baffone, "Antagonistic Activity of *Lactobacillus acidophilus* ATCC 4356 on the Growth and Adhesion/Invasion Characteristics of Human *Campylobacter jejuni*," *Current Microbiology* 64, no. 4 (April 2012): 371–78, doi:10.1007/s00284-012-0080-0.

20. Pedro A. Jose and Dominic Raj, "Gut Microbiota in Hypertension," *Current Opinion in Nephrology and Hypertension* 24, no. 5 (September 2015): 403–09, doi:10.1097/MNH.0000000000000149.

21. Jia Luo, Tao Wang, Shan Liang, Xu Hu, Wei Li, and Feng Jin, "Ingestion of *Lactobacillus* Strain Reduces Anxiety and Improves Cognitive Function in the Hyperammonemia Rat," *Science China Life Sciences* 57, no. 3 (March 2014): 327–35, doi:10.1007/s11427-014-4615-4.

22. Christina L. Ohland, Lisa Kish, Haley Bell, Aducio Thiesen, Naomi Hotte, Evelina Pankiv, and Karen L. Madsen. "Effects of *Lactobacillus helveticus* on Murine Behavior Are Dependent on Diet and Genotype and Correlate With Alterations in the Gut Microbiome," *Psychoneuroendocrinology* 38, no. 9 (September 2013): 1738–47, doi:10.1016/j.psyneuen.2013.02.008.

23. Valentina Taverniti and Simone Guglielmetti, "Health-Promoting Properties of *Lactobacillus helveticus*," *Frontiers in Microbiology* 3 (2012): 392, doi:10.3389/fmicb.2012.00392.

24. Javier A. Bravo, Paul Forsythe, Marianne V. Chew, Emily Escaravage, Hélène M. Savignac, Timothy G. Dinan, John Bienenstock, and John F. Cryan, "Ingestion of *Lactobacillus* Strain Regulates Emotional Behavior and Central GABA Receptor Expression in a Mouse via the Vagus Nerve," *Proceedings of the National Academy of Sciences of the United States of America* 108, no. 38 (September 20, 2011): 16050–55, doi:10.1073/pnas.1102999108.

25. Ibid.

26. Natalia Pedersen, Nynne Nyboe Andersen, Zsuzsanna Végh, Lisbeth Jensen, Dorit Vedel Ankersen, Maria Felding, Mette Hestetun Simonsen, Johan

Burisch, and Pia Munkholm. "Ehealth: Low FODMAP Diet vs *Lactobacillus rhamnosus* GG in Irritable Bowel Syndrome," *World Journal of Gastroenterology* 20, no. 43 (November 21, 2014): 16215, doi:10.3748/wjg.v20.i43.16215.

27. John R. Kelly, Andrew P. Allen, Andriy Temko, William Hutch, Paul J. Kennedy, Niloufar Farid, Eileen Murphy, et al., "Lost in Translation? The Potential Psychobiotic *Lactobacillus rhamnosus* (JB-1) Fails to Modulate Stress or Cognitive Performance in Healthy Male Subjects," *Brain, Behavior, and Immunity* 61 (March 2017): 50–59, doi:10.1016/j.bbi.2016.11.018.

28. Shelly A. Buffington, Gonzalo Viana Di Prisco, Thomas A. Auchtung, Nadim J. Ajami, Joseph F. Petrosino, and Mauro Costa-Mattioli, "Microbial Reconstitution Reverses Maternal Diet-Induced Social and Synaptic Deficits in Offspring," *Cell* 165, no. 7 (June 16, 2016): 1762–75, doi:10.1016/j.cell.2016.06.001.

29. S. E. Erdman and T. Poutahidis, "Probiotic 'Glow of Health': It's More Than Skin Deep," *Beneficial Microbes* 5, no. 2 (June 1, 2014): 109–19, doi:10.3920/BM2013.0042; Bernard J. Varian, Theofilos Poutahidis, Brett T. DiBenedictis, Tatiana Levkovich, Yassin Ibrahim, Eliska Didyk, Lana Shikhman, et al., "Microbial Lysate Upregulates Host Oxytocin," *Brain, Behavior, and Immunity* 61 (March 2017): 36–49, doi:10.1016/j.bbi.2016.11.002.

30. T. Kamiya, L. Wang, P. Forsythe, G. Goettsche, Y. Mao, Y. Wang, G. Tougas, and J. Bienenstock. "Inhibitory Effects of *Lactobacillus reuteri* on Visceral Pain Induced by Colorectal Distension in Sprague-Dawley Rats," *Gut* 55, no. 2 (February 2006): 191–96, doi:10.1136/gut.2005.070987.

31. Douglas B. DiRienzo, "Effect of Probiotics on Biomarkers of Cardiovascular Disease: Implications for Heart-Healthy Diets," *Nutrition Reviews* 72, no. 1 (January 2014): 18–29, doi:10.1111/nure.12084.

32. J. J. Jeong, J. Y. Woo, K. A. Kim, M. J. Han, and D. H. Kim, "*Lactobacillus pentosus* Var. *plantarum* C29 Ameliorates Age-Dependent Memory Impairment in Fischer 344 Rats," *Letters in Applied Microbiology* 60, no. 4 (April 2015): 307–14, doi:10.1111/lam.12393.

33. Kamini Ramiah, Carol A. van Reenen, and Leon M. T. Dicks, "Surface-Bound Proteins of *Lactobacillus plantarum* 423 That Contribute to Adhesion of Caco-2 Cells and Their Role in Competitive Exclusion and Displacement of *Clostridium sporogenes* and *Enterococcus faecalis*," *Research in Microbiology* 159, no. 6 (July 2008): 470–75, doi:10.1016/j.resmic.2008.06.002.

34. K. Niedzielin, H. Kordecki, and B. Birkenfeld, "A Controlled, Double-Blind, Randomized Study on the Efficacy of *Lactobacillus plantarum* 299V in Patients with Irritable Bowel Syndrome," *European Journal of Gastroenterology & Hepatology* 13, no. 10 (October 2001): 1143–47.

35. D. Benton, C. Williams, and A. Brown, "Impact of Consuming a Milk Drink Containing a Probiotic on Mood and Cognition," *European Journal of Clinical Nutrition* 61, no. 3 (March 2007): 355–61, doi:10.1038/sj.ejcn.1602546.

36. A. Venket Rao, Alison C. Bested, Tracey M. Beaulne, Martin A. Katzman, Christina Iorio, John M. Berardi, and Alan C. Logan, "A Randomized, Double-Blind, Placebo-Controlled Pilot Study of a Probiotic in Emotional Symptoms of Chronic Fatigue Syndrome," *Gut Pathogens* 1, no. 1 (March 19, 2009): 6, doi:10.1186/1757-4749-1-6.

37. Alison C. Bested, Alan C. Logan, and Eva M. Selhub, "Intestinal Microbiota, Probiotics and Mental Health: From Metchnikoff to Modern Advances: Part III—Convergence Toward Clinical Trials," *Gut Pathogens* 5 (March 16, 2013): 4, doi:10.1186/1757-4749-5-4.

38. Noriko Komatsuzaki and Jun Shima, "Effects of Live *Lactobacillus paracasei* on Plasma Lipid Concentration in Rats Fed an Ethanol-Containing Diet," *Bioscience, Biotechnology, and Biochemistry* 76, no. 2 (2012): 232–37, doi:10.1271/bbb.110390.

39. L. V. McFarland and P. Bernasconi, "*Saccharomyces boulardii*. A Review of an Innovative Biotherapeutic Agent," *Microbial Ecology in Health and Disease* 6, no. 4 (January 1, 1993): 157–71, doi:10.3109/08910609309141323; Mario Guslandi, Gianni Mezzi, Massimo Sorghi, and Pier Alberto Testoni, "*Saccharomyces boulardii* in Maintenance Treatment of Crohn's Disease," *Digestive Diseases and Sciences* 45, no. 7 (July 1, 2000): 1462–64, doi:10.1023/A:1005588911207.

40. L. Drago, V. Rodighiero, T. Celeste, L. Rovetto, and E. De Vecchi. "Microbiological Evaluation of Commercial Probiotic Products Available in the USA in 2009," *Journal of Chemotherapy* 22, no. 6 (December 1, 2010): 373–77, doi:10.1179/joc.2010.22.6.373.

41. H. M. Timmerman C. J. M. Koning, L. Mulder, F. M. Rombouts, and A. C. Beynen, "Monostrain, Multistrain and Multispecies Probiotics—A Comparison of Functionality and Efficacy," *International Journal of Food Microbiology* 96, no. 3 (November 15, 2004): 219–33, doi:10.1016/j.ijfoodmicro.2004.05.012; Laura Steenbergen Roberta Sellaro, Saskia van Hemert, Jos A. Bosch, and Lorenza S. Colzato, "A Randomized Controlled Trial to Test the Effect of Multispecies Probiotics on Cognitive Reactivity to Sad Mood," *Brain, Behavior, and Immunity* 48 (August 2015): 258–64, doi:10.1016/j.bbi.2015.04.003; C. M. C. Chapman, G. R. Gibson, and I. Rowland, "Health Benefits of Probiotics: Are Mixtures More Effective than Single Strains?" *European Journal of Nutrition* 50, no. 1 (February 2011): 1–17, doi:10.1007/s00394-010-0166-z.

42. Michaël Messaoudi, Robert Lalonde, Nicolas Violle, Hervé Javelot, Didier Desor, Amine Nejdi, Jean-François Bisson, et al., "Assessment of

Psychotropic-Like Properties of a Probiotic Formulation (*Lactobacillus helveticus* R0052 and *Bifidobacterium longum* R0175) in Rats and Human Subjects," *British Journal of Nutrition* 105, no. 5 (March 2011): 755–64, doi:10.1017/S0007114510004319.

43. Laurent Diop, Sonia Guillou, and Henri Durand, "Probiotic Food Supplement Reduces Stress-Induced Gastrointestinal Symptoms in Volunteers: A Double-Blind, Placebo-Controlled, Randomized Trial," *Nutrition Research* 28, no. 1 (January 2008): 1–5, doi:10.1016/j.nutres.2007.10.001.

44. A. Ait-Belgnaoui, A. Colom, V. Braniste, L. Ramalho, A. Marrot, C. Cartier, E. Houdeau, V. Theodorou, and T. Tompkins, "Probiotic Gut Effect Prevents the Chronic Psychological Stress-Induced Brain Activity Abnormality in Mice," *Neurogastroenterology and Motility: The Official Journal of the European Gastrointestinal Motility Society* 26, no. 4 (April 2014): 510–20, doi:10.1111/nmo.12295.

45. T. Mimura, F. Rizzello, U. Helwig, G. Poggioli, S. Schreiber, I. C. Talbot, R. J. Nicholls, P. Gionchetti, M. Campieri, and M. A. Kamm, "Once Daily High Dose Probiotic Therapy (VSL#3) for Maintaining Remission in Recurrent or Refractory Pouchitis," *Gut* 53, no. 1 (January 1, 2004): 108–14, doi:10.1136/gut.53.1.108.

46. H. J. Kim, M. Camilleri, S. Mckinzie, M. B. Lempke, D. D. Burton, G. M. Thomforde, and A. R. Zinsmeister, "A Randomized Controlled Trial of a Probiotic, VSL#3, on Gut Transit and Symptoms in Diarrhoea-Predominant Irritable Bowel Syndrome," *Alimentary Pharmacology & Therapeutics* 17, no. 7 (April 1, 2003): 895–904, doi:10.1046/j.1365-2036.2003.01543.x.

47. Ajit Sood, Vandana Midha, Govind K. Makharia, Vineet Ahuja, Dinesh Singal, Pooja Goswami, and Rakesh K. Tandon, "The Probiotic Preparation, VSL#3 Induces Remission in Patients With Mild-to-Moderately Active Ulcerative Colitis," *Clinical Gastroenterology and Hepatology* 7, no. 11 (November 2009): 1202–09.e1, doi:10.1016/j.cgh.2009.07.016.

48. Paolo Aureli, Lucio Capurso, Anna Maria Castellazzi, Mario Clerici, Marcello Giovannini, Lorenzo Morelli, Andrea Poli, Fabrizio Pregliasco, Filippo Salvini, and Gian Vincenzo Zuccotti, "Probiotics and Health: An Evidence-Based Review," *Pharmacological Research* 63, no. 5 (May 2011): 366–76, doi:10.1016/j.phrs.2011.02.006.

49. J. Boudeau, A. L. Glasser, S. Julien, J. F. Colombel, and A. Darfeuille-Michaud, "Inhibitory Effect of Probiotic *Escherichia coli* Strain Nissle 1917 on Adhesion to and Invasion of Intestinal Epithelial Cells by Adherent-Invasive *E. coli* Strains Isolated From Patients With Crohn's Disease," *Alimentary Pharmacology & Therapeutics* 18, no. 1 (July 1, 2003): 45–56, doi: 10.1046/j.1365-2036.2003.01638.x; M. L. McCann, R. S. Abrams, and R. P. Nelson,

"Recolonization Therapy With Nonadhesive *Escherichia coli* for Treatment of Inflammatory Bowel Disease," *Annals of the New York Academy of Sciences* 730 (August 15, 1994): 243–45, doi: 10.1111/j.1749-6632.1994.tb44253.x.

50. W. Kruis, P. Fric, J. Pokrotnieks, M. Lukás, B. Fixa, M. Kascák, M. A. Kamm, et al., "Maintaining Remission of Ulcerative Colitis With the Probiotic *Escherichia coli* Nissle 1917 Is as Effective as With Standard Mesalazine," *Gut* 53, no. 11 (November 2004): 1617–23, doi:10.1136/gut.2003.037747.

51. M. Möllenbrink and E. Bruckschen, "[Treatment of chronic constipation with physiologic *Escherichia coli* bacteria. Results of a clinical study of the effectiveness and tolerance of microbiological therapy with the *E. coli* Nissle 1917 strain (Mutaflor)]," *Medizinische Klinik (Munich, Germany: 1983)* 89, no. 11 (November 15, 1994): 587–93.

52. Jonathan Nzakizwanayo, Cinzia Dedi, Guy Standen, Wendy M. Macfarlane, Bhavik A. Patel, and Brian V. Jones, "*Escherichia coli* Nissle 1917 Enhances Bioavailability of Serotonin in Gut Tissues Through Modulation of Synthesis and Clearance," *Scientific Reports* 5 (November 30, 2015): 17324, doi:10.1038/srep17324.

53. Peter J. Whorwell, Linda Altringer, Jorge Morel, Yvonne Bond, Duane Charbonneau, Liam O'Mahony, Barry Kiely, Fergus Shanahan, and Eamonn M. M. Quigley, "Efficacy of an Encapsulated Probiotic *Bifidobacterium infantis* 35624 in Women With Irritable Bowel Syndrome," *American Journal of Gastroenterology* 101, no. 7 (July 2006): 1581–90, doi:10.1111/j.1572-0241.2006.00734.x; Liam O'Mahony, Jane McCarthy, Peter Kelly, George Hurley, Fangyi Luo, Kersang Chen, Gerald C. O'Sullivan, et al., "*Lactobacillus* and *Bifidobacterium* in Irritable Bowel Syndrome: Symptom Responses and Relationship to Cytokine Profiles," *Gastroenterology* 128, no. 3 (March 2005): 541–51, doi: 10.1053/j.gastro.2004.11.050.

54. Natalia Pedersen, Nynne Nyboe Andersen, Zsuzsanna Végh, Lisbeth Jensen, Dorit Vedel Ankersen, Maria Felding, Mette Hestetun Simonsen, Johan Burisch, and Pia Munkholm. "Ehealth: Low FODMAP Diet vs *Lactobacillus rhamnosus* GG in Irritable Bowel Syndrome," *World Journal of Gastroenterology* 20, no. 43 (November 21, 2014): 16215, doi:10.3748/wjg.v20.i43.16215; W. Feleszko et al., "Probiotic-Induced Suppression of Allergic Sensitization and Airway Inflammation Is Associated With an Increase of T Regulatory-Dependent Mechanisms in a Murine Model of Asthma," *Clinical & Experimental Allergy* 37, no. 4 (April 1, 2007): 498–505, doi:10.1111/j.1365-2222.2006.02629.x.

55. Lynne V. McFarland, "Systematic Review and Meta-Analysis of *Saccharomyces boulardii* in Adult Patients," *World Journal of Gastroenterology* 16, no. 18 (2010): 2202–22.

56. A. Venket Rao, Alison C. Bested, Tracey M. Beaulne, Martin A. Katzman, Christina Iorio, John M. Berardi, and Alan C. Logan, "A Randomized, Double-Blind, Placebo-Controlled Pilot Study of a Probiotic in Emotional Symptoms of Chronic Fatigue Syndrome," *Gut Pathogens* 1, no. 1 (March 19, 2009): 6, doi:10.1186/1757-4749-1-6.

57. A. Kato-Kataoka, K. Nishida, M. Takada, K. Suda, M. Kawai, K. Shimizu, A. Kushiro, et al., "Fermented Milk Containing *Lactobacillus casei* Strain Shirota Prevents the Onset of Physical Symptoms in Medical Students Under Academic Examination Stress," *Beneficial Microbes* 7, no. 2 (2016): 153–56, doi:10.3920/BM2015.0100.

58. Kirsten Tillisch, Jennifer Labus, Lisa Kilpatrick, Zhiguo Jiang, Jean Stains, Bahar Ebrat, Denis Guyonnet, et al., "Consumption of Fermented Milk Product With Probiotic Modulates Brain Activity," *Gastroenterology* 144, no. 7 (June 2013): 1394–1401, 1401–04, doi:10.1053/j.gastro.2013.02.043.

59. Kanti Bhooshan Pandey and Syed Ibrahim Rizvi, "Plant Polyphenols as Dietary Antioxidants in Human Health and Disease," *Oxidative Medicine and Cellular Longevity* 2, no. 5 (2009): 270–78.

60. Flore Depeint, George Tzortzis, Jelena Vulevic, Kerry I'anson, and Glenn R. Gibson, "Prebiotic Evaluation of a Novel Galactooligosaccharide Mixture Produced by the Enzymatic Activity of *Bifidobacterium bifidum* NCIMB 41171, in Healthy Humans: A Randomized, Double-Blind, Crossover, Placebo-Controlled Intervention Study," *American Journal of Clinical Nutrition* 87, no. 3 (March 2008): 785–91.

61. Jelena Vulevic, Aleksandra Juric, George Tzortzis, and Glenn R. Gibson. "A Mixture of Trans-Galactooligosaccharides Reduces Markers of Metabolic Syndrome and Modulates the Fecal Microbiota and Immune Function of Overweight Adults," *Journal of Nutrition* 143, no. 3 (March 2013): 324–31, doi:10.3945/jn.112.166132.

62. Kristin Schmidt, Philip J. Cowen, Catherine J. Harmer, George Tzortzis, Steven Errington, and Philip W. J. Burnet, "Prebiotic Intake Reduces the Waking Cortisol Response and Alters Emotional Bias in Healthy Volunteers," *Psychopharmacology* 232, no. 10 (December 3, 2014): 1793–1801, doi:10.1007/s00213-014-3810-0.

63. D. B. A. Silk, A. Davis, J. Vulevic, G. Tzortzis, and G. R. Gibson, "Clinical Trial: The Effects of a Trans-Galactooligosaccharide Prebiotic on Faecal Microbiota and Symptoms in Irritable Bowel Syndrome," *Alimentary Pharmacology & Therapeutics* 29, no. 5 (March 1, 2009): 508–18, doi:10.1111/j.1365-2036 .2008.03911.x.

64. Marloes A. A. Schepens, Anneke Rijnierse, Arjan J. Schonewille, Carolien Vink, Robert-Jan M. Brummer, Linette E. M. Willemsen, Roelof van der Meer,

and Ingeborg M. J. Bovee-Oudenhoven, "Dietary Calcium Decreases but Short-Chain Fructo-Oligosaccharides Increase Colonic Permeability in Rats," *British Journal of Nutrition* 104, no. 12 (December 2010): 1780–86, doi:10.1017/S0007114510002990.

65. Wang Li Scot E. Dowd, Bobbie Scurlock, Veronica Acosta-Martinez, and Mark Lyte, "Memory and Learning Behavior in Mice Is Temporally Associated With Diet-Induced Alterations in Gut Bacteria," *Physiology & Behavior* 96, no. 4–5 (March 23, 2009): 557–67, doi:10.1016/j.physbeh.2008.12.004.

66. Juliet Sutherland, Michelle Miles, Duncan Hedderley, Jessie Li, Sarah Devoy, Kevin Sutton, and Denis Lauren, "In Vitro Effects of Food Extracts on Selected Probiotic and Pathogenic Bacteria," *International Journal of Food Sciences and Nutrition* 60, no. 8 (December 1, 2009): 717–27, doi:10.3109/0963 7480802165650.

67. Ryan Paul Orgeron II, Angela Corbin, and Brigett Scott, "Sauerkraut: A Probiotic Superfood," *Functional Foods in Health and Disease* 6, no. 8 (August 30, 2016): 536–43.

68. Ngoc P. Ly, Augusto Litonjua, Diane R. Gold, and Juan C. Celedón, "Gut Microbiota, Probiotics, and Vitamin D: Interrelated Exposures Influencing Allergy, Asthma, and Obesity?" *Journal of Allergy and Clinical Immunology* 127, no. 5 (May 2011): 1087–94, doi:10.1016/j.jaci.2011.02.015.

69. Aurora Perez-Cornago, Almudena Sanchez-Villegas, Maira Bes-Rastrollo, Alfredo Gea, Patricio Molero, Francisca Lahortiga-Ramos, and Miguel Angel Martínez-González, "Intake of High-Fat Yogurt, but Not of Low-Fat Yogurt or Prebiotics, Is Related to Lower Risk of Depression in Women of the SUN Cohort Study," *Journal of Nutrition* 146, no. 9 (September 1, 2016): 1731–39, doi:10.3945/jn.116.233858.

70. Matthew R. Hilimire, Jordan E. DeVylder, and Catherine A. Forestell, "Fermented Foods, Neuroticism, and Social Anxiety: An Interaction Model," *Psychiatry Research* 228, no. 2 (August 15, 2015): 203–08, doi:10.1016/j.psychres.2015.04.023.

71. Marjukka Kolehmainen, Stine M. Ulven, Jussi Paananen, Vanessa de Mello, Ursula Schwab, Carsten Carlberg, Mari Myhrstad, et al., "Healthy Nordic Diet Downregulates the Expression of Genes Involved in Inflammation in Subcutaneous Adipose Tissue in Individuals With Features of the Metabolic Syndrome," *American Journal of Clinical Nutrition* 101, no. 1 (January 1, 2015): 228–39, doi:10.3945/ajcn.114.092783.

72. L. Brader, M. Uusitupa, L. O. Dragsted, and K. Hermansen, "Effects of an Isocaloric Healthy Nordic Diet on Ambulatory Blood Pressure in Metabolic Syndrome: A Randomized SYSDIET Sub-Study," *European Journal*

of Clinical Nutrition 68, no. 1 (January 2014): 57–63, doi:10.1038 /ejcn.2013.192.

73. Sanne K. Poulsen, Anette Due, Andreas B. Jordy, Bente Kiens, Ken D. Stark, Steen Stender, Claus Holst, Arne Astrup, and Thomas M. Larsen, "Health Effect of the New Nordic Diet in Adults With Increased Waist Circumference: A 6-Mo Randomized Controlled Trial," *American Journal of Clinical Nutrition* 99, no. 1 (January 1, 2014): 35–45, doi:10.3945/ajcn.113.069393.

74. James E. Gangwisch, Lauren Hale, Lorena Garcia, Dolores Malaspina, Mark G. Opler, Martha E. Payne, Rebecca C. Rossom, and Dorothy Lane, "High Glycemic Index Diet as a Risk Factor for Depression: Analyses From the Women's Health Initiative," *American Journal of Clinical Nutrition* (June 24, 2015): ajcn103846, doi:10.3945/ajcn.114.103846.

75. Felice N. Jacka, Eivind Ystrom, Anne Lise Brantsaeter, Evalill Karevold, Christine Roth, Margaretha Haugen, Helle Margrete Meltzer, Synnve Schjolberg, and Michael Berk, "Maternal and Early Postnatal Nutrition and Mental Health of Offspring by Age 5 Years: A Prospective Cohort Study," *Journal of the American Academy of Child and Adolescent Psychiatry* 52, no. 10 (October 2013): 1038–47, doi:10.1016/j.jaac.2013.07.002.

76. Felice N. Jacka, Arnstein Mykletun, Michael Berk, Ingvar Bjelland, and Grethe S. Tell, "The Association Between Habitual Diet Quality and the Common Mental Disorders in Community-Dwelling Adults: The Hordaland Health Study," *Psychosomatic Medicine* 73, no. 6 (August 2011): 483–90, doi:10.1097/PSY.0b013e318222831a.

77. Y. Benno, K. Suzuki, K. Suzuki, K. Narisawa, W. R. Bruce, and T. Mitsuoka, "Comparison of the Fecal Microflora in Rural Japanese and Urban Canadians," *Microbiology and Immunology* 30, no. 6 (1986): 521–32.

78. Tanya Yatsunenko, Federico E. Rey, Mark J. Manary, Indi Trehan, Maria Gloria Dominguez-Bello, Monica Contreras, Magda Magris, et al., "Human Gut Microbiome Viewed Across Age and Geography," *Nature* 486, no. 7402 (June 14, 2012): 222–27, doi:10.1038/nature11053.

79. P. D. Cani, A. M. Neyrinck, F. Fava, C. Knauf, R. G. Burcelin, K. M. Tuohy, G. R. Gibson, and N. M. Delzenne,. "Selective Increases of *Bifidobacteria* in Gut Microflora Improve High-Fat-Diet-Induced Diabetes in Mice Through a Mechanism Associated With Endotoxaemia," *Diabetologia* 50, no. 11 (November 2007): 2374–83, doi:10.1007/s00125-007-0791-0.

80. Swaroop Pendyala, Jeanne M. Walker, and Peter R. Holt, "A High-Fat Diet Is Associated With Endotoxemia That Originates From the Gut," *Gastroenterology* 142, no. 5 (May 2012): 1100–01.e2, doi:10.1053/j.gastro.2012 .01.034.

81. Terry L. Davidson, Andrew Monnot, Adelai U. Neal, Ashley A. Martin, J. Josiah Horton, and Wei Zheng, "The Effects of a High-Energy Diet on Hippocampal-Dependent Discrimination Performance and Blood-Brain Barrier Integrity Differ for Diet-Induced Obese and Diet-Resistant Rats," *Physiology & Behavior* 107, no. 1 (August 20, 2012): 26–33, doi:10.1016/j.physbeh.2012.05.015.

82. Ina Bergheim, Synia Weber, Miriam Vos, Sigrid Krämer, Valentina Volynets, Seline Kaserouni, Craig J. McClain, and Stephan C. Bischoff, "Antibiotics Protect Against Fructose-Induced Hepatic Lipid Accumulation in Mice: Role of Endotoxin," *Journal of Hepatology* 48, no. 6 (June 2008): 983–92, doi:10.1016/j.jhep.2008.01.035.

83. Arthur N. Westover and Lauren B. Marangell, "A Cross-National Relationship Between Sugar Consumption and Major Depression?" *Depression and Anxiety* 16, no. 3 (2002): 118–20, doi:10.1002/da.10054.

84. Jiadong Sun, Hang Ma, Navindra P. Seeram, and David Chapman Rowley, "Detection of Inulin, a Prebiotic Polysaccharide in Maple Syrup," *Journal of Agricultural and Food Chemistry* (September 9, 2016), doi:10.1021/acs.jafc.6b03139.

85. María Luz Sanz, Nikolaos Polemis, Valle Morales, Nieves Corzo, Alexandra Drakoularakou, Glenn R. Gibson, and Robert A. Rastall, "In Vitro Investigation Into the Potential Prebiotic Activity of Honey Oligosaccharides," *Journal of Agricultural and Food Chemistry* 53, no. 8 (April 1, 2005): 2914–21, doi:10.1021/jf0500684.

86. Lynne M. Chepulis, Nicola J. Starkey, Joseph R. Waas, and Peter C. Molan, "The Effects of Long-Term Honey, Sucrose or Sugar-Free Diets on Memory and Anxiety in Rats," *Physiology & Behavior* 97, no. 3–4 (June 22, 2009): 359–68, doi:10.1016/j.physbeh.2009.03.001.

87. Mustafa Kassim, Mouna Achoui, Marzida Mansor, and Kamaruddin Mohd Yusoff. "The Inhibitory Effects of Gelam Honey and Its Extracts on Nitric Oxide and Prostaglandin E(2) in Inflammatory Tissues," *Fitoterapia* 81, no. 8 (December 2010): 1196–1201, doi:10.1016/j.fitote.2010.07.024.

88. Alan C. Logan and Martin Katzman, "Major Depressive Disorder: Probiotics May Be an Adjuvant Therapy," *Medical Hypotheses* 64, no. 3 (2005): 533–38. doi:10.1016/j.mehy.2004.08.019.

89. Fabienne Laugerette, Jean-Pierre Furet, Cyrille Debard, Patricia Daira, Emmanuelle Loizon, Alain Géloën, Christophe O. Soulage, et al., "Oil Composition of High-Fat Diet Affects Metabolic Inflammation Differently in Connection With Endotoxin Receptors in Mice," *American Journal of Physiology. Endocrinology and Metabolism* 302, no. 3 (February 1, 2012): E374–386, doi:10.1152/ajpendo.00314.2011.

90. Matteo M. Pusceddu, Sahar El Aidy, Fiona Crispie, Orla O'Sullivan, Paul Cotter, Catherine Stanton, Philip Kelly, John F. Cryan, and Timothy G. Dinan, "N-3 Polyunsaturated Fatty Acids (PUFAs) Reverse the Impact of Early-Life Stress on the Gut Microbiota," *PLOS ONE* 10, no. 10 (October 1, 2015): e0139721, doi:10.1371/journal.pone.0139721.

91. Sandrine P. Claus, Hervé Guillou, and Sandrine Ellero-Simatos, "The Gut Microbiota: A Major Player in the Toxicity of Environmental Pollutants?" *Npj Biofilms and Microbiomes* 2 (May 4, 2016): 16003, doi:10.1038/npjbiofilms.2016.3.

92. Veronica L. Peterson, Nicholas J. Jury, Raúl Cabrera-Rubio, Lorraine A. Draper, Fiona Crispie, Paul D. Cotter, Timothy G. Dinan, Andrew Holmes, and John F. Cryan, "Drunk Bugs: Chronic Vapour Alcohol Exposure Induces Marked Changes in the Gut Microbiome in Mice," *Behavioural Brain Research* 323 (April 14, 2017): 172–76, doi:10.1016/j.bbr.2017.01.049.

93. Elizabeth E. Devore, Jae Hee Kang, Monique M. B. Breteler, and Francine Grodstein, "Dietary Intakes of Berries and Flavonoids in Relation to Cognitive Decline," *Annals of Neurology* 72, no. 1 (July 2012): 135–43, doi:10.1002/ana.23594.

94. Tze-Pin Ng, Peak-Chiang Chiam, Theresa Lee, Hong-Choon Chua, Leslie Lim, and Ee-Heok Kua, "Curry Consumption and Cognitive Function in the Elderly," *American Journal of Epidemiology* 164, no. 9 (November 1, 2006): 898–906, doi:10.1093/aje/kwj267.

95. Stefan Bereswill, Melba Muñoz, André Fischer, Rita Plickert, Lea-Maxie Haag, Bettina Otto, Anja A. Kühl, Christoph Loddenkemper, Ulf B. Göbel, and Markus M. Heimesaat, "Anti-Inflammatory Effects of Resveratrol, Curcumin and Simvastatin in Acute Small Intestinal Inflammation," *PloS One* 5, no. 12 (2010): e15099, doi:10.1371/journal.pone.0015099.

96. Patrice D. Cani and Amandine Everard, "Keeping Gut Lining at Bay: Impact of Emulsifiers," *Trends in Endocrinology & Metabolism* 26, no. 6 (June 1, 2015): 273–74, doi:10.1016/j.tem.2015.03.009; Benoit Chassaing, Omry Koren, Julia K. Goodrich, Angela C. Poole, Shanthi Srinivasan, Ruth E. Ley, and Andrew T. Gewirtz, "Dietary Emulsifiers Impact the Mouse Gut Microbiota Promoting Colitis and Metabolic Syndrome," *Nature* 519, no. 7541 (March 5, 2015): 92–96, doi:10.1038/nature14232.

97. Patrice D. Cani, "Metabolism: Dietary Emulsifiers—Sweepers of the Gut Lining?" *Nature Reviews Endocrinology* 11, no. 6 (June 2015): 319–20, doi:10.1038/nrendo.2015.59.

98. Lucio Lombardo, Monica Foti, Olga Ruggia, and Andrea Chiecchio, "Increased Incidence of Small Intestinal Bacterial Overgrowth During Proton Pump

Inhibitor Therapy," *Clinical Gastroenterology and Hepatology: The Official Clinical Practice Journal of the American Gastroenterological Association* 8, no. 6 (June 2010): 504–08, doi:10.1016/j.cgh.2009.12.022.

99. Robert C. Heading, Hubert Mönnikes, Anne Tholen, and Holger Schmitt, "Prediction of Response to PPI Therapy and Factors Influencing Treatment Outcome in Patients With GORD: A Prospective Pragmatic Trial Using Pantoprazole," *BMC Gastroenterology* 11 (2011): 52, doi:10.1186/1471-230X-11-52.

100. Matthew A. Jackson, Julia K. Goodrich, Maria-Emanuela Maxan, Daniel E. Freedberg, Julian A. Abrams, Angela C. Poole, Jessica L. Sutter, et al., "Proton Pump Inhibitors Alter the Composition of the Gut Microbiota," *Gut* (December 30, 2015): gutjnl-2015-310861, doi:10.1136/gutjnl-2015-310861.

101. Charlie T. Seto, Patricio Jeraldo, Robert Orenstein, Nicholas Chia, and John K. DiBaise, "Prolonged Use of a Proton Pump Inhibitor Reduces Microbial Diversity: Implications for Clostridium Difficile Susceptibility," *Microbiome* 2 (2014): 42, doi:10.1186/2049-2618-2-42.

102. B. I. Hirschowitz, J. Worthington, and J. Mohnen, "Vitamin B_{12} Deficiency in Hypersecretors During Long-Term Acid Suppression With Proton Pump Inhibitors," *Alimentary Pharmacology & Therapeutics* 27, no. 11 (June 1, 2008): 1110–21, doi:10.1111/j.1365-2036.2008.03658.x.

103. Louis Bherer, Kirk I. Erickson, and Teresa Liu-Ambrose, "A Review of the Effects of Physical Activity and Exercise on Cognitive and Brain Functions in Older Adults," *Journal of Aging Research* 2013 (2013), doi:10.1155/2013/657508.

104. Lukas Schwingshackl, Benjamin Missbach, Sofia Dias, Jürgen König, and Georg Hoffmann, "Impact of Different Training Modalities on Glycaemic Control and Blood Lipids in Patients With Type 2 Diabetes: A Systematic Review and Network Meta-Analysis," *Diabetologia* 57, no. 9 (September 2014): 1789–97, doi:10.1007/s00125-014-3303-z.

105. Elisabet Johannesson, Magnus Simrén, Hans Strid, Antal Bajor, and Riadh Sadik, "Physical Activity Improves Symptoms in Irritable Bowel Syndrome: A Randomized Controlled Trial," *American Journal of Gastroenterology* 106, no. 5 (May 2011): 915–22, doi:10.1038/ajg.2010.480.

106. Andrew Harkin, "Muscling in on Depression," *New England Journal of Medicine* 371, no. 24 (December 11, 2014): 2333–34, doi:10.1056/NEJMcibr1411568.

107. Orla O'Sullivan, Owen Cronin, Siobhan F Clarke, Eileen F Murphy, Micheal G Molloy, Fergus Shanahan, and Paul D Cotter, "Exercise and the Microbiota," *Gut Microbes* 6, no. 2 (March 24, 2015): 131–36, doi:10.1080/19490976.2015.1011875.

108. Xin-Yun Lu, Chung Sub Kim, Alan Frazer, and Wei Zhang, "Leptin: A Potential Novel Antidepressant," *Proceedings of the National Academy of Sciences of the United States of America*, 103, no. 5 (2006): 1593–98, doi:10.1073/pnas.0508901103.

109. Jonathan Breton et al., "Gut Commensal E. Coli Proteins Activate Host Satiety Pathways Following Nutrient-Induced Bacterial Growth," *Cell Metabolism* 23, no. 2 (February 9, 2016): 324–34, doi:10.1016/j.cmet.2015.10.017.

110. B. C. Finger, T. G. Dinan, and J. F. Cryan, "Behavioral Satiety Sequence "in a Genetic Mouse Model of Obesity: Effects of Ghrelin Receptor Ligands," *Behavioural Pharmacology* 22, no. 7 (2011): 624–32, doi:10.1097/FBP.0b013e32834afee6; Harriët Schellekens, Beate C. Finger, Timothy G. Dinan, and John F. Cryan, "Ghrelin Signalling and Obesity: At the Interface of Stress, Mood and Food Reward," *Pharmacology & Therapeutics* 135, no. 3 (September 2012): 316–26, doi:10.1016/j.pharmthera.2012.06.004.

111. John K. DiBaise, Daniel N. Frank, and Ruchi Mathur, "Impact of the Gut Microbiota on the Development of Obesity: Current Concepts," *American Journal of Gastroenterology Supplements* 1, no. 1 (July 2012): 22–27, doi:10.1038/ajgsup.2012.5.

112. Maria Carlota Dao, Amandine Everard, Judith Aron-Wisnewsky, Nataliya Sokolovska, Edi Prifti, Eric O. Verger, Brandon D. Kayser, et al., "*Akkermansia muciniphila* and Improved Metabolic Health During a Dietary Intervention in Obesity: Relationship With Gut Microbiome Richness and Ecology," *Gut* 65, no. 3 (March 2016): 426–36, doi:10.1136/gutjnl-2014-308778.

113. Chenhong Zhang, Shoufeng Li, Liu Yang, Ping Huang, Wenjun Li, Shengyue Wang, Guoping Zhao, et al., "Structural Modulation of Gut Microbiota in Life-Long Calorie-Restricted Mice," *Nature Communications* 4 (July 16, 2013): 2163, doi:10.1038/ncomms3163.

114. Burke A. Cunha, "Antibiotic Side Effects," *Medical Clinics of North America* 85, no. 1 (January 1, 2001): 149–85, doi:10.1016/S0025-7125(05)70309-6.

115. A. Armuzzi, F. Cremonini, F. Bartolozzi, F. Canducci, M. Candelli, V. Ojetti, G. Cammarota, et al., "The Effect of Oral Administration of *Lactobacillus* GG on Antibiotic-Associated Gastrointestinal Side-Effects During *Helicobacter pylori* Eradication Therapy," *Alimentary Pharmacology & Therapeutics* 15, no. 2 (February 2001): 163–69; Simo Siitonen, Heikki Vapaatalo, Seppo Salminen, Ariel Gordin, Maija Saxelin, Raija Wikberg, and Anna-Leena Kirkkola, "Effect of *Lactobacillus* GG Yoghurt in Prevention of Antibiotic Associated Diarrhoea," *Annals of Medicine* 22, no. 1 (January 1, 1990): 57–59, doi:10.3109/07853899009147243.

116. Erwin G. Zoetendal, Atte von Wright, Terttu Vilpponen-Salmela, Kaouther Ben-Amor, Antoon D. L. Akkermans, and Willem M. de Vos, "Mucosa-Associated Bacteria in the Human Gastrointestinal Tract Are Uniformly Distributed Along the Colon and Differ From the Community Recovered From Feces," *Applied and Environmental Microbiology* 68, no. 7 (July 2002): 3401–07.

CHAPTER 8
1. Paul J. Kennedy, John F Cryan, Timothy G Dinan, and Gerard Clarke, "Irritable Bowel Syndrome: A Microbiome-Gut-Brain Axis Disorder?" *World Journal of Gastroenterology : WJG* 20, no. 39 (October 21, 2014): 14105–25, doi:10.3748/wjg.v20.i39.14105.
2. Siobhain M. O'Mahony. Julian R. Marchesi, Paul Scully, Caroline Codling, Anne-Marie Ceolho, Eamonn M. M. Quigley, John F. Cryan, and Timothy G. Dinan, "Early Life Stress Alters Behavior, Immunity, and Microbiota in Rats: Implications for Irritable Bowel Syndrome and Psychiatric Illnesses," *Biological Psychiatry* 65, no. 3 (February 1, 2009): 263–67, doi:10.1016/j.biopsych.2008.06.026.
3. P. J. Kennedy, G. Clarke, A. O'Neill, J. A. Groeger, E. M. M. Quigley, F. Shanahan, J. F. Cryan, and T. G. Dinan, "Cognitive Performance in Irritable Bowel Syndrome: Evidence of a Stress-Related Impairment in Visuospatial Memory," *Psychological Medicine* 44, no. 7 (May 2014): 1553–66, doi:10.1017/S0033291713002171.
4. E. Stermer, H. Bar, and N. Levy, "Chronic Functional Gastrointestinal Symptoms in Holocaust Survivors," *American Journal of Gastroenterology* 86, no. 4 (April 1991): 417–22.
5. Tamira K. Klooker, Breg Braak, Rebecca C. Painter, Susanne R. de Rooij, Ruurd M. van Elburg, Rene M. van den Wijngaard, Tessa J. Roseboom, and Guy E. Boeckxstaens, "Exposure to Severe Wartime Conditions in Early Life Is Associated With an Increased Risk of Irritable Bowel Syndrome: A Population-Based Cohort Study," *American Journal of Gastroenterology* 104, no. 9 (September 2009): 2250–56, doi:10.1038/ajg.2009.282.
6. Timothy G. Dinan, John Cryan, Fergus Shanahan, P. W. Napoleon Keeling, and Eamonn M. M. Quigley, "IBS: An Epigenetic Perspective," *Nature Reviews Gastroenterology and Hepatology* 7, no. 8 (August 2010): 465–71, doi:10.1038/nrgastro.2010.99.
7. Katri S. Juntunen, David E. Laaksonen, Karin Autio, Leo K. Niskanen, Jens J. Holst, Kari E. Savolainen, Kirsi-Helena Liukkonen, Kaisa S. Poutanen, and Hannu M. Mykkänen, "Structural Differences Between Rye and Wheat Breads but Not Total Fiber Content May Explain the Lower Postprandial Insulin

Response to Rye Bread," *American Journal of Clinical Nutrition* 78, no. 5 (November 1, 2003): 957–64.

8. Petteri Kallio, Marjukka Kolehmainen, David E. Laaksonen, Jani Kekäläinen, Titta Salopuro, Katariina Sivenius, Leena Pulkkinen, et al., "Dietary Carbohydrate Modification Induces Alterations in Gene Expression in Abdominal Subcutaneous Adipose Tissue in Persons With the Metabolic Syndrome: The FUNGENUT Study," *American Journal of Clinical Nutrition* 85, no. 5 (May 2007): 1417–27.

9. Margaret F. Gregor and Gökhan S. Hotamisligil, "Inflammatory Mechanisms in Obesity," *Annual Review of Immunology* 29 (2011): 415–45, doi:10.1146/annurev-immunol-031210-101322.

10. Liam O'Mahony, Jane McCarthy, Peter Kelly, George Hurley, Fangyi Luo, Kersang Chen, Gerald C. O'Sullivan, et al., "*Lactobacillus* and *Bifidobacterium* in Irritable Bowel Syndrome: Symptom Responses and Relationship to Cytokine Profiles," *Gastroenterology* 128, no. 3 (March 2005): 541–51, doi:10.1053/j.gastro.2004.11.050.

11. D. B. A. Silk, A. Davis, J. Vulevic, G. Tzortzis, and G. R. Gibson, "Clinical Trial: The Effects of a Trans-Galactooligosaccharide Prebiotic on Faecal Microbiota and Symptoms in Irritable Bowel Syndrome," *Alimentary Pharmacology & Therapeutics* 29, no. 5 (March 1, 2009): 508–18, doi:10.1111/j.1365-2036.2008.03911.x.

12. David L. Suskind, Mitchell J. Brittnacher, Ghassan Wahbeh, Michele L. Shaffer, Hillary S. Hayden, Xuan Qin, Namita Singh, et al., "Fecal Microbial Transplant Effect on Clinical Outcomes and Fecal Microbiome in Active Crohn's Disease," *Inflammatory Bowel Diseases* 21, no. 3 (March 2015): 556–63, doi:10.1097/MIB.0000000000000307.

13. G. Hoarau, P. K. Mukherjee, C. Gower-Rousseau, C. Hager, J. Chandra, M. A. Retuerto, C. Neut, et al., "Bacteriome and Mycobiome Interactions Underscore Microbial Dysbiosis in Familial Crohn's Disease," *mBio* 7, no. 5 (November 2, 2016): e01250-16, doi:10.1128/mBio.01250-16.

14. Wei Wang, Liping Chen, Rui Zhou, Xiaobing Wang, Lu Song, Sha Huang, Ge Wang, and Bing Xia, "Increased Proportions of *Bifidobacterium* and the *Lactobacillus* Group and Loss of Butyrate-Producing Bacteria in Inflammatory Bowel Disease," *Journal of Clinical Microbiology* 52, no. 2 (February 2014): 398–406, doi:10.1128/JCM.01500-13.

15. César de la Fuente-Núñez, Fany Reffuveille, Evan F. Haney, Suzana K. Straus, and Robert E. W. Hancock, "Broad-Spectrum Anti-Biofilm Peptide That Targets a Cellular Stress Response," *PLOS Pathogens* 10, no. 5 (May 22, 2014): e1004152, doi:10.1371/journal.ppat.1004152.

16. S. N. Salem and K. S. Shubair, "Non-Specific Ulcerative Colitis in Bedouin Arabs," *Lancet* 289, no. 7488 (March 1967): 473–75, doi:10.1016/S0140-6736(67)91094-X.

17. Charles N. Bernstein, Sunny Singh, Lesley A. Graff, John R. Walker, Norine Miller, and Mary Cheang, "A Prospective Population-Based Study of Triggers of Symptomatic Flares in IBD," *American Journal of Gastroenterology* 105, no. 9 (September 2010): 1994–2002, doi:10.1038/ajg.2010.140.

18. Hans-Christian Deter, Wolfram Keller, Jörn von Wietersheim, Günther Jantschek, Rainer Duchmann, Martin Zeitz, and German Study Group on Psychosocial Intervention in Crohn's Disease, "Psychological Treatment May Reduce the Need for Healthcare in Patients With Crohn's Disease," *Inflammatory Bowel Diseases* 13, no. 6 (June 2007): 745–52, doi:10.1002/ibd.20068.

19. F. C. Dohan and J. C. Grasberger, "Relapsed Schizophrenics: Earlier Discharge From the Hospital After Cereal-Free, Milk-Free Diet," *American Journal of Psychiatry* 130, no. 6 (June 1973): 685–88, doi:10.1176/ajp.130.6.685.

20. A. De Santis, G. Addolorato, A. Romito, S. Caputo, A. Giordano, G. Gambassi, C. Taranto, R. Manna, and G. Gasbarrini. "Schizophrenic Symptoms and SPECT Abnormalities in a Coeliac Patient: Regression After a Gluten-Free Diet," *Journal of Internal Medicine* 242, no. 5 (November 1997): 421–23.

21. Jessica R. Jackson, William W. Eaton, Nicola G. Cascella, Alessio Fasano, and Deanna L. Kelly, "Neurologic and Psychiatric Manifestations of Celiac Disease and Gluten Sensitivity," *Psychiatric Quarterly* 83, no. 1 (March 2012): 91–102, doi:10.1007/s11126-011-9186-y.

22. G. Kristjánsson, P. Venge, and R. Hällgren, "Mucosal Reactivity to Cow's Milk Protein in Coeliac Disease," *Clinical and Experimental Immunology* 147, no. 3 (March 2007): 449–55, doi:10.1111/j.1365-2249.2007.03298.x.

23. Francisco Cabrera-Chávez, Stefania Iametti, Matteo Miriani, Ana M. Calderón de la Barca, Gianfranco Mamone, and Francesco Bonomi, "Maize Prolamins Resistant to Peptic-Tryptic Digestion Maintain Immune-Recognition by IgA From Some Celiac Disease Patients," *Plant Foods for Human Nutrition (Dordrecht, Netherlands)* 67, no. 1 (March 2012): 24, 30, doi:10.1007/s11130-012-0274-4.

24. Victor F. Zevallos, H. Julia Ellis, Tanja Šuligoj, L. Irene Herencia, and Paul J. Ciclitira, "Variable Activation of Immune Response by Quinoa (*Chenopodium quinoa* Willd.) Prolamins in Celiac Disease," *American Journal of Clinical Nutrition* 96, no. 2 (August 2012): 337–44, doi:10.3945/ajcn.111.030684.

25. Aristo Vojdani and Igal Tarash, "Cross-Reaction Between Gliadin and Different Food and Tissue Antigens," *Food and Nutrition Sciences* 4, no. 1 (2013): 20–32, doi:10.4236/fns.2013.41005.

26. Chihiro Morita, Hirokazu Tsuji, Tomokazu Hata, Motoharu Gondo, Shu Takakura, Keisuke Kawai, Kazufumi Yoshihara, et al., "Gut Dysbiosis in Patients With Anorexia Nervosa," *PloS One* 10, no. 12 (2015): e0145274, doi:10.1371/journal.pone.0145274.

27. Michael E. Benros, Berit L. Waltoft, Merete Nordentoft, Søren D. Ostergaard, William W. Eaton, Jesper Krogh, and Preben B. Mortensen. "Autoimmune Diseases and Severe Infections as Risk Factors for Mood Disorders: A Nationwide Study," *JAMA Psychiatry* 70, no. 8 (August 2013): 812–20, doi:10.1001/jamapsychiatry.2013.1111.

28. Susan C. Kleiman, Hunna J. Watson, Emily C. Bulik-Sullivan, Eun Young Huh, Lisa M. Tarantino, Cynthia M. Bulik, and Ian M. Carroll, "The Intestinal Microbiota in Acute Anorexia Nervosa and During Renourishment: Relationship to Depression, Anxiety, and Eating Disorder Psychopathology," *Psychosomatic Medicine* 77, no. 9 (December 2015): 969–81, doi:10.1097/PSY.0000000000000247.

29. Chihiro Morita, Hirokazu Tsuji, Tomokazu Hata, Motoharu Gondo, Shu Takakura, Keisuke Kawai, Kazufumi Yoshihara, et al., "Gut Dysbiosis in Patients With Anorexia Nervosa," *PLOS ONE* 10, no. 12 (December 18, 2015): e0145274, doi:10.1371/journal.pone.0145274.

30. Esther Nova, Julia Wärnberg, Sonia Gómez-Martínez, Ligia E. Díaz, Javier Romeo, and Ascensión Marcos, "Immunomodulatory Effects of Probiotics in Different Stages of Life," *British Journal of Nutrition* 98, no. S1 (October 2007): S90–95, doi:10.1017/S0007114507832983; Esther Nova, Olga Toro, Pilar Varela, Irene López-Vidriero, Gonzalo Morandé, and Ascensión Marcos, "Effects of a Nutritional Intervention With Yogurt on Lymphocyte Subsets and Cytokine Production Capacity in Anorexia Nervosa Patients," *European Journal of Nutrition* 45, no. 4 (June 2006): 225–33, doi:10.1007/s00394-006-0589-8.

31. F. S. Luppino, L. M. de Wit, P. F. Bouvy, et al., "Overweight, Obesity, and Depression: A Systematic Review and Meta-Analysis of Longitudinal Studies," *Archives of General Psychiatry* 67, no. 3 (March 1, 2010): 220–29, doi:10.1001/archgenpsychiatry.2010.2.

32. The Nutrition Source, "An Epidemic of Obesity: U.S. Obesity Trends," Harvard T.H. Chan School of Public Health, accessed September 9, 2016, www.hsph.harvard.edu/nutritionsource/an-epidemic-of-obesity.

33. Annadora J. Bruce-Keller, Jeffrey N. Keller, and Christopher D. Morrison, "Obesity and Vulnerability of the CNS," *Biochimica et Biophysica Acta (BBA)–*

Molecular Basis of Disease 1792, no. 5 (May 2009): 395–400, doi:10.1016 /j.bbadis.2008.10.004.

34. Annadora J. Bruce-Keller, J. Michael Salbaum, Meng Luo, Eugene Blanchard, Christopher M. Taylor, David A. Welsh, and Hans-Rudolf Berthoud, "Obese-Type Gut Microbiota Induce Neurobehavioral Changes in the Absence of Obesity," *Biological Psychiatry* 77, no. 7 (April 1, 2015): 607–15, doi:10.1016 /j.biopsych.2014.07.012.

35. Johanna Ilmonen, Erika Isolauri, Tuija Poussa, and Kirsi Laitinen, "Impact of Dietary Counselling and Probiotic Intervention on Maternal Anthropo-metric Measurements During and After Pregnancy: A Randomized Placebo-Controlled Trial," *Clinical Nutrition (Edinburgh, Scotland)* 30, no. 2 (April 2011): 156–64, doi:10.1016/j.clnu.2010.09.009.

36. Y. Kadooka, M. Sato, K. Imaizumi, A. Ogawa, K. Ikuyama, Y. Akai, M. Okano, M. Kagoshima, and T. Tsuchida, "Regulation of Abdominal Adiposity by Probiotics (*Lactobacillus gasseri* SBT2055) in Adults With Obese Tendencies in a Randomized Controlled Trial," *European Journal of Clinical Nutrition* 64, no. 6 (June 2010): 636–43, doi:10.1038/ejcn.2010.19.

37. Jill A. Parnell and Raylene A. Reimer, "Weight Loss During Oligofructose Supplementation Is Associated With Decreased Ghrelin and Increased Pep-tide YY in Overweight and Obese Adults," *American Journal of Clinical Nutrition* 89, no. 6 (June 2009): 1751–59, doi:10.3945/ajcn.2009.27465.

38. Ryan J. Anderson, Kenneth E. Freedland, Ray E. Clouse, and Patrick J. Lustman, "The Prevalence of Comorbid Depression in Adults With Diabe-tes," *Diabetes Care* 24, no. 6 (June 1, 2001): 1069–78, doi:10.2337/diacare.24 .6.1069.

39. Elaine Patterson, Paul M. Ryan, John F. Cryan, Timothy G. Dinan, R. Paul Ross, Gerald F. Fitzgerald, and Catherine Stanton, "Gut Microbiota, Obesity and Diabetes." *Postgraduate Medical Journal* 92, no. 1087 (May 2016): 286–300, doi:10.1136/postgradmedj-2015-133285.

40. Camila Moroti, Loyanne Francine Souza Magri, Marcela de Rezende Costa, Daniela C. U. Cavallini, and Katia Sivieri, "Effect of the Consumption of a New Symbiotic Shake on Glycemia and Cholesterol Levels in Elderly People With Type 2 Diabetes Mellitus," *Lipids in Health and Disease* 11 (2012): 29, doi:10.1186/1476-511X-11-29.

41. Se Jin Song, Christian Lauber, Elizabeth K Costello, Catherine A Lozupone, Gregory Humphrey, Donna Berg-Lyons, J Gregory Caporaso, et al. "Cohab-iting Family Members Share Microbiota With One Another and With Their Dogs," *eLife* 2 (April 16, 2013), doi:10.7554/eLife.00458; Julia K. Goodrich, Jillian L. Waters, Angela C. Poole, Jessica L. Sutter, Omry Koren, Ran

Blekhman, Michelle Beaumont, et al., "Human Genetics Shape the Gut Microbiome," *Cell* 159, no. 4 (November 6, 2014): 789–99, doi:10.1016 /j.cell.2014.09.053.

42. Elisabeth Svensson, Erzsébet Horváth-Puhó, Reimar W. Thomsen, Jens Christian Djurhuus, Lars Pedersen, Per Borghammer, and Henrik Toft Sørensen, "Vagotomy and Subsequent Risk of Parkinson's Disease," *Annals of Neurology* 78, no. 4 (October 1, 2015): 522–29, doi:10.1002/ana.24448.

43. Timothy R. Sampson, Justine W. Debelius, Taren Thron, Stefan Janssen, Gauri G. Shastri, Zehra Esra Ilhan, Collin Challis, et al. "Gut Microbiota Regulate Motor Deficits and Neuroinflammation in a Model of Parkinson's Disease," *Cell* 167, no. 6 (December 1, 2016): 1469–80.e12, doi:10.1016 /j.cell.2016.11.018.

44. Filip Scheperjans, Velma Aho, Pedro A. B. Pereira, Kaisa Koskinen, Lars Paulin, Eero Pekkonen, Elena Haapaniemi, et al., "Gut Microbiota Are Related to Parkinson's Disease and Clinical Phenotype," *Movement Disorders: Official Journal of the Movement Disorder Society* 30, no. 3 (March 2015): 350–58, doi:10.1002/mds.26069.

45. Michela Barichella, Agnieszka Marczewska, Roberta De Notaris, Antonella Vairo, Cinzia Baldo, Andrea Mauri, Chiara Savardi, and Gianni Pezzoli, "Special Low-Protein Foods Ameliorate Postprandial Off in Patients With Advanced Parkinson's Disease," *Movement Disorders* 21, no. 10 (October 1, 2006): 1682–87, doi:10.1002/mds.21003.

46. E. Cassani, G. Privitera, G. Pezzoli, C. Pusani, C. Madio, L. Iorio, and M. Barichella, "Use of Probiotics for the Treatment of Constipation in Parkinson's Disease Patients," *Minerva Gastroenterologica E Dietologica* 57, no. 2 (June 2011): 117–21.

47. David L. Hare, Samia R. Toukhsati, Peter Johansson, and Tiny Jaarsma, "Depression and Cardiovascular Disease: A Clinical Review," *European Heart Journal*, November 26, 2013, eht462, doi:10.1093/eurheartj/eht462.

48. Jürgen Barth, Martina Schumacher, and Christoph Herrmann-Lingen, "Depression as a Risk Factor for Mortality in Patients With Coronary Heart Disease: A Meta-Analysis," *Psychosomatic Medicine* 66, no. 6 (December 2004): 802–13, doi:10.1097/01.psy.0000146332.53619.b2; Reiner Rugulies, "Depression as a Predictor for Coronary Heart Disease," *American Journal of Preventive Medicine* 23, no. 1 (July 1, 2002): 51–61, doi:10.1016/ S0749-3797(02)00439-7.

49. Karim El Kholy, Robert J. Genco, and Thomas E. Van Dyke, "Oral Infections and Cardiovascular Disease," *Trends in Endocrinology & Metabolism* 26, no. 6 (June 1, 2015): 315–21, doi:10.1016/j.tem.2015.03.001.

50. Liesbeth Allais, Frederiek-Maarten Kerckhof, Stephanie Verschuere, Ken R. Bracke, Rebecca De Smet, Debby Laukens, Pieter Van den Abbeele, et al., "Chronic Cigarette Smoke Exposure Induces Microbial and Inflammatory Shifts and Mucin Changes in the Murine Gut," *Environmental Microbiology* 18, no. 5 (May 2016): 1352–63, doi:10.1111/1462-2920.12934.

51. Takeshi Kitai, Jennifer Kirsop, and W. H. Wilson Tang, "Exploring the Microbiome in Heart Failure," *Current Heart Failure Reports* 13, no. 2 (April 2016): 103–09, doi:10.1007/s11897-016-0285-9.

52. Julian L. Griffin, Xinzhu Wang, and Elizabeth Stanley, "Does Our Gut Microbiome Predict Cardiovascular Risk? A Review of the Evidence From Metabolomics," *Circulation: Cardiovascular Genetics* 8, no. 1 (February 1, 2015): 187–91, doi:10.1161/CIRCGENETICS.114.000219.

53. Ming-liang Chen, Long Yi, Yong Zhang, Xi Zhou, Li Ran, Jining Yang, Jundong Zhu, Qian-yong Zhang, and Man-tian Mi, "Resveratrol Attenuates Trimethylamine-N-Oxide (TMAO)-Induced Atherosclerosis by Regulating TMAO Synthesis and Bile Acid Metabolism via Remodeling of the Gut Microbiota," *mBio* 7, no. 2 (May 4, 2016): e02210-15, doi:10.1128/mBio.02210-15.

54. Douglas B. DiRienzo, "Effect of Probiotics on Biomarkers of Cardiovascular Disease: Implications for Heart-Healthy Diets," *Nutrition Reviews* 72, no. 1 (January 2014): 18–29, doi:10.1111/nure.12084; Timothy G. Dinan, Roman M. Stilling, Catherine Stanton, and John F. Cryan, "Collective Unconscious: How Gut Microbes Shape Human Behavior," *Journal of Psychiatric Research* 63 (April 2015): 1–9, doi:10.1016/j.jpsychires.2015.02.021.

55. Timothy G. Dinan, Roman M. Stilling, Catherine Stanton, and John F. Cryan, "Collective Unconscious: How Gut Microbes Shape Human Behavior." *Journal of Psychiatric Research* 63 (April 2015): 1–9, doi:10.1016/j.jpsychires.2015.02.021; L. Desbonnet, G. Clarke, F. Shanahan, T. G. Dinan, and J. F. Cryan, "Microbiota Is Essential for Social Development in the Mouse," *Molecular Psychiatry* 19, no. 2 (February 2014): 146–48, doi:10.1038/mp.2013.65.

56. National Institutes of Health, "Gene Linked to Autism in Families With More Than One Affected Child," January 20, 2016, www.nih.gov/news-events/news-releases/gene-linked-autism-families-more-one-affected-child.

57. Peter Good, "Do Salt Cravings in Children With Autistic Disorders Reveal Low Blood Sodium Depleting Brain Taurine and Glutamine?" *Medical Hypotheses* 77, no. 6 (December 2011): 1015–21, doi:10.1016/j.mehy.2011.08.038.

58. National Autistic Society, "Mental Health and Autism," accessed August 14, 2016, www.autism.org.uk/about/health/mental-health.aspx; Katherine M. Magnuson and John N. Constantino, "Characterization of Depression in

Children With Autism Spectrum Disorders," *Journal of Developmental and Behavioral Pediatrics* 32, no. 4 (May 2011): 332–40, doi:10.1097/DBP.0b013e318213f56c; Ovsanna T. Leyfer, Susan E. Folstein, Susan Bacalman, Naomi O. Davis, Elena Dinh, Jubel Morgan, Helen Tager-Flusberg, and Janet E. Lainhart,"Comorbid Psychiatric Disorders in Children With Autism: Interview Development and Rates of Disorders," *Journal of Autism and Developmental Disorders* 36, no. 7 (October 2006): 849–61, doi:10.1007/s10803-006-0123-0.

59. Laura de Magistris, Valeria Familiari, Antonio Pascotto, Anna Sapone, Alessandro Frolli, Patrizia Iardino, Maria Carteni, et al., "Alterations of the Intestinal Barrier in Patients With Autism Spectrum Disorders and in Their First-Degree Relatives," *Journal of Pediatric Gastroenterology and Nutrition* 51, no. 4 (October 2010): 418–24, doi:10.1097/MPG.0b013e3181dcc4a5.

60. Jennifer A. Bartz and Eric Hollander, "Oxytocin and Experimental Therapeutics in Autism Spectrum Disorders," in *Progress in Brain Research, Advances in Vasopressin and Oxytocin—From Genes to Behaviour to Disease* 170, ed. Inga D. Neumann and Rainer Landgraf (Elsevier, 2008), 451–62, www.sciencedirect.com/science/article/pii/S0079612308004354.

61. Elaine Y. Hsiao, Sara W. McBride, Sophia Hsien, Gil Sharon, Embriette R. Hyde, Tyler McCue, Julian A. Codelli, et al., "The Microbiota Modulates Gut Physiology and Behavioral Abnormalities Associated With Autism," *Cell* 155, no. 7 (December 19, 2013): 1451–63, doi:10.1016/j.cell.2013.11.024.

62. Shelly A. Buffington, Gonzalo Viana Di Prisco, Thomas A. Auchtung, Nadim J. Ajami, Joseph F. Petrosino, and Mauro Costa-Mattioli, "Microbial Reconstitution Reverses Maternal Diet-Induced Social and Synaptic Deficits in Offspring," *Cell* 165, no. 7 (June 16, 2016): 1762–75, doi:10.1016/j.cell.2016.06.001.

63. Derrick F. MacFabe, "Short-Chain Fatty Acid Fermentation Products of the Gut Microbiome: Implications in Autism Spectrum Disorders," *Microbial Ecology in Health & Disease* 23 (August 24, 2012), doi:10.3402/mehd.v23i0.19260; Derrick F. MacFabe, "Autism: Metabolism, Mitochondria, and the Microbiome," *Global Advances in Health and Medicine* 2, no. 6 (November 1, 2013): 52–66, doi:10.7453/gahmj.2013.089.

64. Anna Pärtty et al., "A Possible Link Between Early Probiotic Intervention and the Risk of Neuropsychiatric Disorders Later in Childhood: A Randomized Trial," *Pediatric Research* 77, no. 6 (June 2015): 823–28, accessed August 15, 2016, www.nature.com/pr/journal/v77/n6/pdf/pr201551a.pdf.

65. Sydney M. Finegold, Denise Molitoris, Yuli Song, Chengxu Liu, Marja-Liisa Vaisanen, Ellen Bolte, Maureen McTeague, et al., "Gastrointestinal Microflora Studies in Late-Onset Autism," *Clinical Infectious Diseases: An Official*

Publication of the Infectious Diseases Society of America 35, Suppl. 1 (September 1, 2002): S6–16, doi:10.1086/341914.

66. Helena M. R. T. Parracho, Max O. Bingham, Glenn R. Gibson, and Anne L. McCartney, "Differences Between the Gut Microflora of Children With Autistic Spectrum Disorders and That of Healthy Children," *Journal of Medical Microbiology* 54 (October 2005): 987–91, doi:10.1099/jmm.0.46101-0.

67. A. Venket Rao, Alison C. Bested, Tracey M. Beaulne, Martin A. Katzman, Christina Iorio, John M. Berardi, and Alan C. Logan, "A Randomized, Double-Blind, Placebo-Controlled Pilot Study of a Probiotic in Emotional Symptoms of Chronic Fatigue Syndrome," *Gut Pathogens* 1, no. 1 (March 19, 2009): 6, doi:10.1186/1757-4749-1-6.

CHAPTER 9

1. John R. Kelly, Yuliya Borre, Ciaran O'Brien, Elaine Patterson, Sahar El Aidy, Jennifer Deane, Paul J. Kennedy, et al., "Transferring the Blues: Depression-Associated Gut Microbiota Induces Neurobehavioural Changes in the Rat," *Journal of Psychiatric Research* 82 (November 1, 2016): 109–18, doi:10.1016/j.jpsychires.2016.07.019.

2. Shirong Liu, Andre Pires da Cunha, Rafael M. Rezende, Ron Cialic, Zhiyun Wei, Lynn Bry, Laurie E. Comstock, Roopali Gandhi, and Howard L. Weiner, "The Host Shapes the Gut Microbiota via Fecal MicroRNA," *Cell Host & Microbe* 19, no. 1 (January 13, 2016): 32–43, doi:10.1016/j.chom.2015.12.005.

3. Shirong Liu and Howard L. Weiner, "Control of the Gut Microbiome by Fecal microRNA," *Microbial Cell* 3, no. 4 (April 4, 2016): 176–77, doi:10.15698/mic2016.04.492.

4. Stephanie J. Soscia, James E. Kirby, Kevin J. Washicosky, Stephanie M. Tucker, Martin Ingelsson, Bradley Hyman, Mark A. Burton, et al., "The Alzheimer's Disease-Associated Amyloid β-Protein Is an Antimicrobial Peptide," *PLoS ONE* 5, no. 3 (March 3, 2010), doi:10.1371/journal.pone.0009505.

5. Deepak Kumar Vijaya Kumar, Se Hoon Choi, Kevin J. Washicosky, William A. Eimer, Stephanie Tucker, Jessica Ghofrani, Aaron Lefkowitz, et al., "Amyloid-β Peptide Protects Against Microbial Infection in Mouse and Worm Models of Alzheimer's Disease," *Science Translational Medicine* 8, no. 340 (May 25, 2016): 340ra72-340ra72, doi:10.1126/scitranslmed.aaf1059.

6. Roman M. Stilling and John F. Cryan, "Host Response: A Trigger for Neurodegeneration?" *Nature Microbiology* 1 (July 26, 2016): 16129, doi:10.1038/nmicrobiol.2016.129.

7. Zhongyi Chen, Lilu Guo, Yongqin Zhang, Rosemary L. Walzem, Julie S. Pendergast, Richard L. Printz, Lindsey C. Morris, et al., "Incorporation of

Therapeutically Modified Bacteria Into Gut Microbiota Inhibits Obesity," *Journal of Clinical Investigation* 124, no. 8 (August 1, 2014): 3391–3406, doi:10.1172/JCI72517.

8. Jennifer Ackerman, "U.S. Navy Recruits Gut Microbes to Fight Obesity and Disease," *Scientific American,* accessed October 19, 2016, www.scientific american.com/
article/u-s-navy-recruits-gut-microbes-to-fight-obesity-and-disease.

9. Francesco Asnicar Serena Manara, Moreno Zolfo, Duy Tin Truong, Matthias Scholz, Federica Armanini, Pamela Ferrretti, et al., "Studying Vertical Microbiome Transmission From Mothers to Infants by Strain-Level Metagenomic Profiling," *bioRxiv* (October 21, 2016): 81828, doi:10.1101/081828.

FURTHER READING

Blaser, Martin J. *Missing Microbes: How the Overuse of Antibiotics Is Fueling Our Modern Plagues*. Picador, 2015.

Dietert, Rodney. *The Human Superorganism: How the Microbiome Is Revolutionizing the Pursuit of a Healthy Life*. Dutton, 2016.

Enders, Giulia. *Gut: The Inside Story of Our Body's Most Underrated Organ*. Greystone Books, 2015.

Finlay, B. Brett, and Marie-Claire Arrieta. *Let Them Eat Dirt: Saving Your Child From an Oversanitized World*. Algonquin Books, 2016.

Gershon, Michael D. *The Second Brain: A Groundbreaking New Understanding of Nervous Disorders of the Stomach and Intestine*. Harper Perennial, 1999.

Gilbert, Jack, and Rob Knight. *Dirt Is Good: The Advantage of Germs for Your Child's Developing Immune System*. St. Martin's Press, 2017.

Knight, Rob. *Follow Your Gut: The Enormous Impact of Tiny Microbes*. Simon & Schuster, 2015.

Mayer, Emeran. *The Mind-Gut Connection*. Harper Wave, 2016.

Sonnenburg, Justin, and Erica Sonnenburg. *The Good Gut*. Penguin Books, 2016.

Spector, Tim. *The Diet Myth: Why the Secret to Health and Weight Loss Is Already in Your Gut*. The Overlook Press, 2016.

Yong, Ed. *I Contain Multitudes: The Microbes Within Us and a Grander View of Life*. Ecco, 2016.

INDEX

312

ABOUT THE AUTHORS

Scott C. Anderson is a veteran science journalist with specialization in medical topics and computer programming. He was one of the creators of LEGO Island, a computer game, and his work has combined computer programming with medical research. He consults for a company called Freedom Health that studies bacterial health in racehorses and has developed prebiotics for animals and humans. He lives in Hudson, Ohio.

John F. Cryan is professor and chair of the Department of Anatomy and Neuroscience, University College Cork, Ireland, and a principal investigator in the APC Microbiome Institute, a leading-edge institute researching the role of the microbiome in health and disease. He lives in Cork, Ireland.

Ted Dinan is professor of psychiatry and a principal investigator in the APC Microbiome Institute at University College Cork, Ireland. He was previously chair of Clinical Neurosciences and professor of psychological medicine at St. Bartholomew's Hospital, London. He lives in Cork, Ireland.